D1569533

World War I
and the
Cultures of
Modernity

World War I

and the

Cultures of Modernity

Edited by
Douglas Mackaman
and Michael Mays

University Press of Mississippi
Jackson

To our parents, Richard and Clare Mackaman and Tom and Claudia Mays,
for their example, support, and love

www.upress.state.ms.us

Library of Congress Cataloging-in-Publication Data
World War I and the cultures of modernity / edited by Douglas Mackaman and Michael Mays.
    p. cm.
    Includes index.
    ISBN 1-57806-243-8 (cloth : alk. paper)
    1. World War, 1914-1918—Influence. 2. Civilization, Modern—20th century. I. Title:
World War one. II. Title: World War 1. III. Mackaman, Douglas Peter. IV. Mays,
Michael. V. Title.
D523 .W745 2000
909.82—dc21   99-057734

British Library Cataloging-in-Publication Data available

Contents

Acknowledgments

The editors wish to thank the institutions and individuals who have made work on this book a far more manageable task than it otherwise would have been. From the University Press of Mississippi, we have enjoyed encouragement and magisterial assistance from Craig Gill and others whose efforts in our behalf have been considerable and professional. Within the departments of history and English at the University of Southern Mississippi, we have found help of many kinds and in bountiful quantities, too, from our colleagues and friends. Additionally, we express gratitude for the teaching experiences we have enjoyed as faculty in the Honors College at USM, where it has been our great privilege to teach together periodically in a team-taught humanities course for sophomores. Confronting the enormous potential for interdisciplinary inquiry through the challenges of teaching two and even three disciplines together has made us smarter, more humble and more eager to form partnerships like the one that helped to create this book.

As co-directors of the Institute for the Study of Modern Life at USM, we have enjoyed significant financial support from this university. In particular, we thank the Office of the President, the Office of the Vice President for Research and Planning, the College of Liberal Arts, the College of International and Continuing Education and the Honors College for the help its administrators have given to our institute and the efforts needed to make this book become a reality. We would also like to thank the scholars who joined us in Mississippi in 1997 for our conference on the First World War. Their exciting work made the book a pleasure to conceive and assemble, just as the solidarities and friendships that came from that weekend will continue to influence our lives as teachers and scholars for many years to come.

Acknowledgments

Finally, we would like to thank the graduate students in the Departments of English and history at USM who helped us manage every detail related to the 1997 conference. In particular, we note the terrific efforts of Dr. Kathy Barbier, who organized almost on her own not just the conference but the frantic lives of its directors. We wish to note also the aid of Pete Bishop and Joyce Olewski, both of whom helped not just with the conference but with much that went into the book.

Preface
"Unreal City": The Place of the Great War in the History of Modernity

Sandra M. Gilbert

Same old crossing, same old boat,
　Same old dust round Rouen way,
Same old narsty one-franc note,
　Same old 'Mercy, sivvoo play;'
Same old scramble up the line,
　Same old 'orse-box, same old stror,
Same old weather, wet or fine,
　Same old blooming War. . . .

Same old trenches, same old view,
　Same old rats and just as tame,
Same old dug-outs, nothing new,
　Same old bodies out in front,
Same old *strafe* from 2 till 4,
　Same old bloody War.

　—A. A. Milne

[I]n the territory beneath the eye, or hidden by folds in the ground, there must have been—on the two sides—a million men, moving one against the other and impelled by an invisible force into a Hell of fear that surely cannot have had a parallel in this world. It was an extraordinary feeling to have in a wide landscape.

—Ford Maddox Ford

Preface

Among the many curious and disturbing military relics on view in the Imperial War Museum that has (appropriately enough) long occupied the grounds where London's notorious Bedlam once stood is an old-fashioned doubledecker bus, painted olive-drab to blend into the ruinous territory through which its occupants were to be transported. For as if to dramatize the uncanniness of the quotidian into which they had stepped, the soldiers of 1914-1918 were often ferried from the apparent normalcy of the Home Front to the extraordinary hell of the Front in what would otherwise have been the blandest and most ordinary of vehicles—the lumbering buses that plied the streets of the British capitol, knitting homes, pubs, shops, schools and hospitals into a pattern of placid urbanity. Now, dislodged from their peacetime contexts, the buses journeyed as in some bizarre parody of London transport, toward the even more bizarre realm of the trenches.

Yet despite its oddness, such a use of London buses was singularly appropriate, for the intricate network of trenches in which the Great War's combatants were buried alive for four long years itself constituted a kind of grotesque parody of a modern city, as is suggested by some of the names the troops bestowed on key routes or intersections ("Half Moon Street," "Dublin Castle") in the "labyrinth" they inhabited. For the "muddy maze of trenches," declared one Major Owen Rutter, was "Worse to find one's way about in/Than the dark and windy subways/Of the Piccadilly tube are" so that even on the most superficial level it made sense to map them as if they were part of an extended cityscape. But again, the bleak "city" into which the soldiers were bussed was shockingly eerie, indeed, as the historian Eric Leed has explained, *unheimlich*, for this weirdly urban battlefield was "'empty of men' and yet it was saturated with men."[1]

"Trenches rise up, grey clay, three or four feet above the ground," wrote one observer. "Save for one or two men—snipers at the sap-head—the country was deserted. No sign of humanity—a dead land. And yet thousands of men were there," in what another observer saw as "desolate buildings uninhabited by men": they were there "like rabbits concealed" or like furtive dwellers in some nightmare *quartier*. No wonder, then, that Wilfred Owen famously compared No Man's Land to those paradigmatic cities of evil "Sodom and Gomorrah" and "Babylon the Fallen," that Rudyard Kipling called the vast British war cemeteries "the silent cities," and that, as Modris Eksteins notes in this volume, one J. W. Gamble thought that once tourists saw the ruins of Ypres the "ancient ruins of Pompeii . . . will be simply out of it." Just "as the war had marked the arrival of mass culture, mass politics and mass society," Douglas Mackaman and Michael Mays incisively remind us in their introduction here, "so had its course and outcome eradicated for poets, painters and writers the right to follow a pastoral muse."[2]

Armies have always, of course, been traveling communities, so that there is a sense in which a war, any war, can always be figured as a sort of horrifyingly conflicted city, devoted to its own destruction. And, too, the "city of dreadful night" has always itself been a trope for a kind of ultimate social perversion: the hell of human *in*humanity. Dwight Eddins's fine essay in this collection (on Ted Hughes and the Great War) properly points out the relevance of Northrop Frye's theories of "demonic" imagery to the self-wasting of culture so often and so powerfully symbolized through representations of the war's infamous No Man's Land. The "demonic human world," wrote Frye, is archetypally portrayed not only "in its unworked form of deserts, rocks, and waste land" but also as cities "of destruction and dreadful night" as well as "such images "of perverted work" as "engines of torture, weapons of war, armor, and images of a dead mechanism which, because it does not humanize nature, is unnatural as well as inhuman."[3] In the violent psychodrama of our era's first "war to end all wars," however, these longstanding cultural stereotypes came together not with a whimper but a bang, constructing a demonic cityscape that (as Mackaman and Mays rightly claim) was "the epochal event, *the beginning*, of the twentieth century" because it effectively ended the very history that might produce so naive a concept as a "war to end all wars."

As early as 1915, that shrewd cultural analyst Sigmund Freud tellingly meditated on just this issue, remarking that before the war, "he who was not by stress of circumstance confined to one spot, could confer upon himself . . . a new a wider fatherland, wherein he moved unhindered [but] now that civilized cosmopolitan [stands] helpless in a world grown strange to him—his all-embracing patrimony disintegrated. . . . the fellow-citizens embroiled and debased." More recently, the British poet Philip Larkin memorably made the same point in his poignantly memorial "MCMXV," through—interestingly enough—a description of the unwary prewar city, with its "long uneven lines" of volunteers "Standing as patiently/As if they were stretched outside/The Oval or Villa Park . . . Grinning as if it were all/An August Bank Holiday lark":

> Never such innocence,
> Never before or since,
> As changed itself to past
> Without a word – the men
> Leaving the gardens tidy,
> The thousands of marriages
> Lasting a little while longer:
> Never such innocence again.[4]

To be sure, the "moustached archaic faces" of Larkin's beaming enlistees, ingenuously regarding the guns of August as harbingers of a kind of extended "Bank Holiday lark," were very likely visages of working-class city dwellers, while cultivated and urbane, Freud's cosmopolitan traveler, "not by stress of circumstance confined to one spot," needed no such liberation but was instead a connoisseur rather than a prisoner of cities, perhaps a kind of Baudelairean *flaneur*. Both worker and *flaneur*, however, were still at that point denizens of the intricately fascinating and largely prosperous city that Baudelaire saw as the type and image of "modern life" in the nineteenth century. "For the perfect *flaneur*, for the passionate spectator," enthused the French poet in "The Painter of Modern Life," "it is an immense joy to set up house in the heart of the multitude, amid the ebb and flow of movement, in the midst of the fugitive and the infinite," adding, as if in anticipation of Freud's description of the prewar "civilized cosmopolitan," that it is the *flaneur's* special privilege "To be away from home and yet to feel oneself everywhere at home." In particular, this "passionate spectator"–this artist of the quotidian whose scrutiny of "the ephemeral, the fugitive, the contingent" was in some ways to provide a paradigm for the aesthetic not just of Baudelaire himself but of English-language writers from Whitman to Woolf—"marvels at the eternal beauty and the amazing harmony of life in the capital cities, a harmony so providentially maintained amid the turmoil of human freedom."[5]

Yet "Never such innocence again," one is tempted to exclaim, contemplating this passage by the author of *Les Fleurs du Mal*. Never, in any case, so innocent an imagining of the city, of the modern, perhaps even of the *human!* Never, at least in part because the city of the war perhaps permanently contaminated those peacetime cities of which it was a murderous reflection. Static and seemingly interminable, its combatants immobilized in endless miles of trenches on both sides of No Man's Land, the war that began as an "August Bank Holiday lark"–a way of getting out of the workaday city–soon began to feel permanent as a city, with the "Same old bodies out in front,/Same old *strafe* from 2 till 4,/ Same old bloody War"established like a *tour aboli* on the horizon of modernity. Alienating as a massive city, its citizens stripped of peacetime identities and recreated as virtually nameless ciphers, this entrenched city of dreadful night was also alienated *from* what had been "normal" cities, as the notorious gulf between Front and Home Front suggests, with its construction of the Front as a kind of counter-capitol to the capitol itself. Nor was it possible for the citizen of this city to consider himself in a Baudelairean sense "away from home" yet "everywhere at home." On the contrary, as the distinction between Front and Home Front implies, one could never be at home even in what one Canadian balladeer called one's "little wet home in the trench" at the Front even while, dislodged from the now radically defamiliarized Home Front, one could not longer feel at home there either.[6]

Worse still, industrialized and technologized, so that, as Mackaman and Mays put it, "some wicked perversion of the factory system" seemed to have evolved into "the killing fields of the Somme, Verdun and elsewhere," the city of the war looks retrospectively not just like "the negative realization" of those quintessentially urban products "Enlightenment and Industrialization" but also like "the spring board to what 1918 would ultimately lead the world into: a second war where death was still more scientifically and industrially delivered" in the murderous cities of Auschwitz and Bergen-Belsen as well as *to* the cities of London, Dresden, Berlin, and Hiroshima. It was in the first world war's city of death, indeed, that the casualties of technology first became even in death grotesque tools of technology. Writes the historian David Cannadine, "the combat zone might remain littered for weeks with bodies [and] New trenches might be dug through them; parapets might be made of them"–pioneering a grisly efficiency that was to be far more systematically exploited in the concentration camps of the next war.[7] Not only was "the Romantic pastoral . . . quite plainly gone" after the appearance of such cities of the war, the Romantically inspired Baudelairean city was gone too, to be replaced by the "Unreal City" of the Eliotian waste land—

> . . . hooded hordes swarming
> Over endless plains, stumbling in cracked earth
> Ringed by the flat horizon only . . .
> Falling towers
> Jerusalem Athens Alexandria
> Vienna London
> Unreal[8]

And "stumbling in cracked earth" through the damned and doomed city of the Great War the once joyous Baudelairean *flaneur* became a very different figure, a sort of *voyeur maudit*, a desperate spectator/participant, whose wartime observations of "the ephemeral, the fugitive, the contingent" were scribblings in a journal of death whose bleak, ironic precision would influence generations of elegists in every European language. From Henri Barbusse's *Le Feu* and the sketches of Fernand Leger to the grimly anti-pastoral lyrics of Siegfied Sassoon, Isaac Rosenberg, and Wilfred Owen, these joyless anti-*flaneurs* took note of the grisly minutiae out of which the war/city had been built: "the green clumsy legs/High-booted" of one dead soldier, "the red wet thing/I must somehow forget" that was the body of another, the "queer sardonic rat[s]" surrounding the dead, the "monstrous anger of the guns" and "the stuttering rifles' rapid rattle" that helped do the killing.[9] With its bitter allusion to Horace's "It is sweet and proper to die for one's country," Wilfred Owen's famous depiction in *"Dulce et Decorum Est"* of the ephemeral, fugitive and contingent moment of one soldier's death by gas perhaps most vividly illustrates the horror experienced by this new kind of Baudelairean poet-as-*voyeur- maudit*—

> Gas! GAS! Quick, boys!–An ecstasy of fumbling,
> Fitting the clumsy helmets just in time;
> But someone still was yelling out and stumbling,
> And flound'ring like a man in fire or lime . . .
> Dim, through the misty panes and thick green light,
> As under a green sea, I saw him drowning. [*CP*, 55]

But countless other works by this writer and his wartime contemporaries offer comparably bleak and fleeting visions of what we might call "the buried life" in an uncanny city of death where, in the words of Fernand Leger, *"On est entre dans la terre, on est absorbe par elle, on se colle dessus pour eviter la mort qui est partout . . . . On se cache derriere un tue. On vit avec les morts en bon camarade. On ne les enterre meme pas. A quoi bon? Un autre obus les deterrera."* [10]

Soon after the Armistice, Modris Eksteins tells us in the fascinating essay on "War, Memory, and the Modern: Pilgrimage and Tourism to the Western Front" included here, travel firms began planning tours of the now "all quiet" western front. Declared the brochure for one such trip: "BOOK EARLY if you want to see anything of the chaos and debris of War. . . . YOU MUST COME NOW if you want to see anything of the chaos of a modern Battlefield,." for "Trenches and shell holes will disappear and neatly tilled fields will take their place." But though the battlefields were indeed cleansed of the chaos some tour operators evidently considered marketably picturesque, though the cemeteries of the Somme and Verdun are green and calm, we still at least metaphorically inhabit a city of modernity that the Great War built. Musing on Ted Hughes's "Ghost Crabs," Dwight Eddins remarks that in the view of Hughes, whose father was a nightmare-ridden survivor of Gallipoli, it "is as though in the case of the war, the nightmare was made flesh and dwelt among us, proving that no substantial barriers exist between the worst we can imagine and the worst that can happen," for "Far from being the war to end all wars, [World War I] is the war that has never ended and never will." Wrote Hughes–addressing his dead father just ten years ago, in "For The Duration"—

> Your day-silence was the coma
> Out of which your night-dreams rose shouting.
> I could hear you from my bedroom -
> The whole hopelessness still going on,
> No man's land still crying and burning
> Inside our house, and you climbing again
> Out of the trench, and wading back into the glare
>
> As if you might still not manage to reach us
> And carry us to safety.[11]

Have the fathers reached us and carried us "to safety"? Or is "No man's land still crying and burning/Inside our house?" Given the history of our century, the millennial answer to such questions would seem clear: in our post-Great War, post-Holocaust, post-nuclear age, "safety," whatever that might have been, is as far away as the innocent summer of Larkin's "MCMXIV," whose very title–with its archaic Roman numerals–looks as though it ought to be chiseled on a tomb or on the cornerstone of a building in some city of dreadful night. And as himself a kind of belated *voyeur maudit* of the calamity at Gallipoli, Hughes noted (as Eddins points out) the wartime origins of *The Waste Land*, that founding text of modernity, remarking in an interview that T. S. Eliot's "sickness told him the cause" of "the disintegration of Western civilization": "he cleaned his wounds and found the shrapnel."

Whether or not Hughes knew it, Eliot was also at second-hand a *voyeur maudit* of Gallipoli, where Jean Verdenal, the best friend of his student days in Paris, was killed in the "cruelest month" of April, 1915. Not far from this battlefield where "modern life" revealed one of its true meanings–not far from the trenches sardonically named (according to John Masefield, one of Hughes's predecessors in the laureateship) "Half Moon Street" and "Dublin Castle"–the ruins of Troy had stood, another "Unreal City" providing a different, more conventionally heroic paradigm of combat.[12] But the all too real "Unreal City" of Eliot's neurasthenic bad dreams is really more like the one in which, metaphorically speaking, we still live–or anyway (to put the case more hopefully) *have been* living for almost a century.[13] "[S]o many,/I had not thought death had undone so many," laments the speaker of *The Waste Land*. So too would speak the hapless and hopeless *flaneurs* of the Great War, as this volume, with its many perceptive examinations of *World War I and the Cultures of Modernity,* dramatically demonstrates.

Introduction
The Quickening
of Modernity

Douglas Mackaman and Michael Mays

Everywhere in the hills above the Verdun sector of the Meuse River, there are signs of how the landscape was tortured by the German offensives of 1916. The gently sloping green lawns of Verdun's mammoth graveyard have the torture enmeshed in not just calm and sadness but also in a perspective whose sweep seems to stretch to forever. There, the memorial to the unknown soldiers of this sector's campaign reaches skyward in an architectural style that seeks to balance how far down the hillside the tens of thousands of marked graves stretch. Are there 50,000 entombed? Are there twice that number? Are they all unknown? One stops to ask these and other questions of a janitor or anyone who might know. This architectural and landscaped complex of memorialization is one kind of modern site of cultural and political meaning. It is a destination. It asks to be seen and to be counted. It has parking space for busses, and close to it is a small café with sandwiches and drinks. To see the national and communal forests from the ossuary's hillside, planted after the armistice to clean with nature what civilization had ruined—and to see how odd and stunted the stands of these trees look still—is to know something about the permanence of the First World War.

But one knows of this permanence, too, by snaking along the small highways that cut through these failed forests, watching the ground undulate and offer up its black moss and stumped essence from shallow trenches to a sunshine that can pierce at least the edge of such a woods. Slow driving here pays off, in that there are so many signs of the tiny French towns that never grew back when the 1914-1918 war was over. Road signs, even, which announce that one is in a town only to announce in a matter of yards that one has left that same town. These other markers of modern memory are no less appropriate or moving than such destinations as the Verdun fortifications or the graveyard itself, for one sees them on the fly—in that most modern of all ways—through the lens of a car window as one drives along more easily than memory and its weight ought to allow. Obliterated but for a pair of highways signs and an earth laden with shards of what these miniature worlds were before their burial, the dead towns of Verdun are said to attract no birds. The tourists come instead, and in steady if not so large numbers they tramp over the sites of battle and final resting places of the dead, scavenging for rusted war relics and otherwise plumbing what depths they wish to, searching for a war's physical and emotional remnants on the ground and inside of themselves.

Searches of a more scholarly sort have been the stuff of much contemporary work by historians and literary critics, whose varied interrogations of "modernity" and "post-modernism" have fueled lively debates within academe and beyond it. These discussions have sought to define the meanings of modernity and its different modes, just as they have endeavored to situated the First World War within the shifting terms of what the modern age has been.[1] In traditionalist readings of these issues, what had been Romanticist in aesthetics prior to 1914 did not emerge intact after 1918. On the contrary, just as the war had marked the arrival of mass culture, mass politics and mass society, so had its course and outcome eradicated for poets, painters and writers the right to follow a pastoral muse. These scholarly polemics have recently found their challengers, among them works which show how Romanticist sensibilities persevered and even found invigoration after 1918 precisely because it was so urgent to reckon with death on a large scale and to render its ubiquity somehow special, sacred and of nature.[2] Others have explored related assessments of the modern condition with respect to the First World War, particularly in terms of those ideas of progress, humanism, science and technology which for so long had been the identifying features of western modernity. In these studies of "total war" and how science, administration and progress were fused together with barbarous results—such that some wicked perversion of the factory system became the killing fields of the Somme, Verdun and elsewhere—scholars have given the Great War to its readers and students as not just the negative realization of Enlightenment and Industrialization but also as the spring board to what 1918 would ultimately lead the world into: a second war where death was still more scientifically and industrially delivered and after which the Romantic pastoral was quite plainly gone.[3]

Scholarly and popular interest in World War One today, which has recently witnessed the publication of several acclaimed novels, the writing of many popular histories, Hollywood films either wholly or partly about 1914-1918 and a recent B.B.C./P.B.S. mini series devoted to the war, is a noticeable departure from what was long a focus on World War Two. Indeed no event in modern life, certainly no event of such monumental scope, was so quickly superseded as was the 1914-1918 war. Which is not to say, of course, that the conflict has seen anything less than fairly steady scholarly interest since the 1920s. Nor is it to suggest that the combatant nations of Europe failed after 1918 to appeal to the war's impact on the world as they shaped new polities or adjusted old ones. But however deeply the 1914-1918 war had etched the horrors of bleak "trenchscapes" and ghastly barrages into the imaginations of those who had been there, or lost young men in them, Dresden and Hiroshima and Auschwitz would inscribe more indelibly and monstrously a worse set of scenes only two decades later. And emerging from the ashes of that second war was a world that Europeans before the first one would not have known. The "great powers" that had collaborated to form a network of military alliances prior to 1914 were, after 1945, reduced to tangential importance with the rise of a "bi-polar" ordering of international affairs. Similarly, the earnest confidence of that earlier age, which refused to collapse—F. Scott Fitzgerald's Dick Diver tells us these weights meant next to nothing, and he may be right—under the grim forebodings of Nietzsche or the anti-enlightenment epistemology brashly announced in the works of Stravinsky, Picasso, Marinetti, Barrès and so many others, succumbed after World War Two to the more pertinent existentialism of Sartre and deBeauvoir.[4]

The first war set adrift survivors who had lived too long "eye deep in Hell," young men wandering the streets of large cities and small towns physically maimed and, worse, psychically shattered, yet there still remained after 1918 a sense that some understanding of this horrible tragedy could eventually be gained. Virginia Woolf, whose readers were given ample reason to hate the medical experts presiding over the ruin of shell-shocked Septimus Smith, could leave open the possibility in *Mrs. Dalloway* that the wracked shell of a soldier could restore *something* by making himself die.[5] Not even this minuscule consolation could endure the second war, however, after which survival itself became the question posed by such figures as Primo Levi, Tadeusz Borowski, and Bruno Bettleheim. These and scores of others who endured the death camps were left, not to live with, but to live *out* Camus's meditations on the absurdity of life and the meaning of suicide, devoid of any illusion that their deaths might restore anything of what had been systematically stripped from them.

Inasmuch as each historical age seeks to secure a sense of its own permanence through contemporary and ongoing historicizations, it is hardly surprising that a cold war generations of historians and critics, coming of age in the turbulent wake of the Second World War, should have identified the middling decades its middling decades as the crux of the Twentieth Century. All that those twenty years before and after the mid-century mark had produced by way of an international order and cultural system amounted to argument enough about what the century had meant and wherein resided its significance. That interpretation of high modernity's chronological loci was understandable, given both the barbarity of the second war and the high degree to which its outcome would challenge more than a generation of people after 1945 to forget it. Finally, of course, it seemed to many who had lived through both wars that the political, cultural and social forces mobilized during the first one were the very causes of the second conflict.[6] It was hardly a stretch, even, to question if there has in face been two separate wars, when it felt so much to so many as though 1919-1939 had been merely two decades of interregnum in another century's Thirty Years War.

But if the Second World War eclipsed 1914-1918 in our collective memory, and made us neglect its centrality in the shaping of a distinctively modern consciousness, political, social, and cultural tensions at the end of the twentieth century have brought us forcibly back to the defining crises of the century's beginning. Eight decades later, the tensions between consolidation and fragmentation, assimilation and autonomy, the collective and the individual, remain as brutal and acrimonious as ever. And with Bosnia and Kosovo back in their knotty relevance, even as nationalisms are supposed to be ending in a new Europe ordered by ever more economic and political unity, we have not just a multi-polar world again, but, moreover, a set of political and cultural tensions all but begging us to recall the 1914-1918 war and measure very deliberately its multiple meanings. Thus as we herald the "return" of Europe at the millenium's end we would do very well to note not just that the recent and ongoing wars in southeaster Europe but also that minority and hybrid national and ethnic communities elsewhere still clash with bureaucratic demands for linguistic unity, conformity in the classroom and otherwise audible calls for "France First" or "Germany for Germans." Skinhead movements and the resurgence of fascistic politics and the horrors of "ethnic cleansing" demand that we notice, too, that brutishness continues to loom large as a political culture, countering forcefully the implications of an ongoing revolution in ideas about race, gender and sexuality.

Now returned to us at this century's end, the First World War resonates still as the *Great* War precisely because it seemed to so shockingly and completely shatter what the "bourgeois century" built but could not sustain.[7] Designated as an apocalyptic moment of transition from one world to another not just by many who endured it but also by scholars who have taken the eras around it as the terrain of their expertise, the 1914-1918 war ought also to be studied closely with respect to its own experiential terrain. How did those human beings, social groups and cultural formations which went either eagerly or otherwise into war inhabit the world of the conflict and crawl or march or flee or never return again from it? The experience of the war and its own generations, oddly—in that so many decades are gone between then and now—remains among the more important histories of that era yet to write. And in writing this history we can hope to learn some of the more crucial lessons still to come from studying the conflagration, chief among these to what degree the war was either an intensification of the already-existing conflicts wrought by modernization or a pivotal break in the history of humanity.

After 1918, there would emerge a pervasive sense that society and culture had, to borrow from Yeats, "changed, changed utterly," becoming unrecognizable, irreconcilable, and ages away from the world before. Pondering a photograph of himself taken the year before the war began, Pat Barker's Billy Prior captures a sense of the feeling shared by soldiers and civilians alike, who had for 1,500 days made lives out of war : "Why does it look so long ago?" he asks. [8] Historicizing his lived experience and reckoning with what is in his view was the cataclysm of the war," Billy tells us "Oh, dear me, we *are* living through a period of terribly rapid social change, aren't we?" Profoundly aware of a jarring change that is still so much unfolding, Barker's soldier asks us "whether there aren't periods when people do become aware of what's happening, and they look back on their previous unconscious selves and it seems like decades ago. Another life." Hemingway had struck a similar chord, in writing that heroism and chivalry were not just absent from the after-war world, they were banished from writing, just as Woolf noted that certain raptures from before the war had settled into being inaccessible feelings, "that one used to have."

For many writers and their contemporaries, of course, the feeling of living in historically-redefining times had begun with the war's first summer, when it seemed to so many Europeans that combat might indeed be just the short, sharp shock that would bring vitality back to a tired order and otherwise resolve some of the turmoil, frenetic spirit and boredom which modernity at the end of the bourgeois century had occasioned but not fully ordered. The German assertion of *burgfrieden*, which was matched in France with the proclamation of *union sacrée*, would welcome the war with a facade of unity, behind which still lurked anxieties about violence in politics, incomprehensibility in the arts and the still unmastered social structures that industry and urbanization had produced in Europe. Although exalting initially in the belief that victory would be swift and certain, the combatant nations would feel the euphoria of August 1914 fall away quickly enough, to be replaced by stalemate, hunger, boredom, and the charnel house of shell holes and entrenchments that would be called the western front and devour in a few short years 7,000 casualties each day of the war.

This book is about how the war was lived and understood by the soldiers and civilians whose lives it came to organize and define. Our optic onto these enormous matters is necessarily one which views the war from a multiplicity of academic perspectives. Indeed essays in this volume have grown out of a conference that was hosted by the Departments of History and English on the campus of the University of Southern Mississippi. In attendance at the November 1996 meeting were scholars from disciplines that ranged from film studies, to literature and history. Joined in the common project of weighing the ways and means of World War One as well as a consideration of its cultural, political and literary legacies, the conference participants debated in their research and even more at the round table that ended the proceedings why they were moved by the war to study it and how work in the future might best be framed, so as to contribute to a broad and vigorous understanding of this war and its importance to the history of our times. All the participants offered insight and challenge in the work they brought to the conference. We have chosen the essays for this book because of how well they argue with each other and otherwise engage with the "interdisciplinarity" we think a scholar's conversation on the war requires.

Few questions loom larger in any social history of Europeans in the half century before 1914 than those related to class and identity formation. Focusing on shifting attitudes toward morality and sexuality, both Regina Sweeney and David Simpson explore how the war experience cast into crisis what had seemed to be the well built construction of bourgeois mores in France and Britain. Studying military and civil government censorship of songs, performances and even sheet music, Sweeney exposes an anxious world of administrators and prudes who worried simultaneously about how music might erode morale and also give an unwanted shock to France's middle-class morality. Moreover, Sweeney assesses how wartime restrictions on entertainment and culture gave edgy ministers of culture and stewards of public taste a unique opportunity to strike out at the venues, artists and industries of entertainment that had been beyond the pale of their authority prior to 1914. Simpson similarly reveals how prewar attitudes toward sexuality, male virility and prostitution were cast into sharp relief by the British experience in the First World War. Exploring diverse military and civilian opinions related to soldering and male sexual desire, for example, the author shows how prostitution was understood in certain circles to be an important and even patriotic matter of men's hygiene. How soldiers could find the health that sexual release promised them was no easy matter, however, as Simpson's essay shows in its close analysis of regulatory efforts related to prostitution and the spread of venereal disease. For if the essay reprises for critical study Victorian and Edwardian calls for manly self control, Simpson shows even more that where chastity left off a regulated and medically sanctioned sexuality picked up.

The war as a crystallizing force in the world's press toward modernity is in part the focus of the essays by James Daughton and Jeffrey Smith. Both of these authors explore how the war served to *process* the rise of mass cultural forms that were well in evidence long before 1914. Examining the wartime fortunes of cartoons, posters, and post cards, these authors show how experiences of combat, fear and hope were communicated through and mediated by important implements of mass culture. These essays tease out tensions related to the expanded public sphere that followed the rise of mass culture in European society, just as they assess censorship and wartime constraints on the flow of information and ideas. Moreover, they reveal how unebbing the tide of mass cultural exchange continued to be during the war, even when the concept of total war took precedence over longstanding traditions of the free exchange of ideas. Suggesting, too, a partial revision of the traditionally drawn dichotomy of the home front and the battle front for 1914-1918, Daughton and Smith still appraise the trenches and their civic counterparts as being distinct from each other in vitally important ways.

Janet Watson's essay, which has gender and Britain as its thematic and national foci, critically interrogates the history of women and ideas about them in wartime England. In "The Paradox of Working Heroines: Conflict over the Changing Social Order in Wartime Britain, 1914-1918" Watson argues powerfully that the post war place of English and European women was never far from the thinking of those who allowed them to work and assume the status of home front combatants during the war. Even more, Watson reveals how class triumphed over sisterhood in British attitudes toward women's work, inasmuch as so many middle-class women felt that their servants ought to forsake the lucrative work of the munitions industry for the necessary labors that domestic servants had long done inside of Victorian and Edwardian homes. Assessing how as a collectivity the domestic servants who did munitions work were well received and respected, Watson shows how the flight of servants pitched the middle class into a wartime crisis over the terms of its domestic identity.

This war's geographic sweep astonished its contemporaries, in the same way that its survivors were surprised to see how differently it had been "intellectualized" in the midst of its occurrence. The essay by Geoffrey Jensen, "Dangerous Neutrality: Spain, the Great War, and Modern Catalan Nationalism," serves to remind us not just of the war's vast sweep over the world's map but also that nations beyond the shadow of the trenches had their own important and unique investments in the war. Because of their peripheral status, "small nation" nationalists like the Catalans, as Jensen argues, often understood the war as much in terms of tradition and civilization as they did any kind of purely geopolitical struggle. Douglas Mackaman's essay, "Regaining the "Lost Provinces": Textual Battles for Alsace-Lorraine in the First World War," takes a "small nations" approach to this great conflict, too, focusing on the literary and administrative efforts of the French to argue their position on the fate of post-war Alsace and Lorraine, those territories of France which the Germans had seized in the wake of the 1870 war and administered thereafter as belonging to the *Reichsland*. Exploring popular histories and the travel books in which those histories were contained, Mackaman assesses the narrative tone and techniques used by

Introduction

travel writers whose goal it was to render the history of Alsace and Lorraine after a Romanticist, nationalist and French fashion.

The essay by Gregory Barnhisel studies Ezra Pound's central place in literary Modernism in America and Europe. Unlike his contemporaries who would claim membership in a generation that was lost in the first war, Pound appears in Barnhisel's work as a poetic profiteer of the conflict. Exposing how the war rendered indispensable marketing techniques that before 1914 would have been anathema to writers whose livelihoods were rooted in a patronage system, Barnhisel gives us Pound and his small-press cohorts hard at work, not just writing poetry of an avant-garde bent but also crafting their publications to immediately become scarce and thus much sought artifacts. With the war as a vehicle of sorts, therefore, Pound experienced both the most creative writing era of his life and also an impetus to produce limited runs of his books and employ other marketing ploys that echoed techniques used in the increasingly sophisticated world of mass market book trading.

If contemporaries made use of the war to their own ends, the generation that followed responded with ever more interpretive eagerness, mostly out of necessity. Dwight Eddins's essay opens up a discussion of the legacy of the war between generations, asking us to see through the dark and sore eyes of those who were there, to walk with those who must walk every day the rutted ghost road that is the modern survivor's inexpressible memory lane, and to bear witness without sentimentality— or any easy search for cathartic release—to what the world still must mean, even when the shelling rains have past. Eddins shows us how sons and daughters, in poetry and fiction and around holiday tables or even more in the slices of everyday life when nothing special is there, have in themselves an unending if often unclear reaction to a war that took their parents as wholly as can ever happen, while leaving them alive after 1918 to be heard, reacted to, fought against or otherwise made sense of.

Modris Eksteins' "War, Memory and the Modern: Pilgrimage and Tourism to the Western Front" is an essay, too, very much about remembrance, forgetting and generations. Charting the eagerness of the tourist industry to market and sell the western front, before it could grow grass again or otherwise be joined back to the natural and civilized worlds its barbarisms had so assailed, Eksteins takes us on an emotional pilgrimage to where the war was fought and where thousands of military cemeteries, large and minuscule, stand silent, forever. If Eksteins thoughtfully explores what tourism meant and did not mean to those first sojourners to Verdun and elsewhere of the 1920s, his tour of these traveler's motives is set squarely in the grid of modernity's icy irony. Peronne, that city in the Somme sector that passed so often back and forth from being French to German, announced in a voice that Eksteins respects very much that those who would see the ravished city and its shattered centrum would do best to "not be angry, only amazed." And so Eksteins holds his own temper well and asks us to do the same, as he reveals not that the meanings of World War One are to be read in the little messages left by visitors in the guest registries kept by all the cemeteries but, rather, that the war and the issues related to its meanings are no longer easily or plainly articulated by anyone, anywhere. Against every shred of heartfelt connection to this war of the worlds that Eksteins can discover, the author finds a massive counterweight of evidence to suggest that the war is gone. For out of so many school buses that park next to the war museum that has been established in Peronne, which lies at the heart of what was the Somme sector of the war, emerge teenagers who will walk with an angst or levity unconnected to the great inferno that burned and belched this place so completely from one world to another, to sign their presence quickly, disinterestedly: "lots of death . . . why was it and do we care?"

"A beginning," the literary critic Edward Said has written, "constitutes an authorization for what follows from it." Originating in the shrouded mist of circumstance and historical vicissitude, a beginning emerges only reflectively, providing the focal point for a retrospective ordering or understanding, for some degree of rationale, however tenuously asserted. Thus every beginning also marks a departure, as it establishes a discontinuous relationship with its multiple precedents. The Great War is just such a beginning. And thus the interest in modernity so prevalent now as we approach the century's end—whether motivated by millennial anxiety, or merely a predilection for accounting, a need to take stock of where we have been— has sent us back, circularly, to the epochal event, *the beginning*, of the twentieth century. But what this book reveals is not that authentic or immutable claims to the origins of modern life or literary Modernism are to be found in and around the years 1914-1918 and the ways according to which the world lived war then. Rather we contend that with the Great War came the quickening of modernity and its political, social, cultural and literary attributes. And so our project privileges process and experience over origins, assessing as it does how the lives of people who knew that war physically and inside of themselves were midwives to a modernity that had not been theirs to conceive nor would be theirs to present proudly to the other generations, to us.

World War I
and the
Cultures of
Modernity

La Pudique Anastasie

Wartime Censorship and French Bourgeois Morality[1]

Regina Sweeney

◆◆✕◆◆

In the spring of 1915, Henry Moreau submitted his song "Réveil nocturne" to the Censorship Office of the Paris prefect. Much to the songwriter's dismay, the examiner banned the second of three verses because of its "lewd" characteristics. (Hinting at sexual antics, the lyrics told of a married couple who stayed in bed instead of going down to the shelter during a zeppelin warning.) Moreau did not hesitate to respond, insisting in a long letter that the second verse's "suggestive allusion" was "skillfully hidden." Unsure, the primary censor then turned to the Paris police prefect, who disagreed with Moreau's interpretation and declared the entire song *non visée*—which meant it could no longer be performed anywhere in Paris or, in fact, anywhere in the rest of France. When Moreau sent a second letter with a new version, he carefully explained that he feared losing his royalty income, and he threatened to get help from his friends in the government. The prefect responded simply that the entire piece was "one continual innuendo" (*sous-entendu*) and maintained his ban. We have no indication that Moreau ever got his visa.[2]

What should we make of French authorities and *chansonniers* arguing over the merits of song lyrics, particularly lewd ones, in the midst of their enormous, bloody struggle to remove the Germans from northeast France? And why were hundreds of old and new songs declared unsuitable as part of the wartime system of musical censorship? This exchange over "Réveil nocturne" represented an unusual case only in

3

the composer's verbosity and unveiled threat. Otherwise, it followed the general course of the 16,000 or so songs submitted to Parisian officials during the four-and-a-half years of war.[3] The system itself, however, reveals much about specific worries surrounding entertainment and the more complicated issue of what "appropriate" civilian behavior was in wartime.

In the case of cultural censorship on the homefront, a pre-war agenda intersected with wartime demands, where the war added urgency to earlier concerns.[4] At stake was the power to create or impose representations—representations which could affect the legitimacy of the government, the reputations of military leaders or the treatment of soldiers. French censors, on the one hand, encouraged a pro-war ethos (or the *union sacrée*, broadly defined) which would lend total support without interfering with politics. On the other hand, pursuing an older bourgeois ideology, officials worked to uplift or to civilize the social tenor of the *cafés-concerts* and music halls.[5] They sought to create upright, moral citizens. These were not, however, two separate agendas. They converged in a new link drawn between public morality and civilian morale. As the government minister Aristide Briand declared in front of Parliament in 1916, "the moral behavior of the country is at least as important as cannons and guns. . . ."[6]

Yet, World War I scholars have often used the word "morale" in reference to civilians unreflectively, partly because government officials and other well-known figures of the time utilized it so often. The amorphous concept of civilian "morale" was actually constructed as the war unfolded, in part by French authorities who judged that "total" war required total commitment, and that if morale weakened on the home front the soldiers could lose. Whereas 1914 made enthusiasm and obvious anti-German expressions the order of the day, 1917 found humorous grumbling complimenting stalwart patience. Under these circumstances, patriotism dictated correct appearance, behavior, gestures and song selections for all citizens.[7] The concepts of good morale and high morals became entangled, and it is this combination in comparison to the Army's less involved approach which this essay will explore.

[2.1] The Blue Pencil's Powers

The large, complicated machinery of censorship, affecting most public expression, was activated when the French Assembly declared a state of siege in early August 1914. New regulations multiplied, as did new bureaucratic offices.[8] Despite an astonishingly smooth mobilization, the government did not hesitate to turn to censorship and surveillance—both well-used nineteenth-century techniques—to guarantee public order and support. The procedures embraced all media from songs and theater pieces to newspapers and books. Having begun promptly in August 1914, censorship of entertainment continued on past the Armistice until October 1919.[9]

4

In the case of Parisian song production and performance, historical precedence and limited personnel supported the use of a centralized civilian structure; thus in August 1914, the Military Governor of Paris turned the responsibility over to the Parisian Prefect of Police.[10] For Paris and its suburbs, a list of all songs for music halls, fundraising benefits, and public concerts had to be submitted to censors. This meant that officials reviewed approximately 300 new songs each month, although directors, composers and performers also constantly resubmitted songs with or without modifications in an attempt to change a censor's mind. While it is unclear how many censors were employed, the criteria for songs appears to have been centrally controlled. In over 200 cases sent to the prefect on appeal all except one came from just one civil servant, a Monsieur Martin. The prefect himself dealt with questionable cases and met with disgruntled composers or directors.[11]

The immediate and relatively smooth imposition of the machine reflected not only the current government's wish to eliminate all subversive activity but also a collective memory of how the censoring mechanism had worked. The *cafés-concerts* and theaters had only shaken off censorship in 1906, just eight years before the war began, and the wartime procedures were fundamentally the same as those used throughout the early Third Republic.[12] In 1914, directors, performers and especially writers once again took up the ritual of submitting pieces and negotiating for visas.[13]

As the song examiners sharpened their pencils, they worried about any song, poem, or text which was to be used in a performance, not hesitating to expunge specific words, refrains, or whole verses. Although the examiners showed the greatest care with the texts, they gave some attention to melodies. For example, they protected sacred tunes such as the "Marseillaise" or the Belgian national anthem, "La Brabançonne," from ridicule. With an acute sensitivity to public performance, officers also attended dress rehearsals to evaluate the costumes, sets and gestures. Police agents would then visit shows periodically to insure compliance with the censors' rulings, and could, if necessary, request new modifications or impose a fresh ban.[14] In one case, in March 1915, a district officer withdrew a visa for the song "Le Beau Grenadier" after a random visit revealed the use of obscene gestures.[15] During another patrol, an agent discovered that a loud crash of cymbals at an opportune moment drowned out the last syllable of a verse which led to lascivious interpretations—the song was henceforth prohibited.[16] Thus, although the censors strove in their analyses of lyrics to divine "subversive" performances, hidden meanings and possible audience reactions, as we shall see, the inspections were essential for evaluating a song's delivery and effect. And performers' patriotic intentions did not assuage officials' concern over the audience's own interpretation.[17]

Overall, censorship was hardly an exact science, and it was difficult to make perfectly consistent decisions. An historian works from either faint pencil marks which give clues about the "inappropriate" words or questionable meanings, or from the emphatic blue lines which may have crossed out a verse only to designate it "Bon" (good) at a later date. Some written correspondence between officials and music-hall participants still exists, but much of the negotiating was done verbally. Although we do not have detailed memos listing the censors' objectives, their surgical approach allows us to piece together the puzzle.

The one serious exception to this system was in the trenches where military officers controlled songs by soldiers.[18] The army's process was almost completely decentralized, except for the most serious cases which reached top officials.[19] Aware of the possibilities for disorder and subversion, the authorities established stiff penalties including confiscations and arrests which became most important in 1917 with the troop mutinies. But the front was enormous, and solitary singing and performances were far more informal there than in most Parisian cases, so that soldiers quickly created and recreated pieces without submitting them to any censor.

The dissimilarity also reflected deeper structural differences between the army and civilian spheres. Kenneth Silver has argued that because soldiers lived in a more formally disciplined environment both physically and in terms of their objectives, they were given a less restrained ideological space. As long as they kept performing their duties, the army was not overly concerned with their cultural expressions. But "for the civilian population of relatively free individuals whose social hierarchy is (compared to the military's) tenuous and almost ineffectual, ideology and propaganda are the necessary means by which all collective action is affected. While the feelings or attitudes of the individual soldier are negligible to the structure of the army, those of the civilian are essential to his deportment and are therefore carefully scrutinized and controlled on the home front."[20] Although accurate about the looser space soldiers inhabited, especially when they occupied front-line trenches, Silver underestimated the army's concern for the soldiers' thoughts or politics. The military did promote patriotic organizations such as the *Théâtre aux Armées* or the *Théâtres du Front* to affect soldiers' thoughts and to firm up morale, particularly while soldiers were in rest (*repos*) areas.

Silver has not, however, exaggerated the intense attention given to civilians' potentially subversive behavior—especially in Paris. The capital city sat in a peculiar spot throughout the war, because of its central role in French politics and culture and its closeness to the army zone. During much of the conflict, although less so in the first year, it held an unstable mix of civilians, soldiers, and foreigners.[21] Once war began, worry over citizens' morale translated into an official distrust of certain places and times, particularly of public gatherings. But this concern was not completely new; authorities, for example, had long watched for seeds of discontent or moral corruption to grow in the fertile spaces of the *cafés-concerts*. The police understood the fluid environment of performance, where improvisation occurred on a nightly basis and where new names and causes became the latest target of musical satire.

What the war called for, however, were propagandistic materials and practices which required irrefutable clarity and didactic messages. After all, one had to know precisely who the enemy was and why one was fighting. The French songs of the *belle époque*, on the contrary, were anything but fixed, and their ambiguities—pauses, ad lib variations or nonsense syllables—posed a threat which had to be eliminated. *Chansonniers'* double entendres also did not suit wartime when loyalty was supposed to be obvious and transparent. In the eyes of officials, the stakes had risen, and the uncertainty of songs became a serious threat.

[2.2] Politics and War Don't Mix

The censors' political goals were most obviously war-related, while their social agenda was more complicated. Not surprisingly, French censors of all media reacted very sensitively to representations of the war: its aims, progress, and participants. Song censorship paralleled other media and supported the broadest government goals. Authorities promoted the war by permitting materials with positive views of soldiers and the High Command, and by limiting criticism.[22] The examiners carefully monitored the treatment of current events and attempted to prevent songs from being too satirical and from interfering with government policy. In one case, the censor vetoed a song which anticipated the Italians' entry into the war in 1915, since the song might have put pressure on a potential ally.[23] Not even patriotically well-intentioned aspersions directed at Rolland Romain, or "those who for Switzerland have departed," could be assured of approval, and Monsieur Martin did not hesitate to question one song because he feared "it was a bit satirical for the Republic."[24] This control of the "political" was to carry into the postwar years; in February 1919, for example, the police chose to ban a song called "le Suffrage Universel" because of what they termed its "inopportune" and "political character."[25] The war had combined these two adjectives making partisan political views no longer appropriate.

Similarly, examiners worked to protect the reputations of political figures and to divert the course of pre-war complaints. An old reproach about the absence of the naked truth (*la Vérité nue*) in Parliament, while naked bodies prevailed on theater stages, became unacceptable, and the President of the Republic could no longer offer to show his "Loupillon," whatever it might be, to a woman.[26] In addition, a ban on most proper names was supposed to keep songs in music halls from directly reprimanding leaders, and when music-hall directors included older, pre-1914 songs on their programs, a slew of deputies' names had to be removed.[27]

Although military officials also kept watch for politically subversive materials, and in particular for those which sounded defeatist or divisive, decentralization and greater overall latitude led to much more political satire in trench songs and newspapers. Audoin-Rouzeau has argued that "the attitude of the military authorities was extremely variable at all levels of the hierarchy" and was both "intermittent" and "pragmatic."[28] As a result, soldiers were permitted to create and hear things civilians could not. One anonymous piece, called simply "Chanson," appeared in the trench newspaper *La Fusée* in November 1916 with a trenchant attack against the neutral powers and the Germans. The lyrics berated the worst bystanders—the Swiss, the Dutch, the Greeks, and of course the Yankees. Such a political denunciation would surely not have reached a Parisian stage.[29] The army's flexibility towards soldiers' complaints reflected government officials' disparate agendas and responsibilities, as well as the difference in audience.

Whereas the civilian censors seemed most edgy about the reputations of civil politicians, possibly because singers and comics had always enjoyed attacking Parisian figures, they also carefully monitored the presentation of the new stars—the military leaders and the strategically vital *poilus* (the name given to the French infantrymen). Composers were welcome to praise or compliment officers' selfless and intelligent leadership, but they could not show a general's vanity or ambition—the honorable "bâton d'maréchal," for instance, was to be earned (*gagner*), not coveted (*viser*).[30] An early version of the popular tune "Ils ne passeront pas" offered admiration for the generals Castelnau, Maunoury, and Joffre; then by 1918 the composers had simply changed the names with Clemenceau now happily sandwiched between Foch and Maréchal Joffre (who by then had been quietly removed from power), with General Pétain appearing as the one who had "freed Alsace and Lorraine."[31] This eulogistic discourse marked a sharp departure from the acrimonious debates of fin-de-siècle France, when the army had been attacked as reactionary and unreliable in its defense of the Republic, and when royalists' celebratory lyrics had defended the military against radical (or Republican) contamination. Somewhat ironically, it was now soldiers at the front who had greater leeway to criticize officers—albeit for a limited audience.

Meanwhile, a rhetorical shift in song lyrics as well as in other media occurred quickly and, in many cases, spontaneously in representations of French soldiers. They proved to be fearless in the face of German weaponry and eager to find glory.[32] Censors contributed to this martial renaissance by forcing significant changes, for instance, in the popular pre-war genre of the *comique-troupier* in which French soldiers had been humorously portrayed as unceasingly naive and even stupid. A song such as "Bon soldat" by Louis Bousquet and Henry Mailfait, which in all likelihood had been written before the war, lost three verses since it made fun of dying for glory.[33] Instead, authorities sought to reinforce proper soldierly behavior. Tunes which sang of soldiers retiring quietly from war with minor wounds or of a friendly encounter between a *poilu* and the Kaiser could not be tolerated.

Within the Parisian musical world, the examiners targeted one other potentially political set of songs, those which were too realist or too rabid. They did not want to provoke public emotions, but instead strove to encourage or to manage "moderate" levels of patriotism, while not allowing room for violent outbursts or "defeatism." In other words, they wanted controlled dedication.[34] In part, this was because French officials could not ignore the lesson of the Franco-Prussian conflict—that war begat social and political upheaval. The management meant constantly patrolling the borders of discourse on such subjects as combat, life in the trenches, the government, and the allies in order to signal what expressions now sat out of bounds. With the inventiveness of popular and mass cultural forms, the censors had to stay alert. Even well-intentioned lyrics, not to mention the most rabid nationalist tunes, could suffer a censor's displeasure. Consequently, despite the seemingly obvious benefits of atrocity propaganda, not all descriptions of German war crimes were approved. In 1914 as a result of reports attributing falling morale to such stories, the Minister of War "asked all prefects to instruct [newspaper] editors 'in the future to avoid detailed descriptions of acts of cruelty committed by the Germans; repeated accounts of this type might have a deleterious effect on the morale of the population. . . . '"[35] The song censors followed suit.

Expressions of grief, distress or anger also had to remain within acceptable limits, according to this policy. A successful war effort required proper public sentiment and deportment, and songs would show the way. Therefore, the song "l'Embusqué" which condemned a mother for encouraged her son to shirk his military duty was defined as "too realistic," in part because, even though criticism of shirkers might have been viewed as beneficial in discouraging unpatriotic behavior, officials worried more about setting off public anger over divisive issues.[36]

Taken all together, the web of rules regarding politics and influential figures aimed to depoliticize public entertainment in the sense of lessening active participation, discussion or division. It was not that political events or ideas were not present; clearly the war was a topic of songs, and political leaders and the allies could be applauded. But the political spectrum was to be covered over, and criticism was carefully contained. The censors' labors also helped maintain the *union sacrée* in political terms. In fact, a joke about how difficult it would be for brawling politicians to preserve the *union sacrée* after the war could not get past the blue pencil.[37] Justified by wartime imperatives, the censor's campaign represented a significant undertaking, since in attacking trenchant satire it sought to eliminate the stock and trade of many singers. It also had important implications for social politics, in that it undermined elements of a popular culture—for example, the political criticism in songs—which had been central to working-class life.

[2.3] Strengthening Cultural Mores—Chapter and Verse

For the authorities, however, to depoliticize or ensure a pro-war stance was not enough. The war also gave them an opportunity to expand earlier efforts to mold the music halls to their tastes and values. This ideological project involved cleaning up language, fostering a discriminating sense of humor, and teaching appropriate behavior. The promotion of "good taste" spread middle-class values and undermined a positive working-class culture, as part of what Pierre Bourdieu would call the "symbolic work of fabrication of groups."[38] This pre-war strategy moved forward, now intricately tied to the war effort. The goal of civilian morale dictated attention to morality.

But how explicit was the class dimension to censorship or the attempt to impose representations? There are some obvious clues which lead one to characterize the overall project as bourgeois. The term "bourgeois" obviously represents a rather broad category, and the censors were only a small portion of the government. But the use of the term is suggested first because the struggle had originated prior to the war and on the part of dominant social groups, and, second because the language of the enterprise reveals a sense of social hierarchy in the need to "raise up," improve, or clean out lower, undesirable sites or habits. More specifically, examiners barred anti-bourgeois sentiments from songs, suppressing references to "nasty landlords" (les mauvais propriétaires), the "bigshots" (les gros), or a song title such as "Bourgeois Rapaciousness" (Rapacité bourgeoise).[39] In the name of the union sacrée, they also intended to efface bitter class divisions both in wartime society and, more remarkably, in French history.

Officials faced a difficult challenge, however, refashioning perceptions of working-class identity. Throughout the long nineteenth century, workers had rallied around lyrics describing the hardship of unemployment or strained relationships with the boss (patron), and these songs represented an integral part of working-class culture.[40] With its pervasiveness, the repertoire could not easily be eliminated. Censors still allowed general descriptions of a harsh daily life, but they erased bitter sentiments or calls for action against a ruling class or against factory owners. One 1912 melody, "Y a qu'le populo!," could evoke the virtues of the working class including their labor and their repopulation, but could not belittle aristocrats as "nothing other than / sons of ragpickers / grooms [thief in slang] or bootmakers / whom Napoleon created."[41] Gaston Montéhus and Aristide Bruant's repertoires, both of which had taken up the lower classes' cause in the pre-war years, were carefully reviewed and often modified. Whereas police had long worried about subversive intentions and the provocation of dangerous behavior, now the examiners had free rein to work on the details.

All of this depended on rewriting French history, favoring some episodes and excising others. Predictably, the censors placed great significance on revanchism, or the French objective of recapturing the lost provinces of Alsace and Lorraine, which a whole spate of songs from the nineteenth century fed. In this nationalist depiction, all classes were unified and encouraged to fight—especially the workers.[42] Representations of the French Revolution proved to be particularly problematic, especially because of the fear that war sparked revolution and popular insurrection. The best scenario from a censor's point of view shrewdly praised the tough and stalwart Parisians, without recalling their role in storming the Bastille. In the song "la Baïonnette" by A. Montagard, for example, singers feted the beloved weapon for its many achievements including the great battle of Valmy, but could not honor the bayonet's assistance the "bon peuple en sabots" in getting rid of the "ancien régime."[43] In another song, the popular objective of fighting for "egalité" had to be changed to "la patrie," neatly reflecting the primacy of nationalism.[44]

Moreover, the censors' efforts to bolster the bourgeois position were not limited to explicitly political topics of revolution and class conflict. A far more sensitive struggle focused on cultural mores (*moeurs*), or standards of behavior in the broadest sense.[45] Taste was a site of class struggle as aesthetics were socially constructed and as certain language, gestures and practices were defined as legitimate and others as vulgar or immoral.[46] Take, for example, how Monsieur Martin explained his objections to the song "Rapacité bourgeoise": "Even the title, which seems to encompass a whole category of citizens under the same uncivil label, appears too violent. The song is not itself obscene, but rude (*grossière*) in tone . . . ."[47] While the censor was certainly unhappy with the portrayal of individuals with such a clear class identity, he was also bothered by the song's "somewhat coarse (*gros*) effect." Being immersed in a long, deadly struggle did not permit civilians to lose their civility.

If one wished to encourage the correct values and to raise cultural taste, how did one begin? Most comprehensively, it was a matter of defining higher standards. In a January 1915 memo concerning a program at the *Théâtre Belge*, Mr. Martin worked to do just that. First, he noted the overall high "quality" of the schedule, then he summarized the cases of crude or stupid lyrics: "This program has a literary and moral quality *somewhat superior* to the average. Out of 36 numbers, 15 are proposed without reservation for approval. These are patriotic songs, comic songs referring to the war or sentimental songs. Seven are suggested without reservation for refusal of the visa, as being coarse or indecent."[48] He then asked the prefect for assistance in evaluating a third set which included "sentimental songs with a hint of triviality or ribaldry, or humorous songs which, although decent, disarm the most severe judge with their stupidity. One among them . . . has absolutely no intelligible meaning." The best examples, in Martin's opinion, exhibited a mix of morality, erudition and patriotism, assuming recognizable norms for all three. The worst, while not obviously unpatriotic or defeatist, were condemned as indecent, or simply too idiotic.[49] In addition, part of raising previously deficient standards included modifying audiences' sense of humor.[50]

The mission to reform audiences' sensibilities involved two interrelated tasks: the suppression of "popular" language and the elimination of explicit sexual de-

11

scriptions and lewd double entendres.[51] In the first case, "vulgar" language was purged. Terms, which might otherwise be considered colorful, earthy vernacular, were deemed improper, unbecoming (*malséant*), stupid or crude (*grossière*). Descriptions of body parts, or scatological humor were also no longer acceptable. Words such as *fesses* (buttocks), *faire pipi* (urinating), *miches* (breasts) or any use of *queue* (tail) drew forth the blue pencil.[52] If the censors disliked references to body parts, then erotic parts were even worse. Having a singer croon about "the dazzling breasts where one could get tipsy" or "a mouth where kisses dozed" was too much.[53]

Much of what the censors objected to involved some sort of transgressive behavior, which they defined as immodest and inappropriate. Audiences were not to have the opportunity to laugh at accidental substitutions of food and excrement or chamberpots and tea.[54] Name calling also became "unseemly," eliminating such age-old, useful insults as *cochon* (pig, bastard), *salaud* (bastard, swine), *couillon* (cretin, idiot) or *charogne* (slut, bitch—even when they referred to William II.[55] Here, censors were not just removing "colorful" language, they were also undermining a traditional political tactic from the world of popular culture. Before the war, *cafés-concerts* had offered an arena for social politics and now authorities moved against both the political idiom of the lower classes and any expressions of conflict.

Even more widespread and troubling was the ubiquitous sexual humor of the French *cafés-concerts* which heavily taxed the censors' crusade to promote decency. Earning the nickname "la pudique Anastasie," the censors repeatedly designated songs as indecent (*indécente*), "licentious" (*libertine*), or smutty (*grivoiserie*).[56] With great ingenuity, however, composers devised a wide variety of double entendres using everyday objects and activities, for instance, "his bird" and her "cage," musical instruments like accordeons or castagnettes, or women cultivated like gardens. They also used nonsense syllables or pauses at crucial moments, as we saw in the earlier example where playing cymbals at the right moment changed an innocent verse into an offensive one.

Because of the use of double entendres, suggestive gaps or gestures, examiners often found themselves fighting semiotic uncertainty and silliness at the same time, and time after time, censors worked to eliminate ambiguities. As one newspaper censor Paul Allard remarked, officials fought a running battle against "the allusions and the innuendoes"; the censor "cut even *the intention* of having an ambiguous rhyme heard . . . in the well-known game of slippery rhymes."[57] Many cases obviously rested on the censors' understanding of the audience, or their fashioning of an audience's sexual *imaginaire*. At times, examiners believed that even if they themselves could not think of the obscene interpretation, the audiences' skills were even more prodigious. Nothing could be taken at face value. What had been considered simply silly or funny before the war was now judged disrespectful and damaging for morale. The French cause was weakened by a distracting or subversive immorality.

The censors had one last important task—to get songs to teach proper deportment; after all, this was a time when one's appearance or behavior had political, as well as social, implications. We have already seen their concern with suitable expressions of grief or anger, and in the case of Henri Moreau's song, with which we began, the offending couple's defiance of the air-raid rules did not help Moreau's case. With its pencils, the government tried to draw a clear line between respectable or patriotic behavior and improper or treasonous conduct, and songs provided a helpful forum because lyrics constantly addressed everyday life. In just one example, examiners blocked a song which celebrated alcoholic beverages and complained about the banning of absinthe.[58] As censors began their war work, they moved to buttress the bourgeois marriage and endorse repopulation while quashing representations of prostitution, adultery and other examples of gratuitous sex.

They hoped to reinforce the sanctity of marriage by discouraging adultery which they tied directly to morale—since soldiers would suffer if their wives betrayed them.[59] This bourgeois, familial ideal included clearly conservative gender roles with dutiful wives and hard-working, virile husbands. Not surprisingly, a pre-war song in which a French soldier had tried to learn the "song of love" and could not get higher than "do re mi" was *non visée*.[60] Since examiners did not like explicit descriptions of sex or sexual parts, allusions to the size or shape of male genitals were banned along with hidden references to castration or masturbation—popular pre-war double entendres.[61] Interestingly, as part of the encouragement of family, and the strengthening of civilian morale, the censors worked to protect the reputation of women. Thus many older lyrics which had seriously criticized women's nature and had expressed violence against women were eliminated.[62]

As should be clear by now, the censors were rarely comfortable with explicit sexual scenes regardless of the moral content, but they were strictest on gratuitous sex. This put a serious crimp in the pre-war repertoires, since performers could no longer dwell on lost virginities, seductions, or creative striptease. "Voilà la Parisienne!" which had received a visa in November 1904 met with a different response once the war had reset the semiotic parameters. The censors reacted with powerful strokes against verses which described Parisian women's erotic undressing or calm explanations of how they had lost their virginity before their wedding night.[63]

This management of morality on stage turned out to be quite difficult and complicated, since, despite all their efforts, the censors were confronted with thousands of popular representations which associated women's sexual benevolence with raising soldiers' morale. These wartime songs played off of the pain of separation and the loneliness of trench life, and made sex a compensation or reward for fighting. Here, the censors' pre-war and wartime objectives diverged, and the savvy *café-concert* veterans knew how to adapt the many modes of eroticism in popular culture to gain approvals of their songs. The most virtuous erotic scenario had soldiers on leave meeting and marrying eligible women.[64] And examiners could support lyrics about prostitutes who were nice to soldiers, were then rehabilitated and married a *poilu*. Overall, the censors found it far easier to veto song lyrics with questionable morality when the context had nothing to do with the war. But these same situations reappeared in songs about the *poilus'* leaves and were endorsed.[65]

The topic of repopulation proved to be especially troublesome. Examiners found themselves caught between wanting to further the cause of nuptials and impeccable moral virtue or promoting procreative activities whatever the moral costs.[66] Moreover, the war had made the government efforts to advance the pronatalist campaign even more urgent.[67] In most instances, references to soldiers going home on leave to make (*fabriquer*) the class of '35 or '36 posed no problems, since "On travaille pour la République" (One works for the Republic).[68]

The Army did not suffer this contradiction, since military officials readily accepted obscene language and sexual ribaldry in marching songs, at troop concerts, or in trench newspapers as a means of intensifying proper aggressive attitudes. As one memo from the military archives explained, although directors of rest camps were responsible for supervising the content and performance of songs, they were not to be overzealous, since soldiers were men, not "little girls."[69] Older regimental refrains had often joked about soldiers, pretty women and drinking, and pre-war military teachings recommended a repertoire of bawdy songs and broad jokes (*gaudrioles*) for morale.[70] Soldiers themselves also quickly turned to creating their own erotic song texts and musical revues, as well as sexually explicit trench memorabilia.[71] Thus, jokes about efforts at repopulation flourished along with lyrics describing the provocative possibilities of what *marraines* (the wartime penpals) had to offer soldiers. Given the army's focus on soldiers' morale, it willingly promoted a discourse on virility to create vigorous combatants.[72] This put greater pressure on Parisian officials with regard to pre-war tunes and composers creating and sending material to soldiers.

[2.4] Historical Precedents

As I have argued, World War One did not invent the elites' fears of popular entertainment nor their attempts to reform it. Although the French had had a very long history of Rabelasian language and humor, the culture also had a more recent record of righteousness or anxiety towards it.[73] France had experienced repressive political and cultural censorship up to 1881, except for brief revolutionary periods, and continuing fears of political unrest and sedition were deeply rooted in the events of the 1870s.[74] When the Third Republic's liberalized regime established greater political liberties in 1881, the surveillance system for cultural materials and performance remained intact. According to one historian, "the government," assisted by "prominent bourgeois residents and politicians," "gave force to bourgeois sensibilities by censoring songs and plays that were too politically threatening or too racy."[75]

This campaign had not attacked singing or performance per se, nor was it strictly a negative response to modernity. Officials had actually recognized singing as an effective pedagogic method and embraced singing's multi-faceted nature which could encourage memory and literacy, while it instilled discipline and the correct ideology.[76] But not all singing was equally salutary, and government officials and bourgeois commentators of fin-de-siècle France showed great concern over the "contamination" of French music by the *cafés-concerts* and over the stubborn persistence of "popular" songs.[77] Eugen Weber's work, especially, has highlighted the Third Republic's project to refine tastes by getting rid of "doggerel" as an entree into acquiring wider cultural breeding and good taste as well as the correct political views.[78] In the end, a cultural or civilizing agenda with strong social overtones reinforced the political pedagogy.

By the early twentieth century, however, the intense fear of subversive politics had been gradually outweighed by an increasing anxiety over French citizens' morality. And the pre-war years had witnessed countless battles over pornography and definitions of obscenity.[79] More specifically, Susanna Barrows has argued that "by the closing decades of the nineteenth century, the great fear of politics disappeared from the culture of the cafe; in its fading shadow grew the great fear of sexual license." As the government took increasing steps to regulate "erotic pleasure" and expand surveillance of the suspicious spaces, it also "attacked the ribald and rabelaisian spirit long associated with the Gauls."[80] Thus, although there were calls for the dismantling of censorship, many supporters had argued for the need to protect citizens, especially women and children, from the vile effects of immoral songs, dances, posters and jokes. It was this anxiety over public morality which was absorbed into the wartime discourse. Moreover, the prevailing atmosphere in the Great War stretched the police's mandate, resulting in stricter and more inflexible rules than had been used prior to 1914. Since all songs, old and new, had to be submitted, many pre-war pieces which had received a visa before 1906 could not pass through the wartime matrix of values.

[2.5] Supporting the War, Supporting Themselves— The Composers' Response

In the end, how well did this system work? Did composers and performers readily conform to it? Clearly, the industry recognized the government's agenda and cooperated—more or less. But the negotiation of changes formed an integral feature of the censorship system, caused in part by the recurring ambiguities and by performers' ability to circumvent the rules.[81] Most songwriters, however, showed a great willingness to modify the texts, gestures or costumes according to the censor's instructions, and continually proclaimed their high level of patriotism while also worrying about their livelihood and dependence on a specific repertoire. At times, the economic realities of the industry led to insistent dickering over visas, especially because the public closely identified many performers with their repertoire and losing specific numbers hurt individuals.[82]

A common tactic used by composers was to attach the adjective "patriotique" to their songs when they sought leniency. Paul Weil, in his fight for "Ferdinand de Bulgarie," questioned the prefectoral decision by highlighting his own fundamental contribution to the war effort: "Our manner of fighting certainly does not have the value of that of the young men who have the good fortune, because of their age, to be at the front; but the benefit of our songs cannot be disputed as each day our brave wounded men applaud us in the hospitals of Paris where we do our duty. Even in the workshops, where we go to give a little distraction to the courageous wives and daughters of those mobilized, our singing has the honor of being appreciated . . ."[83] One could hardly find a clearer defense of the music-hall industry's self-appointed role. The industry had come of age at the turn of the century, but had still faced criticism. Once the war began, its members sought to achieve respectability through patriotic contributions.

Along with promoting their own potential role in the war effort, many songwriters appear to have understood the opposition, as posited, between patriotism and obscenity. In Jean Bastia's argument over his song "Zeppelinades," he found it "intolerable to think" that the censor had confused his patriotic work with other indecent materials. The composer lashed out specifically at the examiner who had compared his work "to some empty production in a *café-concert* . . . with its base goal of pleasing the public by throwing out an obscene word," and who had thus done an "injustice" to Bastia's "artistic conscience." Bastia, who ran the cabaret "le Perchoir" and was a central figure in the Parisian music-hall world, applauded the censors' goals, claiming that he too had "the keenest desire to see the level of art and integrity raised" in the "entertainment halls" (*salles de spectacle*).[84]

On the other hand, one songwriter, a Monsieur Pinel, tried a different tactic which still answered to the prevailing atmosphere of cultural chauvinism—he justified his song by calling it "*gauloise*" and pointing to the French tradition of humor. This term's use highlighted the blurred line between obscenity and earthiness which had bedeviled government debates before the war, and writers, performers, and editors were well aware of the controversial grey area's existence.[85] Just as Pinel tried to convince the prefect that his lyrics had not reached the level of "suggestiveness of many other authorized songs," Moreau, the composer of "Réveil nocturne" with whom we began, argued that the censors' ruling seemed to be more stringent than the pre-1906 regime.[86] Nevertheless, both Pinel and Moreau were insisting on the relative purity of their "modest" songs.

The authorities' willingness to negotiate signified a certain assurance, since throughout the war a greater public consensus existed in support of cultural censorship than of political. An outcry against interference in newspaper reporting on political grounds began almost immediately in late 1914, and the government struggled to defend its position. No such campaign against official prerogatives grew up around the censorship of songs, musical revues or postcards.[87] Thus even as political censorship eased up in late 1917 with the arrival of Georges Clemenceau as Prime Minister and Minister of War, the control of cultural products and performance continued.[88]

At the same time, following the severe unrest of the army mutinies in May and June of 1917 and with General Pétain in command, the army tightened its rules and surveillance. In June, for example, Pétain ordered the confiscation of all copies of the tune "la Terre Nationale" following the arrest of two colporteurs near the front. In this case, the song had been printed in Paris and then hidden between "nationalist songs" "with a patriotic imprint." He directed that "an active surveillance be exercised by the Censor on songs and other printed materials being peddled, which under the cover or appearance of patriotic songs, constitute a mode of pacifist propaganda, if not the incitement to disobedience."[89] An itinerant singer was also arrested in Montbéliard near the front, with an inventory which included the song "Tragique Ballade des Tranchées" which depicted the soldiers' desperate feelings in the spring of 1917 and criticized official propaganda.[90] Troops were punished for singing the "Internationale" as well as other subversive songs as part of the 1917 mutinies.[91] The soldiers' own popular culture had allowed expressions of dissent to grow by 1917 and forced the Army to clamp down. From then on the army moved more in line with the homefront's censorship practices and objectives. A united government went on the offensive with Clemenceau and Pétain working together. Beginning with the repression of the mutinies, the Army hunted down subversive revolutionary ideas and defeatism at the front, and Clemenceau initiated a vigorous campaign against *embusqués* (shirkers) and defeatism on the home front. In contrast to the military, however, the Parisian censors had benefited from familiarity with the ritual of cultural censorship and a ready legal structure—their quick response in 1914 was hardly a surprise, nor was it negligible. It is clear that police, songwriters and performers all recognized the potential power and malleability of song lyrics in performances. One sees a responsiveness to the goals and a willingness on the part of the *artistes* to follow the guidelines, if only to keep their repertoires intact—all of which also suggests severe self-censorship. Silence, however, is difficult, if not impossible, to measure.

[2.6] Conclusion

As the system in Paris moved smoothly along in late 1915 and early 1916, government reports confidently claimed that "dramatic adaptations of our national hymns at the theaters, and patriotic songs or satires of our enemies at the music halls, have served to sustain the public;" "in each case, they [the police] have almost always succeeded in eliminating any licentiousness in the works and unwholesomeness in the performances."[92] The same report, however, noted that as management changed hands, some music-hall directors had not felt bound to an earlier agreement (of November 1914) between police and directors and had "systematically organized shows without elevation and without patriotism." This telling comment hinted at continual haggling. Techniques of resistance remained, as songwriters and performers kept pushing at the boundaries of satire and the "appropriate."

Despite the fact that the entrepreneurs often tried the censors' patience, one should not lose sight of their pro-war zeal. Having focused too narrowly on "official," or government-produced propaganda, WWI scholars have failed to appreciate how widespread and compelling "unofficial" efforts were. Much of the ingenuity and energy for promoting the war on the home front came from private individuals and commercial interests including entertainers. This should hardly be surprising if one understands the vitality of modernity in the *belle époque*. But if individuals out paced the government in their enthusiastic expressions, one cannot discount the role French officials played in dictating the terms of discourse in the public and commercial sphere. Officials in WWI set the ground rules which defined the borders of appropriate language and sentiments for soldiers and civilians, and at times reined in unofficial ventures. The project also extended past determining what could or could not be said in order to dictate proper behaviors.

Obviously, much of the state's power derived from earlier nineteenth-century developments as did the bourgeois project of purification. But scholars have often assumed the government knew what it was doing from the war's start. Examining how the enemy was represented shows us this was not always the case. A flood of anti-German representations appeared at the start of the war, but officials soon discovered that too much nationalist ferocity or zealousness was possible. They learned how to conduct a total war both militarily and politically as they went along.

Defining the war as "total" gave liberal, democratic states such as France greater powers to control the public sphere which in this case involved pursuing older social agendas. As taste was constructed socially and politically, "patriotism" acted as the yardstick. The operations of the social struggle became more explicit because of the extensive wartime powers and the sense of urgency. The war also allowed more rigid standards because officials, and others, argued that morally upright citizens

18

made for stronger civilians. They could also insist that cleaning up *French* popular culture contributed to the strength of the national fabric.

Moreover, just as *fin-de-siècle* modernity fed the pro-war cultural energy, older criticisms of culture came into play. In Germany, as censors carried into the war a broad suspicion or dislike of mass entertainment, they attacked it as foolish, immoral, wasteful and as "unseemly frivolity."[93] French officials came from a different cultural matrix. They believed in the excellent possibilities offered by singing and entertainment for improving the morale of civilians and soldiers. A suitable patriotic song could create cohesion and hope, rallying people and sustaining their energy. Authorities combated the "unseemly," but not necessarily the "frivolous," since some offerings were judged good clean entertainment. The government made itself the arbiter in deciding how far such efforts went.

In the end, the process and goals of censorship produced essentially conservative effects and help to explain why the French "stayed the course," as well as how they experienced the war. We should not underestimate the overall effects of depoliticizing vital public spaces at this moment. Censorship put authorities in a more secure position by dampening political discourse, discouraging questions and lessening popular interference. To understand the French experience during the war, one can not just ask why there was so little defeatism or why the French did not give up.[94] We must also consider the lack of criticism and the slow rate of change in political and military strategies. Censorship clearly contributed to both.

Morale and Sexual Morality Among British Troops in the First World War

David Simpson

The assumption that the upper levels of the British military hierarchy, in seeking to maintain military morale, approved of and even encouraged extra-marital sexual intercourse by soldiers, is a common one among historians. Indeed, it is considered so self-evidently true by those writing on topics concerning the British army and sexual activity that it is never supported by evidence, but merely asserted as support for other, larger arguments. One historian has written that senior British officers "as a caste regarded army morale as contingent on sexual activity."[1] Another, writing on the controversy over military access to regulated French brothels during the First World War, has written that denying such access "would have defied the conventional wisdom, which held that an army's morale was dependent on frequent sexual contact and its health, on the medically certified brothel."[2] This assumption about the British military leadership is often part of a more general one about the nature of military masculinity: that military men, always and everywhere, associate frequent heterosexual sex with virility and, therefore, with military prowess. This assumption begins to fall apart, however, when one looks at evidence about the views of sexual morality among the highest ranks of the British military. Depending on the historical period investigated, historians' conventional wisdom on this topic is at best a half truth; at worst it is entirely incorrect. By the first decades of the twentieth century, if not earlier, it is likely that views of sexual morality among the British military leadership differed little from those of most upper and middle class British civilians, and that, even during the First World War, they could be described as typically "Victorian."

Although the image of the dissolute and promiscuous regular soldier, recruited from the dregs of the working class, was familiar enough to nineteenth century Britons to be a stereotype, there had been, since the 1850s, a number of missionary movements, largely organized by evangelicals, aimed at improving Tommy Atkins' health, living conditions, and morality. A particular concern of those who sought to reform the army in the aftermath of the Crimean war, both within and without the military, was with social, medical, and other non-military conditions in the army. By ameliorating soldiers' environments, by assuring them of clean, well-lit barracks, and access to wholesome entertainment, invigorating sport, and religious counsel, even the most humbly born soldier, it was hoped, could be transformed into a model of British virtue. Improved morals, in turn, would make better soldiers, and, ultimately, an army that could be assured of victory.[3] By the early twentieth century, although the old stereotype of military wantons persisted in some quarters, the British Tommy for most Britons was no longer one of the nation's unpleasant embarrassments, but a symbol of the vitality of the British imperial race. With the outbreak of the Great War in 1914, and the rush of thousands of volunteers to the colors, this desire to see the British soldier as representing Britain's best was only increased.

It was thus with some dismay that many Britons greeted evidence that, from very early on in the war, Tommy had reverted to his more debauched past. The first indication to reach the public's notice of a deterioration of morals was the large number of young women who found their way to garrison towns and to the Channel port cities where soldiers embarked for France. Some of these women were professional prostitutes. Most, it seems, were not, but were simply teenage girls, some as young as 14, who were attracted by the excitement, and the soldiers, they found there. Many attributed the sexual liaisons between these girls and soldiers to misplaced war enthusiasm. By "going with" soldiers, the young women were "doing their bit" for the war. In their way, these girls and young women were simply twentieth-century versions of the camp followers who could be found in the train of any significant congregation of soldiers before they had been reformed away in the late nineteenth century.

Later on in the war, London became notorious both for solicitation of soldiers by street prostitutes and for casual sexual encounters between soldiers and civilian women. London was the most popular destination for soldiers on leave from the western front, especially for colonial soldiers. Leave trains were said to be met by swarms of young women searching for potential companions, and many Londoners complained that Hyde Park had become an open-air brothel. If these were not evidence enough to Britons that their soldiers were fornicating in unacceptably large numbers, the rate of venereal diseases (considered a direct measure of illicit sexual activity) among members of the British Expeditionary Force was.[4]

The First World War was not the first time that the problem of solicitation of soldiers by prostitutes had come to the notice of the British public. The Contagious Diseases Acts of the 1860s had sought to decrease the rate of venereal infection among soldiers and sailors by setting up a system of regulation and medical inspection of prostitutes in certain garrison and port towns. Prostitutes in these towns found to be infected with a venereal disease could detained in hospital for up to nine months while a cure was attempted. Women's organizations opposed the Acts, arguing that they represented a legal double standard, holding women accountable for the spread of disease while letting the men involved go free. Social purity organizations blasted the Acts as a medically ineffective state regulation of vice. A twenty year campaign against the Acts by both finally succeeded in getting them suspended from operation and then completely abolished.[5] The complementary arguments of the feminists and the evangelicals worked, in part, because they corresponded with the movement to reform the morals and social conditions of soldiers. Both groups seemed to argue that soldiers should be held to the same legal and moral standards as every one else.

It is in the renewed debate over soldiers, prostitutes, and venereal disease, this time during the Great War, that contemporary attitudes toward soldiers' sexuality—by both civilians and the military—can most easily be read. In discussing the root causes of venereal disease, civilians in and outside of government expressed not just dismay over soldiers' fornication, but confusion about why they were doing it. Temptation by prostitutes was the most common explanation. The number of women soliciting soldiers on the streets of London became a scandal that elicited letters to the Times, questions in Parliament, denunciation by the Archbishop of Canterbury, and discord between the British government and the governments of Canada, Australia, and New Zealand, whose soldiers were believed to be at greatest risk in London because of their higher pay relative to British soldiers. The constant invitations to sex by these women, many observers believed, tested the self-control of even the most chaste soldier. Loss of self-control, in fact, found its way into almost every musing about the moral failings of soldiers.

The evidence given in 1920–1 to an independent commission on the prevention of venereal disease in Britain is perhaps the most frank and detailed account of the public debate over soldiers and venereal disease of the time. The transcript of the testimony to the commission is witness to the contemporary centrality of self-control in the determination of sexual morality. The commission had among its members or witnesses the foremost medical men and women of the time interested in the problem of V.D., as well as prominent clergymen and military officers. Despite a wide variation in views about how best to prevent the spread of venereal diseases, the members and witnesses seem to agree almost entirely in their presuppositions about the nature of male sexuality. Although many of the members of the commission acknowledged a wide variation in sexual temperament among men, "one man is virile, and another like stone," as one of the members put it, the "sexual instinct" was nearly universal in men, seething beneath the surface, and kept in check only with effort, practice, and education. The following exchange between Sir Alfred Pearce Gould, of the commission, and Dr. Charles Gibbs, surgeon to the London Lock Hospitals, is typical:

Gould: "Have you any evidence to support the view that chastity or unchastity of man and woman depends upon their self-control?

Gibbs: "I should say it is entirely dependent on it."

Gould: "It is not temperament, but self-control?"

Gibbs: "Self-control and education entirely."[6]

Both men and women were thus in need of self-control to check their passions, but it was, as several witnesses pointed out, easier for women because their sexual instinct was weaker than men's. Some claimed that a woman's sexual appetite scarcely existed before marriage, at which time it was brought to the surface. Even after marriage, women's passions could go dormant for long periods of time if there were no outside stimuli to arouse them. Men, with stronger natural drives, were less able to submerge their sexual passions. Any undue temptation could thus cause a man to lose his unstable veneer of civilized behavior. This perceived difference between men and women goes some way to explaining the tendency of commentators to blame the women involved instead of men when discussing illicit sex by soldiers: women should know better, they believed, than to provoke the sexual beast that lurked in the heart of nearly every man.

There were several things other than temptation that could thwart the development or maintenance of self-control. Drink and drunkenness were often seen as the most important of all allies of temptation. The hypothetical scenario most commonly described by those trying to explain soldierly fornication featured a soldier who meant to keep straight, but had one drink too many, lost his self-control, and fell victim to a mercenary temptress. Lectures to soldiers on the dangers of sexually transmitted diseases nearly always contained warnings that drunkenness was the first step to careless fornication which then, inevitably, according to the warnings, led to venereal disease. Worries about drunkenness among soldiers and its probable end in V.D. was, in part, the motivation behind the restriction of public house hours in Britain during the war. Similarly, Lord Kitchener, early on in the war, issued a public plea for civilians to refrain from the alcoholic "treating" of soldiers. The American army, later on in the war, was so convinced of the connection between intoxication, sex, and venereal disease, that any soldier returning to camp in an intoxicated condition was given emergency prophylactic treatment to prevent the development of V.D.[7]

There were others at the time, however, who questioned the necessary connection between drink and fornication. Colonel L. W. Harrison, the Royal Army Medical Corps' senior expert in venereal diseases during the war, claimed that a large proportion of those in venereal hospitals were, in fact, teetotalers. They amounted to 34% of the venereal cases in one military hospital.[8] Another R.A.M.C. officer attributed only 11.7 per cent of a sample of 886 venereal cases to the influence of alcohol.[9] The popular association of drink and sex, however, was probably something more than simply an expression of contemporary anxieties about loss of self-control. That drunken soldiers often engaged in fornication while on leave is undoubted; that drink was the sole reason they did so is another question. Drink and sex were probably so strongly associated, even if there was no necessary causality between them, because they were both activities soldiers traditionally engaged in while on leave.

Self-control could be similarly undermined by dwelling on impure thoughts, contemplating one's genitals excessively, associating with depraved characters, or by being bored and desiring stimulation. Keeping soldiers' minds and bodies chastely occupied was the prime reason behind moves, both before and during the war, to provide improved access to "wholesome recreation," for soldiers. In keeping soldiers' concentration on sport or education, they would have no opportunity to be misled by impure mental processes. A correspondent to the *British Medical Journal* in 1917 provided one pseudo-medical explanation of the way in which thought alone could lead to loss of sexual self-control: "The imagination can summon glands into activity, and, as a reaction, the glands charged with secretion can stimulate the mind's activity in certain directions. This is the foundation on which rests the moral objection to suggestive books, posters, entertainments, and such like."[10]

The strength of a man's sexual self-control could also, according to many explanations, vary according to his social class. Whereas men of the upper and middle classes were considered capable of developing the requisite self-control to remain chaste, if necessary, many believed most working-class men lacked this capacity. Environmental factors were often used to explain this discrepancy: the close quarters and lack of privacy of most working class homes meant that working-class men got an early and decidedly unromantic introduction to sex. Poverty, hardship, and poor education could also thwart the normal development of self-control. Some believed the poor and working class to be hereditarily incapable of chastity; their resulting over-population both a symptom and cause of their class status.

Because of the fragile nature of male sexual self-control, education of both youth and soldiers about the dangers of sex would thus have to tread a careful line, with enough information to clearly spell out the risks without being explicit enough to engender dangerous desires. Those opposed to making condoms and other forms of prophylaxis available to soldiers in order to prevent the spread of V.D.,[11] claimed that the very knowledge that such devices were available would tend to promote illicit intercourse. In the army in particular, this thinking went, official sanction of prophylactics would make men think that fornication was acceptable and was even expected of them. One private physician in giving evidence to the Special Commission on Venereal Disease claimed that several young soldiers suffering from sexually transmitted diseases had come to him and insisted that they would not have gone wrong if they hadn't been assured that prophylactics would make them safe. This claim, however, was met with some skepticism among the commission's members. In fact, for every witness to the commission claiming that knowledge of prophylaxis was dangerous, there was one who believed that increased knowledge of the dangers of promiscuous sex and the ways to prevent infection would instead instill greater sexual caution.

Sexual morality, then, was constructed not of denying the existence of sexual passions, as the stereotype of Victorian and Edwardian views of sex would have it,[12] but their control by the higher faculties. Through mental and spiritual training, the base, animalistic drives of sex could be thwarted. "By education," as one of the commission members stated, there could be produced "such a veneration for the opposite sex as will lift them from sexual intercourse on to a different plane."[13] The appeal of many moral campaigners, and others who sought to impress the young about sexual continence, was to the young Briton's sense of chivalry. Moral strength and self-control had the same basis, according to their view, as the military strength of the medieval knight. One can see this equation of military and moral qualities in the proliferation of medieval, knightly imagery in late nineteenth and early twentieth century boys' didactic literature, including the writings of Lord Baden-Powell, the founder of the Boy Scouts. This view of man, as both angel and beast, "an intelligent being mounted on a spirited horse," as one writer put it,[14] may seem out of place in the supposedly libertine 1920s. Indeed, although after the unexpected brutality of the war overt references to medieval knighthood had diminished, the image of manliness and gentlemanliness had changed very little. The belief that chivalry and self-control were the essence of a gentleman expressed, for example, by the members of the Special Committee on Venereal Disease in 1920, seems little different than one that would have been held 50 or 60 years before. It is some ways more strict, since it is clear that the commission members would ideally hold all British men to this standard of morality, not just the supposedly educable middle and upper classes.

There is also a consensus among the commission members and witnesses, even among those most willing to countenance the widespread distribution of prophylactics to curb the spread of venereal diseases, that fornication is inherently injurious to society at large. "I think it is a great disaster to the nation, to any nation," testified Manchester's chief medical official, "to have general promiscuous intercourse."[15] Even Ettie Rout, the founder of the New Zealand Volunteer Sisterhood, who would greet A.N.Z.A.C. soldiers arriving on leave in Paris with prophylactics and information about regulated brothels, called "promiscuous relationship . . . entirely wrong and anti-social."[16] The actual mechanism by which extra-marital intercourse could cause the downfall of society is much more often assumed than described. J. G. Adami, a Canadian military venereologist, comes close to offering an explanation in arguing that if the family is the basic unit of society, and extra-marital intercourse damages the family, then fornication is anti-social. The dilemma for Adami was that man's sexual appetite, which, according to him was naturally polygamous, and which "the individual in his heart of hearts knows to be in itself natural and desirable," had not yet adapted itself to man's social needs.[17] That contradictions exist between what social codes demand and what the individual desires is evident in many commentators, like Adami, on sexual promiscuity. Many lament that the lag between the age of sexual maturity and the time of realistic economic opportunity for marriage was so great. This unfortunate state of the world leads some to believe that the only moral solution would be to develop state-sponsored provisions that would make early marriage more economically and socially viable. Others, holding this hope to be unrealistic, urge, as Adami puts it, the end of "the old regime of silence, concealment and taboo" about sex and venereal diseases, and the pragmatic distribution of prophylactic knowledge to ameliorate the worst excesses of the period between sexual and economic maturity.[18]

The first decades of the twentieth century were a period of great anxiety about all questions surrounding reproduction, including venereal disease and contraception, not just in Britain, but throughout Europe and North America. What is revealed in the public debates on these topics are fears about the physical strength of nations, based on the quantity and quality of their population, and anxieties about national weakness, under-population, and degeneration. Those who expressed these fears can generally be divided into two complementary groups: those who saw the threat to the nation from promiscuous intercourse as primarily a moral threat, and those who saw it as a threat to the nation's physical strength. For those concerned with Britain's moral strength, extra-marital intercourse, even without the transmission of V.D., lead inevitably to the deterioration of the nation's moral tone which, in turn, would lead to both a loss of spiritual superiority against the country's rivals and, eventually, a national physical deterioration. The other group differed in their arguments more in emphasis than in substance. For them, it was the nation's physical strength that was undermined by promiscuous intercourse, since it produced venereal disease, which damaged not only the reproductive capacity of its initial victims, but, in the case of syphilis, could be passed on to a succeeding generation.[19] Many, especially those influenced by the study of eugenics, also worried that those most likely to engage in promiscuous intercourse, and thus the most likely to produce out-of-wedlock births, were members of the least mentally and physically fit section of the population. Not all of those who warned against "degeneration" were motivated by sinister eugenic fears about the nation's racial fitness, however. Many expressed deep social concerns about the ravages of venereal disease and out-of-wedlock births, particularly among the British working class, and wished to ameliorate the suffering caused by them.

It was thus in the interest of society and the state to discourage fornication, particularly among its soldiers, who represented the cream of its young manhood, and were physically the elite of the race. For many in Britain, as elsewhere in Europe, the Great War was more than just a battle between armed states, but was a struggle among entire peoples, or, as they were termed at the time, "races." Descriptions of this could take on social Darwinist overtones, in which the war was a struggle for the survival of the fittest combatant nation. In this kind of struggle, the entire physical and moral strength of the nation was called upon to be mobilized. Although pro-natalist sentiment was rarely as explicit in Britain as it was in wartime France, there is a sense among the utterances and writings of many British commentators that the sexual capacity of Britons, particularly Britain's soldiers, needed to be mobilized along with their bodies. British soldiers needed to remain morally and physically clean to assure the strength of the nation during the present crisis and to assure the continued strength of future generations. Extra-marital sex by soldiers, and the possible racial degeneration that might be the ultimate outcome of it, was thus not a personal choice with no repercussions beyond those involved, but was, instead, a kind of pathology, even a kind of treason.

At first glance it would appear that the attitude toward extra-marital sex by soldiers was indeed very different among the British military leadership. Brothels regulated by the French government were made available to British soldiers in France from the beginning of the war, and many, although not all, commanding officers encouraged their patronage. The long lines and rowdiness of the "red light" brothels for enlisted men, and the more decorous "blue light" brothels for officers were familiar sights to members of the British Expeditionary Force, if First World War memoirs are to be believed. When soldiers' access to these brothels became a scandal in Britain in the spring of 1918, and there were public calls for them to be declared out of bounds for soldiers, the military leadership was almost unanimous in their desire to keep them within limits for their troops. They greatly resented the intrusion of civilian churchmen, purity campaigners and politicians into an area which they considered their domain.[20] The Contagious Diseases Acts of half a century before had been subject to a similar debate. In the face of criticism by various civilian groups, the military supporters of the acts and their allies responded that, given the sexual drives of soldiers, and the limitations placed on soldiers marrying, regulated prostitution was the most effective way of controlling the spread of venereal diseases among troops. For the same reason, officially sanctioned and inspected brothels for the use of British troops had long been in place in India.[21]

If one looks for explanations of military promotion of brothels and other forms of regulated prostitution among letters, memos, and reports of commanding officers, however, one searches in vain for even the most veiled admission that brothels were necessary for the maintenance of morale. There is, moreover, no hint that they believed that frequent and safe heterosexual intercourse was a requisite activity for maintaining the virility of soldiers. The maintenance of inspected brothels and the access to them by soldiers is almost invariably described in terms of regret. They acknowledged that such a system was immoral, but it was also an unfortunate necessity. Without inspected brothels, it was feared, soldiers would resort to "unclean" street prostitutes, thus increasing the rate of venereal infection, or, worse, resort to seducing respectable girls and women, or even each other, in order to obtain sexual release. Although there was a wide range of opinion among senior military leaders over the ability of soldiers to remain sexually continent, the general attitude seems to have been that while officers, that is, men of the upper and middle classes, could be expected to practice a certain amount of self-control, enlisted men, by and large recruited from the working classes, were constitutionally incapable of doing so. Brothels, therefore, were not considered by the military hierarchy to be essential elements in the maintenance of morale, but were allowed for the practical purposes of limiting loss of manpower from venereal disease, safeguarding respectable women of the neighborhood, and to prevent homosexuality.

Inconsistencies in this general attitude do show up, however. Looking at the situation among British troops in India, for example, can reveal the range of opinions among officers of the regular army before, during, and after the Great War. The twenty years or so before the war saw the attempt by many British social purity organizations to end what they called the "state regulation of vice" in India, that is, the maintenance of officially tolerated and inspected brothels in military cantonments. British officers in India reacted in much the same way as they would in the similar situation in France in 1918. They claimed to have found the most practical way in which to deal with what they believed to be an entirely military problem, and resented the intrusion of outsiders, no matter how benevolent. The reaction of "an unattached unofficial observer," apparently a retired officer, to the campaign is telling. "They're naive," he claims, and "fail to face [the] real situation. It seeks to apply Christian standards to a fundamentally unchristian state of things." It was unrealistic to expect young working class men, only 5 to 7% of whom were allowed to marry according to military regulations, and who were deprived of the association of "good" English women, to submit to "compulsory chastity enforced by law." Such attempts, according to the observer, would only "create a perverted taste for Sodomy from which the Army is at present free."[22]

Perhaps one reason for the sanctioning of prostitution by officers was that many of them took advantage of it themselves. John Baynes, in his study of morale and the Second Scottish Rifles during the First World War, claims that the regular army officers of the battalion fell into one of two groups. The first was made up of those officers who abjured sexual intercourse entirely, for reasons of conscience, religion, upbringing, or lack of interest. In a profession in which marriage was impractical because of the danger and travel involved, not to mention the pressure of colleagues to put the profession of arms before all civil attachments, celibacy certainly had its advantages. Indeed, many officers considered it to represent an ideal of soldierly self-control. The second group included those officers who, although they may have accepted the moral and professional superiority of celibacy, found that they were temperamentally incapable of chastity, and thus sought a release in patronizing prostitutes. Baynes claims that those in this group were often those who objected most strongly when other officers married. "Someone who was a subaltern in the Scottish Rifles before 1914," Baynes writes, "has told me of hearing two members of this group talking in the Mess. One turned to the other and said: 'Have you heard that old So-and-So is getting married—the bloody man?' The other replied: 'Another good officer lost. Well, they won't catch us—we'll whore it out to the end."[23]

Acceptance of soldiers' patronage of prostitutes, was, however, in the decade before the war, no longer going unchallenged even in the military. Lord Kitchener, who had been made Commander-in-Chief of the Indian army in 1903, was an ally of many in the social purity movement, and brought with him to India many of their ideas for moral and physical reform of soldiers' lives. Brothels and prostitutes were no longer officially inspected under Kitchener, although there are indications that such inspections continued unofficially, even, according to some medical officers with experience in India, with Kitchener's connivance.[24] Religious organizations were encouraged to set up recreational facilities where soldiers could go for diversion, and opportunities for sports were increased. Perhaps most importantly, Kitchener did not hold to the view that enlisted men were incapable of remaining sexually chaste. His pamphlet *A Straight Talk to His Men*, distributed to soldiers in India (a similar one would be distributed to all soldiers embarking for France in 1914), could have been written by a social purity activist, or by a member of the Special Committee on Venereal Disease: "Every man can by self-control restrain the indulgence of those imprudent and reckless impulses that so often lead men astray, and he who thus resists is a better soldier and a better man than the man of weak will who allows his bodily appetites to rule him and has not the strength of character to resist temptation and to refuse to follow any bad example he may see before him."[25]

Although many of Kitchener's views can hardly be considered typical of regular army officers of the time (his pamphlet was the object of ridicule by many officers and men during the war), he was not alone in his expectation that all soldiers should be held to high standards of sexual morality. As early as 1907, Kitchener's influence could be seen to have an effect on the moral tone of the army in India. One report wrote of the sexual morality of soldiers in the Indian army: "What used to be looked upon as a matter of course—if not, in the young soldier, as something rather to his credit—is now generally considered bad form."[26] A Government of India report of 1913 indicated a lowering in the amount of drunkenness, gambling, foul language and venereal disease in the previous few years. "There is a great improvement in the general tone of social morality among the troops," it claimed.[27] By the middle of the war, in 1917, the Adjutant General in India could write with some nostalgia, when looking with dismay on the high rate of venereal disease among British soldiers in India during the war, on the high moral tone that "had been inculcated and prevailed in the Army" immediately before the war. In writing a letter of chastisement to commanding officers in India, he writes: "It is therefore disappointing and it must be added disgraceful that such a falling off from the peace standard of morality and efficiency should be found in war time—a time when of all others a soldier, if he be a true soldier, should make every effort to keep himself fit to render service to his King and country. This war will be won by man power; man power depends not so much on actual numbers, as on individual fitness, and fitness is only obtainable by temperance and stern self denial."[28] Although more concerned with the practical problem of man power than his civilian counterparts might have been, the author reveals himself to be well within the dominant, restrictive view of sexual morality that identified illicit sex as anti-social, even treasonous, behavior. Indeed, it identifies the "true soldier" not as sexual predator, but as someone capable of exercising self-control.

The remedies for sexual promiscuity among soldiers were almost identical among both military observers and civilians interested in the subject, such as those on the Special Committee on Venereal Disease. A military report for India in 1916 was typical of army recommendations during the war. It called for: (a) an increase in temperance; (b) greater facilities for recreation; (c) greater keenness for outdoor games; (d) education regarding venereal disease, and (e) the fostering of an esprit de corps, and of a sound public opinion on the subject with a consequently higher moral tone in the units.[29] These goals—keeping the mind occupied by recreation, the promotion of sport as a diversion of sexual energy and as training for the higher faculties of body and mind, such as selflessness and teamwork, and the importance placed on esprit de corps—are typical of the goals of those purity campaigners who sought moral reform within the military for the half century before the Great War. They are also remarkably similar to those expounded by the "muscular Christians" who promoted the cult of games in the public schools, the training grounds of officers and gentlemen. Indeed, the attempt to mold the mind and the spirit by manipulating the body's environment was a common thrust of all Victorian and Edwardian liberal reform. The training of the soldier, even the enlisted man, for self-denial was thus, by the First World War, the same as that for the Victorian and Edwardian gentleman. Moreover, the gap between what was morally expected of officers and men had narrowed, although, perhaps, not closed entirely.

It appears likely, then, that the view of sexual morality by the British military leadership was not too far removed from that held by civilians of the same class and education. It is also likely, however, that British officers, both in Europe during the war and in India, realized that there was a distinction between what they could and should officially expect from their soldiers in the matter of sexual activity, and what was realistic to expect of them. Lord Kitchener's public disavowal of inspection of bazaar prostitutes by military doctors and his private condoning of the practice would give credence to this. It should not be assumed, however, that such a privately made distinction was necessarily a mark of hypocrisy. Rather, it was a way for the military leadership to deal with conflicting external pressures in a politic manner, one that upheld expected moral values while allowing local medical officers to control venereal disease in the way they best saw fit. If the military leadership countenanced regulated brothels in France and India, it was more for fear of the practical consequences of their absence rather than an indication that they approved of them morally. If they resented intrusion of purity campaigners into their arrangements, it was more because of a traditional hostility to civilian interference in military life than it was a disagreement with them on the basic points of sexual morality.

What, finally, would average soldiers have thought on the topic of sexual morality? Written evidence on this is very scattered, but if reports of actual practice are any guide, soldiers were somewhat less concerned with sexual chastity than their commanders. Baynes claims that "most soldiers were ready to have sexual intercourse with almost any women whenever they could."[30] The restraining influences of religion, guilt, and sexual ignorance were, he argues, much less common in enlisted men than among officers. Sexual contact between soldiers on duty in France and French women, however, was apparently uncommon. As one British veteran memoirist has written, "the officers could always have a day out in such towns as Amiens, Bethune, or Poperinghe; and in the French villages, the local farm girls always seemed ready to do their best to solve the mens' [sic] problems, but their numbers were insufficient."[31] An historian of the Canadian army in the war claims that throughout Canadian soldiers' memoirs and letters home, they insisted that the few women found in areas near the front were sexually unappealing.[32] Language barriers could also thwart courtship between French women and English-speaking soldiers, and the patronage of prostitutes was often prohibitively expensive for poorly paid rankers.

If the times and places of sexual contacts of soldiers can be assumed to approximate the times and places in which they acquired venereal disease, then sexual contact was most often with women met while on leave, and more often with so-called "amateur prostitutes"—those who accompanied soldiers in order to be entertained, given gifts, or simply for their own sexual satisfaction, than with common prostitutes. The only other sexual contact possible would have been masturbation or homosexual contact between soldiers. It is impossible to determine exactly how common these forms of sexual activity were, since few men would consciously leave records of their involvement in them. Masturbation, however, was even more frowned upon than extra-marital intercourse at the time and there is no indication in memoirs or medical reports that homosexual activity was widespread. Homosexual transmission of venereal disease, for example, is never mentioned in even the frankest military or medical records on V.D. In fact, the only time homosexuality is mentioned is to deny that it ever presented a problem. This may have been naïve, but the lack of privacy in the trenches or in billets would have made undetected masturbation or homosexual contact very difficult indeed. The homoerotic aspects of soldierly comradeship during the war, most memorably described by Paul Fussell, have, perhaps, been overstated. At least it must be remembered that "homoerotic" does not necessarily mean "homosexual." Desmond Morton has cautioned about such homoeroticism that "the implication of homosexuality is more apparent now than it may have been to men in 1917."[33] It is possible, however, that soldiers and their officers systematically looked the other way when they detected or suspected homosexual activity, and what happened between men on leave is anybody's guess, but without concrete evidence on the topic it must remain an open question.

Would men in the ranks have made an equation between sexual activity and morale, even if their officers hadn't? Baynes claims that "as far as the average private soldier of the 2nd Scottish Rifles was concerned I do not believe that sex had any bearing on morale at all, except that he might consider himself a bit hard done by if he had to go too long without having intercourse."[34] Without using the term "morale," however, soldiers may have referred to something close to it when considering and talking about sex. By the very nature of some of the questions posed to doctors by the Special Committee on Venereal Disease, it seems likely that there was an entirely separate discourse about sex among enlisted men and younger officers that had nothing to do with the moral and medical considerations of their superiors. Every witness to the commission, for example, was asked if chastity were consistent with the maintenance of health. Not surprisingly, all witnesses responded that chastity and health are perfectly compatible. What the question implies, as do discussions of the same topic elsewhere, is that there was a certain body of popular opinion that believed that sexual activity was, for men at least, a necessary prerequisite to maintaining health, strength, and vigor. One military witness claimed that among the non-commissioned officers in particular this view held sway, and that they would encourage young soldiers to fornication because it would make men of them. As Dennis Winter has written, "the infantry were largely working men and it was part of the working-class ethic that good health required a regular lay. By convention, much sexual experience was available at home to lads between the ages of thirteen and eighteen."[35] Many soldiers apparently held, moreover, in a belief that was probably part bravado and part grim reality, that one was not a real soldier until he had had a few doses of gonorrhea.

That lectures given to soldiers during the war about the dangers of promiscuous sex almost invariably started with the injunction that fornication was "unnecessary" supports concluding that the belief that is *was* necessary was widespread among soldiers or, at least, that it was often used as an excuse for sexual indulgence. These lectures could vary widely in their sophistication and usefulness. At their worst they were used to frighten soldiers into chastity by telling the horrors of disease and sin. An exchange reported by G. Archdall Reid, who served in the Royal Army Medical Corps, between him and his orderly who had just returned from such a lecture, reveals that such tactics sometimes missed their mark.

—"What sort of lecture was it?"

—"Very good lecture, sir. The usual sort."

—"What did he say?"

—"He said venereal disease was God's punishment for sin."

—"Well, what of it?"

—"The men are saying, sir, that it can't be sinful to go with virgins and respectable married women."[36]

Reid, along with many civilian and R.A.M.C. doctors, ridiculed religiously oriented venereal lectures as completely ineffective, and his anecdote has all the markings of a fictional exchange related to prove a point. He was, however, probably correct in his estimation of the effectiveness of a religious appeal to chastity. Baynes claims that while a significant percentage of officers could be expected to hold strong religious beliefs, religious devotion among the rank and file was intermittent, at best.[37] This was true even after several decades of civilian evangelizing among soldiers. Moreover, the low esteem with which most military padres were held by troops during the war probably made them less effective messengers of the dangers of venereal disease than the generally well-respected medical officers. There are other reports, however, that such lectures did frighten some men into chastity, and that anxiety about venereal disease was common.

It seems likely, though, that the lectures, and beliefs about sexual morality, whether held by civilian churchmen and purity campaigners or by their own superior officers, were not so much disagreed with as much as simply ignored. It is likely that under pressure of service at the front and the near daily prospect of instant grisly death, the polite rules of sexual morality were discarded along with organized religion and naive jingoism, because, in practical terms for a soldier at the front, they were all only so much "eyewash." Ettie Rout wrote of colonial soldiers, "the ordinary Australasian soldier—particularly the Australian—does not deliberately intend to be vicious. He is simply and frankly pagan, and his attitude, as far as I can understand, is—I'm hanged if I'll give up a single desire in me till I know why."[38] The arbiters of morality, sexual and otherwise, became for soldiers less the traditional social structures back home, and more soldiers' immediate comrades and their own desires.

In all of their discussion of fornication by soldiers, whether in testimony to committees, in medical journals, or in government communications, there is no indication by those taking part in the debate that soldiers might have sex simply because it was pleasurable or because it allowed them, however temporarily, to forget the horrors of war. That is, in looking for the pathology of sex, these observers overlooked that it is immensely entertaining. In describing soldiers' war-time attachment to musical halls and sports, J. G. Fuller concludes: "They had, though, learned from long experience that it was better to concentrate on pleasure than hardships, that the best way to render tolerable the worst of conditions was to make a joke of them, that moments of escape, such as games and concerts could provide, should be exploited to the full."[39] Such a description could also be used to describe sexual activity by soldiers.

Perhaps, then, sex did have something to do with soldiers' morale. If so, it came more from the bottom of the military hierarchy up than vice versa. If there was a belief that frequent sexual intercourse was a necessary component of health and military strength, it found credence less among the leadership of the army than among enlisted men. The rhetoric of sexual morality of the military leadership, as with most doctors, politicians, and clergymen, held to very strict standards of behavior. The easy assumption that unbridled sexual activity on the part of soldiers is an essential and unchanging part of the military ethos thus merits reexamination, particularly for the period of the First World War. Anything but the most cursory glance at the evidence suggests that, despite the traditional association of war with masculine sexual power, the thinking by military men on the subject of sex was much more nuanced and varied than many historians have suggested. Although the institutional culture of the military was often distinct from civilian culture, necessarily in many ways, its separation from the larger national culture can be overstated. This is particularly true of the period of the Great War, during which the British army firmly established itself not as a dangerous institution alien to the traditions of the nation, but as a truly national army that represented Britain's cultural and political ideals.

Sketches of the *Poilu's* World
Trench Cartoons from the Great War[1]

James P. Daughton

On a cool morning in the early autumn of 1915, a French infantryman leaves his post at the western front for a few days at home, *en permission*. The *poilu's* eyes remain fixed on the trenches as he walks away. He takes with him heavy souvenirs of battle: German helmets, weapons, and a large, unexploded shell. By evening, he arrives at the homefront, in the midst of his previous life, where his wife and children excitedly await his train. The wife hugs and kisses her husband while the younger children fight for their father's attention; the aloof older son, proudly donning his father's cap, is fascinated with a real shell brought from the front. At home, with the children asleep, the wife puts on her nightgown, climbs into bed and awaits her husband. She seductively props her head on thick pillows and awaits her husband, then gasps when she notices him, fully-clothed, already asleep on the floor beside the bed. The next morning, the *poilu* entertains himself by playing with his children. But when the play gets rough, the soldier takes out his rifle, and brandishes a dagger. Losing control of himself, he kicks a chair, and knocks the couch over, pinning his son beneath it. His wife yells at him to stop, and chases him out of the house. Later that afternoon, while peacefully working in the garden, the wife smells a terrible stench. She takes hold of her child when she notices the *poilu* hunched behind some potted plants, defecating in the *feuillées*. The next day, the *poilu* returns to the front. Having left his war souvenirs at home, the *poilu* carries supplies for his battalion and a couple bottles of wine.

35

Figure 1. "En Permission", from *Le 3ème Bataillon*, no. 17, 24 September 1915.

The story of this nameless infantryman's trip home appeared as a cartoon in a French trench newspaper, *Le 3ème Bataillon* (no. 17, 24 September 1915). "En Permission"(Figure 1) is narrated almost completely with pictures, each drawing depicted with humor and playfulness. The huge shell, the children starved for attention, the wife's facial expressions of shock, horror and disgust, and the *poilu*'s mindless behavior are all exaggerated for comic effect. The stupidity of the soldier—his inability to distinguish between the "habits" and "regulations" of trench life and the enjoyment of civilian comforts—lends a farcical element. And word plays, such as the imprint *Fabrication Boche* on the shell and the sign *Feuillées* in the garden, add subtle humorous touches. Cartoons such as "En Permission" offered men at the front what must have been a much needed, if brief, moment of amusement. Yet the narrative of "En Permission" also candidly portrays the detrimental psychological consequences of the war experience on the combatant. Along with death, the fear of returning home from the war permanently scarred, physically or psychologically, caused the *poilu* constant anxiety. Behind the comedy of this cartoon, lies the story of a soldier so accustomed to war that he literally brings remnants of its destructiveness home with him. Even after reuniting with his wife and children—two symbols of the home front—the soldier is unable to abandon his trench habits. His detachment from civilian life is so complete that, when he returns to the front, he brings with him no visible souvenirs from home, just supplies.[2] Cartoons such as "En Permission" were not simply humorous distractions. They provided both cartoonists and readers the opportunity to reflect on and communicate the attitudes and emotions of the *poilu*, and the wider soldier community at the front. Rather than revealing specific personal views of the war, trench cartoons offer sketches of the beliefs, concerns, and daily desires—the mentalité—of the common *poilu* in the trenches. But, as such, do cartoons suggest anything new about this character so often discussed in historical literature on the Great War?

A substantial amount of recent scholarship has attempted to recreate the mental world of the average infantryman of the First World War.[3] The literature, diaries, and letters of soldiers describe individuals' first-hand experiences of the war—fear, boredom, frustration, death—often in vivid detail. But these sources pose a number of problems. Literature and memoirs are prone, in the words of Eugen Weber, to "rancorous exaggerations."[4] When and where were diaries and letters written, why and for whom? Were they spontaneous outpourings of thoughts and feelings, or rather carefully crafted, and limited to certain facets of the soldier's experience so as to ease the concerns of loved-ones?[5] A somewhat different kind of source is offered in trench journalism. Stéphane Audoin-Rouzeau has persuasively shown that trench journalism, in the French case, differs from memoirs and letters because the unidealized views of daily life published in trench papers were written not only *by* soldiers, but *for* them as well.[6] Although many trench papers claimed principally to offer troops momentary amusement, they also offered soldiers the opportunity to rewrite the glorified stories of heroism—the *bourrage de crâne* (literally "head-stuffing", or "eyewash")—published in the national press. The scrutiny of the soldiers who read the papers encouraged authenticity of reporting. Trench journals, according to Audoin-Rouzeau, presented "opportunities for self-expression," fulfilling "the fighting troops' desire to rise above the daily misery of war, to bear witness, and to regain some dignity through writing."[7] Editors and staffs of trench papers, though often not located in the front-line trenches, were in constant contact with their readership, and responded to *poilus'* "concerns, interests, grievances and hopes."[8]

Though his analysis of trench prose journalism is exhaustive, Audoin-Rouzeau chose not to examine trench cartoons, which appeared in the majority of trench papers.[9] In fact, trench cartoons are a unique kind of source, functioning differently from prose journalism on a number of levels. By definition, cartoons offered a communal, rather than individual view of the war. Though a single cartoonist draws a cartoon, in order to be successful—that is, to be funny, ironic, satirical—the cartoon's theme must be immediately recognizable to the reader. The reader must see the topic of the cartoon as authentic, as having some relation to a situation, thought, or fantasy that has been witnessed, experienced, or imagined by the reader. For this reason, the theme, more than quality of drawing or wittiness of text, is the key to a cartoon's success.[10] Once the subject is established, cartoons subvert or distort the real situations or emotions for comic effect. This fact requires cartoonists to be especially sensitive to their readers' perceptions of and attitudes toward those situations. In subverting daily life at the front, trench cartoons usually reveal two—and sometimes more—sets of *poilu* sensibilities. For example, in the case of "En Permission", though the cartoon speaks to anxieties over the *poilu's* return from the front, it also reveals a keen understanding of the comforts of home life, and the different forms of behavior typical to military and civilian life. The humor of this cartoon depends upon the reader comprehending not only why the *poilu* might sleep on the floor (trench habit), but also the fact that he *should* very much want to sleep in the bed (a cherished luxury of the homefront). In this case as well as others, the trench cartoon reveals aspects both of soldiers' attitudes toward the war experience, and their perception and appreciation of the norms of civilian life.

Though it is difficult to assess the reception of individual cartoons, in general, trench cartoons were popular with their readership. Some papers reserved an entire page (out of a four page lay out) for cartoons, while others had a number of cartoons spread throughout the journal. And at least two papers, *Face aux Boches Illustré* and *L'Image*, published cartoons exclusively. The prevalence of these cartoons suggests soldiers' desire to reproduce and utilize in the trenches all the forms of expression available to civilian French society. Cartoons, and drawings more generally, gave trench papers an aesthetic, visual sophistication similar to mass-produced papers printed in Paris or other cities. Though technological limitations usually prohibited the reproduction of photographs, most trench papers included drawings, such as portraits of soldiers, sketches of military equipment, and landscapes. But the inclusion of cartoons not only allowed trench editors to recreate, within limits, the look and feel of civilian newspapers. The cartoon itself had a particularly rich history in pre-war French society, from popular cartoons of the Revolutionary period, to the political satire of Daumier and the cartoons of mass-produced newspapers such as *L'Illustration*. Cartoons enabled *poilus* to portray and give meaning to the new experiences of the war through a well-known and popular cultural medium.

Trench cartoons, like the papers in which they appeared, were produced under a variety of circumstances shaped by the location of the cartoonist in relation to the front, the volatility of fighting in his area, and the role of his battalion in the war. Further, trench cartoons were created by individuals of varying talent and acumen, including amateurs who produced rudimentary sketches, and, more commonly, skilled artists who created elaborate drawings and scenarios. Although certain cartoons offered vivid personal responses to the miseries of war, what is perhaps more striking is the repetition of common subjects in trench cartoons from diverse parts of the war. This consistency was in part due to the fact that soldiers were frequently replaced, relieved, shifted from front-line trenches to secondary, support trenches, as well as to different areas of the front as dictated by military strategy. This constant moving from one position to another meant that a large number of soldiers shared the same wide range of experiences during the war. As a result, most trench papers published cartoons drawing on a set of experiences: combat, life in support trenches, work duty near the front, and home leave.

Cartoon themes also did not change substantially over time, though a few chronological generalizations can be made. For instance, the theme of the enemy, and French *versus* German national characteristics were more prevalent during the first half of the war, and considerably less common after 1917. Similarly, cartoonists increasingly turned to the topic of *poilu* trench life, the *embusqué*, *la permission*, and the pleasures of the homefront as the war progressed, from 1916 to the end. Again, the nature of the war on the western front explains much of this chronology. From the first months of 1915 until the so-called war of movement resumed after the second battle of the Marne in July 1918, life at the front was fairly consistent for most soldiers. The ideal of *tenir* ("to hold") largely guided French military strategy. French soldiers built trenches and assumed a defensive stance in the hopes of slowly wearing down the enemy. Besides pitched battle, the *poilu*, therefore, faced many hours interacting with comrades, doing daily chores and manual labor, avoiding boredom, and reflecting on trench life and the war.[11] The repetition of certain themes in cartoons suggest that they both reflected and helped articulate a kind of trench community which emerged after 1915. Cartoons helped define and reinforce standards of behavior in the trenches, by portraying pastimes, spreading jokes, and even examining accepted moral codes.

Cartoons, as well as the papers in which they were printed, were cultural products of this trench community. As the war progressed, cartoons drew on *poilu* daily activities and experiences for subject matter, giving voice to and perpetuating a complex set of soldier attitudes, emotions, and anxieties. The sensibilities of this trench community were not shaped solely by the harsh experiences of war, but were also influenced by French society from which *poilus* came, and with which *poilus* interacted throughout the war. Cartoons indicate the difficulties *poilus* faced in reconciling their contrasting attitudes, emotions and moral values regarding a variety of topics, such as the enemy, the myriad experiences of daily life at the front, women, *embusqués*, and the comforts of civilian life. Rather than providing specific insights into the *poilu*'s every fear, thought, and belief, trench cartoons were most successful at reflecting and perpetuating general *poilu* concerns.

Three aspects of *poilu mentalité* were especially well depicted in trench cartoons. First, trench cartoons were not limited to a portrayal of trench life as a one-dimensional, never-ending life of misery. The monotony interspersed with terror which characterized much of trench life was relieved occasionally in periods of rest, trips home, and even dreams. Cartoons defined the *poilu*, and portrayed his daily thoughts and feelings in a variety of activities, from hand-to-hand combat to getting drunk. Although the image of the *poilu* was common in national publications, trench cartoonists created a more socially and psychologically nuanced version of the *poilu* than the boyish, playful image of the homefront.[12] Second, cartoons suggest that *poilus* made moral judgements about themselves, the enemy, the allies, colonial soldiers, and various members and activities of the homefront.[13] In conceptualizing *poilu* moral values, the metaphor of geography is instructive. In trench cartoons, the *poilu* was held in highest esteem, morally righteous, risking his life, defending the nation. The importance of the *poilu*'s role as soldier was never questioned. Cartoonists most clearly establish this by using the enemy as a foil. Beyond the trenches, however, *poilus* envisioned a range of moral value based on citizens' distance—in both mind and body—from the front. In general, those who supported the war effort in practice and spirit were revered in trench cartoons, while those who feared or ignored it were ridiculed. Within this scheme, there were further distinctions, shaped in part by considerations of class, gender, and less commonly, race. For example, as will be shown in more detail, cartoonists did not treat even the most frivolous women of the homefront as vindictively as their wealthy, male *embusqué* counterparts. In this sense, cartoons broke down the apparent dichotomy of front *versus* homefront into more subtle moral categories. And third, even though trench cartoons chastised the fun-loving ways of urban elites, they also celebrated, if not exalted, the very comforts of civilization the elites enjoyed. The luxury of home life represented both a tool with which to critique the indifferent civilian, and an object of *poilu* desires and even fantasies. Although cartoons functioned very differently from official propaganda, they in some cases shared similar ends. Trench cartoons did not glorify the war experience, nor did they rely on simple symbols such as *devoir* or even *La France*. But, morally, in cartoons and propaganda alike, the *poilu* symbolized a national moral ideal. And, further, by reproducing images of civilization,

Proposition malhonnête . . .

Guillaume offrirait la paix!!!!

Figure 2. "A Dishonest Proposition", from *Le Petit Echo du 18e Territorial*, no. 58, 19 December 1915.

represented not by national icons, but by the simple comforts of civilian life, cartoons reminded *poilus* of the necessity of war in terms they could appreciate, encouraging them to continue fighting.

{4.1} The Enemy: A Foil Unquestioned by Soldiers and Propagandists Alike

Representations of the enemy in trench cartoons suggests that *poilus* did not dismiss all of the characterizations of official propaganda. Both cartoons and propaganda treated the enemy as a foil to the righteousness of the *poilu*. This similarity reveals the difficulties in separating the representations of *bourrage de crâne* from what might be considered more "authentic" *poilu* representations. Cartoons about the enemy commonly depicted German soldiers as barbaric and dishonest criminals, or as stupid weaklings, lacking the discipline to fight. For example, *Le Petit Echo du 18e Territorial* (no. 65, 6 Feb. 1915) printed three drawings of German treachery: a blimp raiding a town, a German submarine prowling the oceans, and a smiling German soldier walking away from a child he has just shot. In another issue of the same paper (no. 58, 19 Dec. 1915), German diplomatic cunning was depicted in a drawing of Kaiser "Guillaume" offering a "dishonest proposition" of Peace (Figure 2). This Peace is not the traditional female icon of youth, grace and beauty, but a pudgy old woman, battered, missing an arm and a leg. Around her neck hangs the German iron cross, and her skirt is decorated with skulls and bones. Behind "Guillaume's" back is the blunt tool used to shape this Peace. These cartoons particularly resemble official propaganda because they play on the fears, not of the *poilu*, but of the nation: the vicious German troops, the wily German government. The victims of German aggression are not soldiers, but rather the nation and its civilians, particularly women and children.[14] But by victimizing only the innocent, the *poilu* was the unmentioned savior of these cartoons—honorable, brave, just. The soldier was not motivated by self-interest, defending himself. Rather, the *poilu* was selfless, the nation's defender, symbolizing France's hope.

Other cartoons drew on familiar generalizations and symbols of national differences in order to contrast morally and culturally the two sides at war. On the front page of *Le Mouchoir* (no. 29, 11 June 1916), under the heading "The Two Crosses," is the image of a German soldier crouched in a threatening position, a torch in one hand and a bloody dagger in the other. Confronting him, a noble *poilu* stands tall, protecting a terrified woman and child behind him. As though the imagery is not clear enough, the artist labeled the German as "Murder", the Frenchman as "Honor." A cartoon in *L'Image* (no. 21, 1917) portrays a German soldier as "The Grim Reaper" on horseback with a large sickle. Two issues of *L'Echo de Tranchéesville* (no. 5, 19 August 1915, and no. 6, 26 August, 1915) use images of women to exemplify German baseness and French dignity. In the first of these cartoons, "Parisian life at the front" is a beautiful woman in a gown: with an olive branch in one hand, and a sword in the other, she glides over broken German helmets in No Man's Land. The following week, a much less glamorous woman, wearing a gas mask, and spraying chemicals symbolizes "Berlin life at the front." Images of women commonly

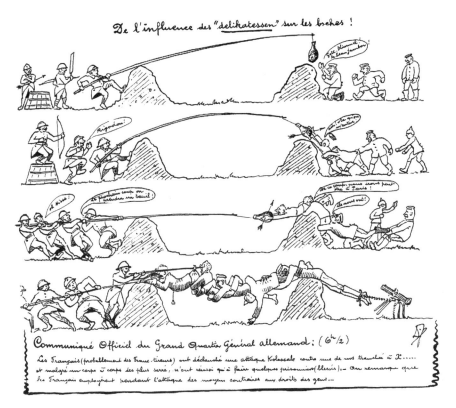

Figure 3. "The influences of the *delikatessen* on the boches", from *Face aux Boches Illustré*, no. 11, July 1916.

represented the differences between French and German cultures in official propaganda: the French "Marianne" was graceful, beautiful, refined (though often frivolous), while "Germania" was barbaric, severe, disciplined, masculine.[15]

The helpless buffoon was another common type used in representing the German soldier. For example, in one cartoon, a German soldier holds his aching feet, crying, "Damn, I cannot march any more, Paris is too far!" (*La Barbe . . . Leé*, n.d.) In a cartoon from *Face aux Boches Illustré* (no. 11, July 1916) entitled "The influence of the *delikatessen* on the *boches*" (Figure 3), French soldiers cast a long fishing pole across No Man's Land, using a ham as bait. A German falls for the trick with an enthusiastic "Gott, Himmel! A beautiful ham!" As he grabs hold of the ham, a *poilu* shoots an arrow from his trench, piercing both the ham and the German's hands. The *poilus* reel in their German catch, bringing *boche* after *boche* as more enemy soldiers join the futile tug of war. In the end, the French capture a string of Germans, along with their machine gun. This cartoon is strikingly similar in tone to national newspapers

43

and official propaganda which reported the ineffectiveness of German fighting at the beginning of the war. In October of 1914, the *Petit Parisien* claimed that "our troops laugh at machine-guns now. . . . Nobody pays the slightest attention to them." And in November, the *Journal* commented, "Bluff, rubbish and double Dutch—that's how to sum up that famous science from across the Rhine."[16] This *bourrage de crâne* was meant to suppress French national fears of being defeated by the enemy—an understandable anxiety considering that initial German advances, curtailed only at the Marne, left the German army entrenched well within the French border. The *delikatessen* cartoon addresses these same concerns, but with the added dimension of the *poilu*'s resourcefulness: French ingenuity can be more effective than German treachery, French plotting (the fishing pole) will overcome German brutality (the machine gun).

Even though some cartoons resembled propagandists' images of the enemy, trench cartoonists often embellished these types with subject matter important to *poilus*. Trench cartoons like "The influence of the *delikatessen*" spoke to an exclusively *poilu* anxiety: the fear of German weapons technology. The carnage and butchery of modern warfare caused anger and despair in the trenches. One machine gun equaled the fire power of sixty men with repeating rifles; hand grenades and artillery could kill a number of men at once; mustard gas blistered the skin and lungs, and caused temporary blindness.[17] In a cartoon with the caption "Fritz goes little by little" (Figure 4) in *Le Gafouilleur* (no. 26, 1 May 1917) these fears were projected onto the enemy. Here, "Fritz" is being blown apart, piece by piece. In this sense, the cartoon was a kind of rallying cry, encouraging men to keep fighting, suggesting that it was just a matter of time before Fritz was either fully dismembered, or retreated. But rather than using traditional images of *devoir* and honor, this cartoon appealed to soldiers' own understanding of war. Maurice Genevoix's *Les Eparges* uses imagery eerily similar to the cartoon's: "Increasingly often, as we became more weary, feverish images were thrown up among the shell bursts: of jumping up with our bodies in fragments; of falling back onto the parapet with broken backs . . . ; of being headless, our heads torn off in a single blow, like Grondin . . . whose head came rolling down to us. . . ."[18] The cartoon's graphic violence contrasts with the lyrical caption beneath it, a nostalgic axiom about departure:

> To leave is to die a little
> We leave a bit of ourselves
> Always and everywhere. . . .

In the context of Fritz's predicament, "to leave a bit of oneself" is no metaphor. Although this cartoon expressed anxieties specific to *poilus*, it also offered hope: the imminent destruction of the enemy. Though cartoons such as this did not exhibit the false optimism of eyewash, the *message* of trench cartoons about the enemy was

Fritz s'en va peu à peu , Oui.....

Mais !   *Partir, c'est mourir un peu*
On laisse un peu de soi-même
A toute heure et dans tout lieu.....

Figure 4. "Fritz goes little by little", from *Le Gafouilleur*, no. 26, 1 May 1917.

little different from the official propaganda: the *Boches* are cunning and murderous, or stupid and misguided, and they threaten the French nation. Either conception justified their defeat by the superior "civilization" of the French. *Poilus*, therefore, clearly did not dismiss all assumptions of official propagandists. But trench cartoons were not simply propaganda; rather, they employed and adapted types popular in the wider, national community, and recontextualized them by giving them new forms that spoke more directly to veterans of the front, appealing to their sensibilities. Unlike propagandists, whose pro-French message was the end in itself, trench cartoonists employed images of the enemy as foils in order to begin to define the complexities of *poilu* identity, especially the *poilu*'s moral position.

[4.2] The *Poilu* and the Trench Community

If the *Boches* were clearly defined by trench and "official" images as bloodthirsty and hateful, then who was the *poilu*? In national typology and trench cartoons alike, the French soldier represented values in opposition to the enemy: the *poilu* was brave, self-sacrificing, honorable—the defenders of the nation. But it is clear from other trench cartoons that *poilu* self-perception was not limited to national expectations. Trench cartoons portray the attitudes, fears and desires not of heroes, but of ordinary men. The *poilu mentalité* was shaped not by individual social or economic background, or political views, but by experiences, emotions, and thoughts shared in the first line, in reserve trenches, *au repos*, and *en permission*. Trench cartoons gave meaning to, and perpetuated a coherent definition of the trench community.

Trench cartoons, like other sources from the trenches, were apolitical: military decisions were never questioned, and national politics rarely critiqued.[19] Infrequently, cartoons satirize the inefficient administration of the war. For instance, in *La Bataillon* (no. 56, 11 April 1916), a cartoon portrays fat soldiers squeezing into tiny uniforms, while thin men don tent-sized fatigues. And in a cartoon in *Le Canard Dieppois* (no. 15, 20 September 1916), a nurse asks a doctor, who is seated at a desk, when the war will end. The doctor answers cynically: "When we run out of paper." Neither of these cartoons openly criticized specific culprits, rather they expressed a general frustration that the welfare of the *poilu* was in the hands of a distant bureaucratic machine. Practical reasons very likely determined the lack of politics in trench papers. Although military officials looked kindly on trench papers, they would have viewed such open criticism as dangerous to morale, if not insubordination.[20] Further, papers that adopted an ideological stance risked alienating members of their readership. Political discussions tend to divide people; trench papers aimed to unify their readership.

Class differences among *poilus*, including distinctions between peasants and urbanites, are rarely mentioned. In *Le Poilu du 37* (no. 2, 2e année, n.d.), two "literary" *poilus* are standing in a trench. One of them is reading a paper, while the other asks, "What's playing at the Odeon tonight?" Although the "literary" type might have been represented as a largely urban, educated, even bourgeois solider, the cartoon does not employ these features for humor. Instead, the irony of the cartoon is derived from the distance between the *poilu*'s interest and his geographical locale. In *L'Echo des Marmites* (no.19, 25 April 1917) (Figure 5), portraits of the types of *poilus* in "La Nation Armée" play on standard caricatures of men of different classes and occupations: from the pointed beard of the *artiste* to the weathered face of the worker, and the cigarette holder of the aristocrat. The cartoonist here draws on the visual types of the wider society. But what is striking about this image is how the individual characteristics of each type are undermined. As a group, these men are identifiable foremost as *poilus*, not just because of the heading *types de poilus*, but because of their dress. Each face is framed by the French infantryman's helmet and the unadorned collar of the military uniform, asserting their collective identity as much as their individual differences. Further, with the exception of "Le Commis Voyageur", each face wears a similar, weary expression.

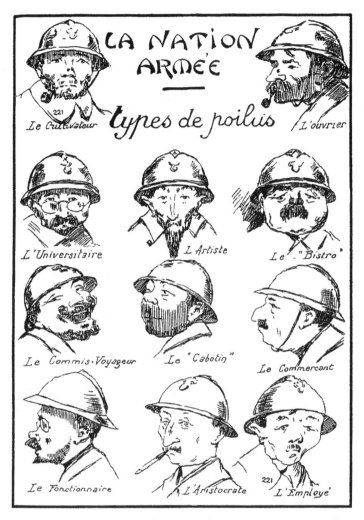

Figure 5. "La Nation Armée", from *L'Echo des Marmites*, no. 19, 25 April 1917.

One distinction, however, is made clear in trench cartoons: the *poilu* is French and white. Black soldiers from the French colonies are portrayed much like the enemy, as stupid and even savage. In *Le Front* (no. 10, 16 November 1916), a black soldier standing guard stops a white *poilu* at a check point, insisting "You can't pass unless you say 'Fontainbleau." Here, by neglecting his job at the check point (by asking for and giving out the pass word), the colonial soldier poses a potential threat to national security. In a series of "Camp Festival" cartoons in *Le Petit Echo du 18e*

Figure 6. "Camp Festival", from *Le Petit Echo de 18e Territorial*, no. 96, 10 September 1916.

Territorial (no. 96, 10 September 1916) (Figure 6), friendly competition between French and colonial soldiers offers the *poilus* a chance to jeer their supposed comrades. In one cartoon, two white soldiers are bent over with laughter as colonial soldiers struggle past in a sack race. In others, the defeat of colonial soldiers in contests such as a foot race and wrestling match asserts the racial superiority of the white competitors. In a drawing called "Danses nègres" two black men, twisted in absurd contortions, are depicted like monkeys, with oversized hands and huge lips. Two cartoons in *Le Bataillon* (nos. 51 and 55, 20 June 1916 and 4 October 1916) equate being black with savagery and brutality. The first tells the story of a white *poilu* who arrives at the trenches, and is painted black by a caricatured black soldier who assures the *poilu* that everyone at the front goes through it. The next picture portrays the *poilu* as a black savage rushing the enemy trenches. A German soldier is so terrified by the approaching vision that he throws up his hands and begs for mercy. A second cartoon represents the cure of the "Maladie Noire"—the disease of becoming black which apparently afflicts white *poilus* who have spent time in the trenches. On one level, this "illness" refers to the filth of trench life. But again the soldiers are not only darkened, they possess caricatured black features and seek a doctor's advice. If mud were the only problem, bathing would be a sufficient cure. Cartoons depicting the barbaric racial attributes of colonial soldiers can be linked to at least two *poilu* anxieties. First, these cartoons express a fear of being brutalized, or made "savage" by the war. Throughout the nineteenth century, orientalist art, literature, and advertising regularly depicted non-Europeans as "savages."[21] This presented cartoonists with a ready-made metaphor. These cartoons played on white French soldiers' anxieties as well. The presence of colonial soldiers in northern France was perceived by *poilus* as a temptation to French women.[22] This was no small threat to *poilus* considering that about half a million colonial soldiers served in the war. Portraying colonial soldiers as ape-like and physically inferior undermined the stereotype of presumed sexual potency. Ultimately, these cartoons defined the *poilu*, and his white community, against the colonial "other" by delineating racially-based differences of behavior both in battle and *au repos*. By exploiting images of colonial soldiers, the cartoonist of *Le Bataillon* suggested that, in the trenches, white soldiers could claim a certain level of dignity, civility, and respectability.

Most trench cartoons illustrated the *poilu* without using foils such as colonial soldiers, often by simply listing *poilu* attitudes and desires. *Poilu* "likes and dislikes" were the topic of a cartoon in *Face aux Boches* (no. 10, June 1916). Likes included hot food, letters, the arrival of relief troops, *la permission*, and especially *le pinard*—the cheap wine which all *poilus* consumed when given the opportunity. Dislikes revealed the ugliness of trench life: mud, lice, rats, shelling, and walking with heavy supplies. Also disliked by the poilu was a period of arduous *repos*. Although *repos* means rest, this time away from the front line was often associated with exhausting work.[23] This attitude is apparent, as the men returning from their "rest" show signs of fatigue, while the men returning from the trenches are plump and content. Though this contrast was exaggerated for humor's sake, it suggests that *au repos* was not always synonymous with an easy post. After the Battle of Verdun only one-sixth of the men in a battalion were to be in the front trenches at one time. This meant that the majority of soldiers were in support roles, in secondary trenches, or working—digging trenches or latrines, or filling sandbags.

Figure 7. "Petition for the well-being of lice", from *Le Bataillon*, no. 69, 24 November 1916.

But *repos* was infrequently depicted in terms of hardship: a cartoon in *L'Echo des Marmites* (no. 22, 5 September 1917) shows *repos* to be a time of comradeship and relaxation. A bath, exercise, and hot food comprise this vision of *repos*; it is a time for men to take walks together, smoke their pipes, and visit with one another. After a mid-day nap, they gather to hear a concert. At times like these, men got to know each other, and younger soldiers learned of the older soldiers' experiences. And *au repos* offered time for the *poilu*'s favorite hobby: drinking *pinard*.[24] *L'Esprit du Cor* (no. 12, 12 January 1918) shows a *poilu* running through mortar fire, risking his life to bring back *pinard* and tobacco for his comrades. *Pinard*'s effects were well documented: *L'Echo des Marmites* (no. 14, 20 October 1916) records "the influence of *pinard* on the *poilu's* morale" with amusing pictures. The *poilu* begins depressed, in the dumps. But after a quart of *pinard*, he is a pacifist; after two, an optimist. Three quarts make him bellicose. After four, he can hardly walk, rendered a "neutralist" by the alcohol. After his "Nth" quart, his face is buried in the mud; he vomits as another *poilu* drags him away. Here, *pinard* helps the *poilu*, first, to express a variety of attitudes toward the war, and, finally, to depart the war altogether, if only in a stupor which lasts a few hours. Just a few quarts of *pinard* are not enough: after three, he is still bellicose, and after four, he still has a stance on the war, even if it is neutral. It is only after his "Nth," when his face is buried in the mud, that he is free of all thought.

Along with the pleasures of free time, the hardships of trench conditions was a central trench cartoon theme. For example, playful cartoons of rats and lice portray the vermin less as foul threats to the soldier's health than as trenchmates. *Le Gafouilleur* (no. 21, 15 February 1917) published a poem called "Homage to Rats" with frolicsome rats dancing around the edges of the page. In another cartoon (Figure 7), lice go on strike, presenting General Joffre with a "Petition for the well-being of Lice." (*Le Bataillon*, no. 69, 24 November 1916) The lice demand that the army "leave the *poilus'* hair alone, so that we don't suffer from the cold of the coming season." However humble, these *poux* are patriots, as one louse chastises another for wearing the despised iron cross. These cartoons confronted the frustrations *poilus* must have felt living with vermin: such filth caused insecurity among soldiers from a society in which soap was increasingly becoming the "yardstick of civilization."[25]

Cartoonists also often depicted the fear of mutilation in humorous and often strikingly frank terms. One particularly blunt cartoon from *Le Front* (no. 8, 16 October 1916) (Figure 8) portrays a *poilu* having both his legs amputated. The soldier, who is sitting up, watching his leg be sawn off, is asked by the doctor, "Am I hurting you at all?" The "true *poilu*" responds, "No, sir, it's just that the sound of the saw sets my teeth on edge." The gratuitous carnage in this cartoon, such as a leg protruding from a bucket by the table, mocks the false image of the stoic soldier who knows no pain. Another cartoon reveals the fear of returning home maimed: a handless, legless man says to a woman, "Yes madam, I had the honor of fighting, and the luck of returning home." (*Le Bochofage*, no. 16–17, November–December 1917) Again, this cartoon directly addressed the concept of honor, and the supposed luck of returning home. Another cartoon expresses the anxiety of losing one's sexual appeal when seriously wounded: a man who is missing both arms and legs, and who has a lurid look in his eye, says to a passing girl, "And since I am more than a trunk . . . *censored*." He is naked except for a phallic-shaped leaf over his genitals. The caption reads, "The future of the French soldier."

Cartoons which focussed on *poilu* life at the front offer a stark contrast to those which portrayed the enemy in often propaganda-like ways. Trench cartoons defined *poilus* as members of an inclusive group of white French men forced to live in harsh

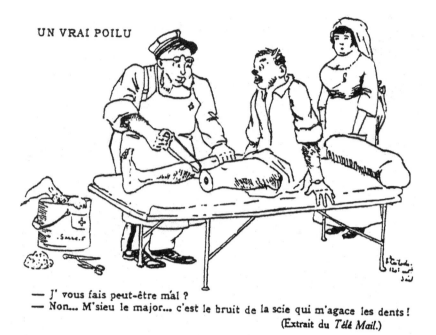

UN VRAI POILU

— J' vous fais peut-être mal ?
— Non... M'sieu le major... c'est le bruit de la scie qui m'agace les dents !
(Extrait du *Télé Mail.*)

Figure 8. "The True *Poilu*", from *Le Front*, no. 8, 16 October 1916.

conditions at the front. References to the enemy and non-French, non-white allies depicted *poilus* in opposition to savagery and stupidity. But it is through the depiction of communal activities that cartoons reveal the more complex, even contradictory attitudes and anxieties of the *poilu*. While cartoons dealing with the enemy did not deny the importance and moral respectability of the *poilu*, cartoons about the difficulties of trench life inherently rejected any suggestion that the task of the soldier was an enviable one. In fact, they at times defiantly asserted the devastating consequences of honor and duty. Images of vermin and mutilation, though both amusing and disturbing, can be interpreted as responses to the playful and carefree *poilu* of homefront publications. But trench cartoons were not defeatist. Through humor, cartoons reinforced the belief that trench conditions could be survived by ridiculing, and even laughing at rats, lice, fatigue, and mutilation. What emerged from these cartoons was a set of sensibilities, more complex than and potentially subversive to the simplified conception of the front found in national propaganda.

[4.3] *Embusqués*: Men Outside the Trench Community.

The attitudes and sensibilities of the *poilu* community were delineated in cartoons about trench life. Yet the limits of the boundaries of this trench community were more fully distinguished by references to Frenchmen outside it. Trench cartoons scorned French men who were perceived by *poilus* to have shirked their responsibility to the nation by not fighting. These cowards were deemed *embusqués*. During the Great War, *embusqué* meant anyone who, in the eyes of *poilus*, had a good post, a safe job. As François Déchelette suggests in his dictionary of *poilu* slang, an *embusqué* could have included just about anyone, depending on who made the accusation. To the *poilu* in a heavily shelled area, a soldier in a less dangerous area might have been called *embusqué*.[26] Cartoons depicting *embusqués*, therefore, were morally weighted, assigning values corresponding to men's involvement in the war effort. For example, on the cover of *Le Mouchoir* (no. 27, 28 May 1916) two *poilus* watch as a sophisticated, higher-ranking soldier walks by with a woman on his arm. One *poilu* says to the other, pointing to the passing soldier's decorations: "My stripes [for continued service]? . . . There they are." The implication of this cartoon is that this soldier has not earned his promotion, though he enjoys the benefits of his status (women in cartoons are invariably attracted to higher ranking men). To these *poilus*, whose tattered uniforms show the hardship they have experienced, the soldier with the woman is an *embusqué*. The suggestion here is that his rank affords him greater access to the comfort of the homefront, as well as greater protection from the dangers of battle. Another cartoon contrasts raining shells at the front with an officer's fear of getting wet in the rain on the homefront. Holding out his hand to feel the drizzle, the officer says to a woman on his arm, "Yes, my dear, it's awful when it rains." (*Le 3ème Bataillon*, no. 24, 12 November 1915) In *L'Echo des Marmites* (no. 16, 1 January 1917) an officer *embusqué* was defined in a cartoon "in which we see the life of the *poilu* and that of the *embusqué*." (Figure 9) Stark contrasts are drawn between the activities of daily life: the *poilu* awakes in a flooded trench, while the officer is brought coffee to his warm bed; the *poilu* gnaws on a bone to the sound of exploding shells, while the officer eats in a restaurant entertained with music. "Le spectacle" means look-out for the *poilu*, but a night at the theater for the *embusqué*. During "l'offensive," the soldier disembowels the enemy, while the city-dweller grabs a waitress from behind. Rank alone certainly did not denote one's status as an *embusqué*. The stripes that each of these *embusqués* wears were also found adorning the sleeves of many *poilus* in trench cartoons.[27] But rank in these particular cartoons was depicted in terms of a class difference as well. The *embusqué* in *L'Echo des Marmites* possesses the standard visual elements of the French *haute bourgeois* typology: he is well-dressed and groomed, has a prominent profile, even a monocle. His tastes are sophisticated: violin music with dinner, then a night out at the theater. He eventually hunts down the traditional object of many a bourgeois fantasy: a barmaid.

Class distinctions were also prevalent in representations of the most hated *embusqué*: the wealthy, secure civilian. In trench cartoons, this *embusqué* epitomized ignorance, laziness, and cowardice. The *embusqué*'s life was one of comfort and self-

Figure 9. "The life of the *poilu* and that of the *embusqué*", from *L'Echo des Marmites*, no. 16, 1 January 1917.

satisfaction; he seduced women and enjoyed the luxuries of well-to-do civilian life, while others defended him and his home. A portrait of the *embusqué* in *Le Bochofage* (no. 5, 25 December 1916) has a plump man sitting in a comfortable chair, his feet propped up, in front of a fire. He smokes a cigar, a glass of brandy and cup of coffee beside him. The *embusqué*'s attitude concerning the war was summed up in a cartoon in *Poil de Tranchée* (no. 2, December (n.d.)) which illustrates the "Proverb of the Embuscade" as "better to hold than to take." One picture depicts the *embusqué* literally holding on to what he enjoys—a cozy life; while another shows a *poilu* crossing No Man's Land, taking an enemy trench. If the *embusqué* does follow the war, he remains oblivious to the irony of his own opulence. One fat civilian sits in front of the fire reading the paper, exclaiming, "These German pigs who are too lazy to go into battle!" (*Le Canard du Boyau*, no. 12, March 1917) In *L'Image* (no. 21, 1917), "Our good civilians" are represented as a well-to-do couple. The woman, dressed for an evening out, asks her husband, "Are you coming, my love?" He answers, gazing at his map, "Impossible. I'm studying our latest offensive."

Another way of lampooning civilian ignorance of trench conditions is the cartoon about civilian visits to the trenches. A cartoon in *Le Front* records "une visite" by a terrified *embusqué* to the front line, and his continued misunderstanding of the war experience even after witnessing it first hand. (no. 1, 1 July 1916) In this cartoon, the civilian arrives dressed in a top hat and long coat. Although he seems afraid of the two *poilus* who greet him, he notes, "I was received in charming fashion." He then "admired the fine work of our soldiers," not realizing the men were digging a latrine. When in the trenches, he puts on his gas mask because he "smelled deadly gas." In fact, around the corner behind him, a *poilu* is defecating. Having skipped dinner, the *embusqué* concludes, "the food was delicious," even though a *poilu* behind him is pulling a dead rat from his tin cup. The cartoon directly derides both "eyewash" and the general misapprehension of civilians in two ways. First, the reporter who visits the trench refuses to report accurately the misery of trench conditions. But also, he clearly expects to find conditions at the front worse than they are, as is clear from his preparedness to witness a gas attack. Two other cartoons in *Brise d'Entonnoirs* (no. 8, February 1917) and *Le Bataillon* (no. 54, 28 July 1916) portray civilians paying admission to see the trenches after the war. The curious civilians come dressed ready for a Sunday promenade. What they find, however, is not a pleasant walk in the park. One man, having climbed into a bunker, runs out screaming, rats nipping at his feet and lice dancing in his hair. Women in elaborate hats and dresses try to run away, though they only sink in the deep mud. A few wise *poilus* watch, amused. In these cartoons, a clear subtext was the knowledge of the *poilu* community, and power derived from it: not only did soldiers comprehend the details of trench life, they were also well aware of civilian attitudes toward the war. This always placed the *poilu* in a position to laugh at, mock, or sit in judgement of civilians.

Civilian ambivalence to the war effort was a source of strong resentment for the *poilu*. In a series of cartoons in three issues of *Le Bataillon*, the tribulations of trench life are contrasted with the relative comforts of home. In the first issue (no. 62, 29 September 1916), there appeared a drawing of fashionable looking men and women sitting around a table in a cafe. In the smoke that billows up from their cigarettes is the image of the trenches, suggesting that their concern for the war is transparent and fleeting. The same issue compared the bombshells of the battlefield with the "bombshells" of the street, in this case a woman flamboyantly dressed. In two following issues, cartoons depicted the passing of the four seasons at both the front and the rear. (no. 63, 6 October 1916, no. 64 20 October 1916). Spring in the city is a time for a man and a woman to meet and fall in love. Summer afternoons bring crowds to outdoor cafes. In the autumn, a couple walks together as leaves fall. And in the winter, a man complains that he can't get his feet warm in front of the fire. The romance and idleness of the year on the homefront makes a striking counter-point to the year at the front: springtime brings a "Dear John" letter; summertime finds him taking a drink during heavy shelling; while the leaves fall at home, more shells fall at the front. By winter, his clothes are tattered, he stands knee-deep in wa-ter, shivering over a candle. Dead rats float by. As a final insult to the *poilu*, when the armistice was announced, the *embusqué* was the first to congratulate himself: for ex-ample, one plump character says to his wife, "Finally dear, WE won the war!" (*Le Bochofage*, Noel, 1918). (Figure 10)

If indeed there were an "enemy to the rear" in the mind of the *poilu*, cartoons sug-gest that it was the villainous wealthy *embusqué*: he represented weakness, fear, in-competence. One cartoon depicted this weakness in a simple caricature of a large dog chasing a small, aristocratic-looking pure breed, saying "Get out, *embusqué*!" (*L'Echo des Marmites*, no. 10, 25 April 1916) This *embusqué* was a foil against which the *poilu* was defined as a common man, who understood duty, served the nation, and resigned himself to self-sacrifice. In this sense, cartoons of the civilian *embusqué* gen-erally critiqued the frivolous ways of the homefront, while they also defined the *poilu* as admirable, morally superior. The civilian *embusqué* presented in trench cartoons represented wealth and comfort: he is the civil servant, the politician's son who stays behind, letting others do the dirty work. There were indeed many men like this. But there were also men who were taken from the trenches to perform essential tasks, such as skilled workers who assembled armaments for the war effort. They, too, were certainly *embusqués* by definition.[28] But the image of the working-class life apparently did not offer the details trench cartoonists sought when depicting the homefront. Soldiers despised the wealthy *embusqué* for having access to what they could only dream of: women, entertainment, a home, comfort—the symbols of civ-ilization.

[4.4] The Elusive Woman: Object of *Poilu* Dreams, Source of Frustration.

Even though cartoons about the *embusqué* described the frustrations associated with trench life and the inequities of military service, they alone did not offer a com-plete picture of *poilu* attitudes toward the homefront. Other aspects of the home-front were central to *poilu* morale at the front. As a cartoon from *Poil et Plume* (no. 13, August 1918) points out, the *poilu*'s "goals of war" were to receive letters and, better still, packages sent from home. And the best goal of all to win was *la perme*

Les Vainqueurs!

"Enfin Bobonne, NOUS avons gagne la guerre."

Figure 10. "Finally dear, WE won the war!", from *Le Bochofage*, Noel 1918.

(leave to go home). Mail was so revered by *poilus* that the "the blessed mailman" is eternalized in stained glass in the "Church of the front"(Figure 11) in a cartoon from *Le Ver Luisant* (no. 13, November 1916). The bearded, saint-like *poilu* wears a long gown and showers letters and packages upon soldiers, sowing happiness throughout the trenches. When no mail arrived for the *poilu*, memories of the homefront penetrated his dreams. One cartoon from *Le Petit Echo du 18e Territorial* (no. 81, 28 May 1916) contrasts trench realities with fantasies about home: rats sniff around a napping *poilu*'s head, but in his dreams he sees beautiful dancers; as a cloud of mustard gas wafts into the trenches, he imagines the intoxicating smells of a home-cooked meal; he feels himself curled in a feather bed, not the hard cot on which he sleeps; and instead of the stench of latrines, he smells imaginary flowers. This cartoon works by contrasting the debilitating hardships of trench life—rats, gas, harsh living conditions—with the mundane comforts of homefront, such as hot food, a bed, flowers. But it also reveals the *poilu*'s tenacity to keep the homefront in his thoughts, even under the most trying circumstances.

Perhaps better than any other, cartoons about women reveal the complexities of the *poilu*'s perception of the war and the homefront. In a cartoon in *Le Canard Diep-*

Figure 11. "The Blessed Mailman", from *Le Ver Luisant*, no. 13, November 1916.

pois (no. 19, 20 Nov. 1916), the conquest of women is as central to the *poilu*'s war aims as the defeat of the enemy. A *poilu* and a woman are in bed together, their clothes strewn on the floor beside them, as if in hurried passion. The woman assures the *poilu*: "Don't worry, *on les aura*." Here, the French soldier's battle cry *On les aura!* ("We will have them!") is used in an erotic context, referring not to territorial conquests, but to sexual ones, as the patient woman responds to the *poilu*'s quick advances. Another cartoon renders "Two good moments" in a soldier's career: running a German through with a bayonet, and kissing a woman. (*Poil et Plume*, no. 3, August 1916) The shift from attacking the enemy to pursuing women is not always as easy as these cartoons suggest, however, and some cartoons express this disappointment explicitly. For example, a cartoon in *Le 3ème Bataillon* (no. 36, 11 February 1916) shows how two *poilus'* judgment has been affected by the war. While walking in town, the two *poilus* fresh from the front see two well- dressed women. They excitedly invite the ladies to meet them that evening. "We'll be here at 8 o'clock," the women respond. But the scheduled rendez-vous reveals that these beautiful dates are not what they appeared: having changed clothes, the "ladies" are in fact two scruffy soldiers themselves. Intense sexual pangs had got the best of the *poilus'* discretion: so excited were the to see someone in a dress, they failed to realize the true gender of their dates. Shocked and appalled by their mistake, the *poilus* hastily retreat.

Leave from the trenches allowed *poilus* to return to the "civilized" world where they could sleep soundly, spend time in cafes, and, most importantly of all, interact with women. In a provocative, sexualized representation of "*la perm*" in *Rigol Boche* (no. 17, 20 July 1915), Cupid, dressed as a mail-boy, delivers to a beautiful young woman news of her *poilu's* homecoming. The woman stands in front of a mirror and small table where bottles of perfume are neatly arranged. Her hand is posed behind her head, accentuating the curves of her body beneath her thin negligee. The bed behind her, draped in a canopy with stacks of pillows and a thick comforter, is an inviting retreat. The woman seems at ease, spending idle hours pampering herself in front of a mirror. Who is this woman who spends her days half-naked? A wife, lover, prostitute? She is a *poilu* fantasy, an idealized vision of the civilian life. What is perhaps most striking about this cartoon is that her comforts are in many ways the gendered equivalents to the cigar, the armchair and the brandy of the *embusqué*. But in this cartoon, there is not a hint of irony or of scorn for this innocent beauty. She lives in a world of delicacy, comfort, solitude, amongst small bottles of perfume, and the haven of her bed. But her close association with luxury is sexually coded, and the presumed recipient of her sexual favors is a distant, but not forgotten *poilu*. She is not only beautiful and alluring, but most important she remains faithful; she exists to pamper and satisfy, and her attention is exclusively reserved for her *poilu*. Rather than resented, her cherished company as well as her dedication to her *poilu* at the front made her the most revered symbol in the trenches.

This symbolic woman was, however, rarely accessible to the *poilu*, and many jokes were wrought from soldiers' fantasies ending in disaster or frustration. A common joke referred to the *marraines*, or "god-mothers"—women who agreed to be pen-pals with soldiers at the front. The *marraine* was frequently the object of men's fantasies: the distant woman inevitably took on seductive characteristics in the mind of the *poilu*. One cartoon exposes these fantasies by portraying a number of *poilus* who, while on leave, have a chance to meet their *marraines*. In one scene, a soldier anxious to meet his lovely pen-pal asks a wrinkled, elderly woman, "Miss Laura won't be long?" Confused, the woman responds, "But I am Laura, my dear god-son." Another *poilu* who has brought a bouquet of flowers for his date, is introduced to a small girl and told: "This is Miss Lulu." In a third scene, a *poilu* yells "But you misled me!" to a large, caricatured African woman. "Pardon me, my heroic boy," she replies, "I told you I had dark features, *very* dark." ["*Pardon, cher héroïque filleul, je vous avez bien dit que j'étais brune, très brune.*"] But this cartoon is not without its serious side: in the center of these drawings, is a young nurse standing beside a body-bag saying, "There's one I'll never get to visit." Anxieties over never returning, or being irreparably changed were often undercurrents in cartoons depicting the return to women and family.

Women's ignorance of the *poilu*'s war experience was also recognized in cartoons, but often with an ambiguous moral message. While women often symbolize sexuality and the comforts of home life, they also could represent frivolity, as well as ignorance of trench conditions. For example, in a cartoon entitled "What one hears on leave," a fashionable woman asks with a coy smile, "Where do you do your daily duty in the trenches?" (*Le Bochofage*, no. 8, 26 March 1917). Another portrays the meeting between a *poilu* and his *marraine*, who complains, "My god-son, I think you gave me a *toto*!" (*toto* being a trench-slang word for lice). The *poilu* sarcastically replies, "Dear Marraine, it is all I have, and I give it to you gladly." This intersection of women's allure and poilu's filth also appears in a cartoon from *Le Front* (no. 3, 1 August 1916) where three well-dressed women stand with bags and boxes labeled "Fashions" in their hands, bragging about their boyfriends at the front:
— Mine's an aviator.
— My poor boy is in an invaded region.
— Which region is that?
— I don't know. He just said, "I've been invaded by *Totos*."
Cartoons such as this demonstrate women's inability to comprehend even the more mundane aspects of trench life, and are another example of soldiers' concern about the degeneration of their personal habits and hygiene.

But trench cartoons did not lampoon even ignorant women with the same harshness as the male *embusqué*. In fact, some cartoons portray women's misunderstanding of trench life more as innocence or even endearing naivete than ignorance or indifference. One woman, in a tearful good-bye at the train station, tells her *poilu*: "And be sure not to sit in any cold drafts." (*Le Front*, no. 14, 16 January 1917) Though this cartoon is certainly not without its irony, the somber atmosphere of this departure scene softens the antagonism which might otherwise be associated with such a misplaced comment. In a similar scene, a man offers consolation: "Don't worry yourself, my love, when I am in Grélines, I will write you long letters." (*Le Canard du Boyau*, no. 10, December 1916) Though this borders the maudlin, it suggests, like the previous cartoon, that sheltering women from the war could be an honorable pursuit. The act of sheltering itself even became a subject to distort for comic results. Another cartoon from *Le Canard du Boyau* shows how downplaying the danger of the war can win women's attention, if not affection. At a bar, a brave *poilu* surrounded by young admirers describes his tour at the front with calculated nonchalance: "Sure, there are lots of mines and bombs, it's true, but you get used to it." (no. 10, December 1916)

After the *poilu* himself, women were the most complex characters in trench cartoons, inhabiting an ambiguous space in the geography of the *poilu*'s imagination. On the one hand, they represented the antithesis of the war: they were beautiful and alluring, refined and gentle. This image of the woman, with her perfume-bottle delicacy, was far removed from the world of rats, lice and shells; they were out of the *poilu*'s reach, both literally and figuratively. She was the symbol of the homefront— a distant place accessible only through letters, packages and the too infrequent leave. But in another sense, women were also constantly *with* the *poilu*, especially in fantasies and dreams. The miseries of trench life did not extinguish the image of the woman from the *poilu*'s mind. Rather, throughout the war, she remained a symbol central to the *poilu*'s self-definition and his assessment of the psychological impact of the war. Her centrality meant she often reflected a variety of soldiers' anxieties. Women who failed to understand the rigors of the trench experience were a source of *poilu* frustration; although the *poilu* did not expect her, and in many case, did not want her to comprehend it. For trench cartoons suggest that soldiers judged a woman's moral value not by her active support of the war effort—for example, in her role as a munitions worker. Rather, poilus judged a woman on how faithful and dedicated, that is, how close in mind if not in body, she remained to her *poilu*.

[4.5] The View from the Trenches: An Enemy to the Rear?

A number of cultural historians have argued that the "us *versus* them" mentality of battle led soldiers in the Great War to understand the conflict as a series of gross dichotomies, such as army *versus* army, trenches *versus* homefront. Further, the ineptitude of military officials and the callous indifference of the civilian population drove soldiers to imagine "an enemy to the rear." Some historians have also argued that soldiers conceptualized the front and homefront in terms of gendered zones: the front represented a male world, the homefront, a female one.[29] In the French case, where soldiers fought on their own soil for the duration of the war, a strict dichotomy is difficult to imagine. Unlike British or German troops, for many Frenchmen, the homefront was within walking distance of the front lines; and considering the extent to which the German army advanced into France at the start of the war, for some French soldiers, "home" was in fact behind enemy lines. Trench cartoons reveal the complexities and contradictions of the physical and symbolic relation between the French front line and the homefront during the Great War. Rather than solidify the dichotomy of trench and homefront, these cartoons depicted overlapping systems of interaction—both real and imagined—between the *poilu* and his home.[30] Though cartoons did define the enemy as a menacing, murderous force, they portrayed the homefront with far more subtlety and ambiguity. The community of *poilus* was often closed, especially to the likes of *embusqués* and non-white colonial troops. But the life of the soldier that emerges in trench cartoons is not one easily associated with dichotomies. Life in the trenches was neither one of undying dedication and heroism, as propaganda often insisted, nor one of unending physical misery and social isolation. The *poilu* was familiar with a variety of occupations and pastimes, from combat to digging latrines, and from playing games to getting drunk on cheap wine. Cartoons also often blurred the physical barriers between home and front. Cartoons often portrayed the daily interactions of soldiers with the civilian life just behind the lines: one *poilu* buying tobacco from a shopkeeper, another waving to girls on a passing train. And soldiers always celebrated the tangible evidence of more distant homes, such as mail, packages, and especially going on leave. The visual element of cartoons also made them particularly effective at recreating *poilu's* imaginary world where front and homefront often mingled: in dreams and fantasies, the smells, sounds, and sensations of home lived in the trenches. The pain and monotony of combat made even the simplest comforts of home more real and more cherished than before the war.

Trench cartoons also reveal a distinct moral code, though not one based on clear dichotomies. The *poilu* did value *l'impôt du sang*—the blood tax paid by a citizen to his country—above all else. Here, the *poilu* was held in the highest regard as he sacrificed everything for the benefit of his countrymen. This was depicted primarily through the use of the enemy foil: against the barbaric and blood-thirsty or stupid and misguided pictures of the enemy, the honorable *poilu* shined as smart, efficient, and honorable. Yet cartoons suggest that *poilu mentalité* was more complex than this *poilu* ideal. These *poilus* thirsted for hot coffee more than glory, and enjoyed a leisurely day of rest more than honor. These soldiers, who drank *pinard* whenever they got the chance, who longed for news from loved-ones, and who fantasized about being home, subverted the military ideal of an effective soldier. But *poilus*, even in cartoons, did not hesitate to acknowledge the importance of their position in the war. A cartoon from *La Musette* (25 February 1918) illustrates the *poilu's* moral vision of the war in terms of distance from combat. The *poilu*, who lives and fights at the front, is deemed a "good" man; the officer, who works at the back of the front, is of "medium" character; and the *embusqué* who hides in the rear is not worth recognizing. A similar, though more complicated hierarchy instructed *poilu* attitudes toward women. The woman on the homefront who stayed close to her *poilu*—wrote him, sent packages, waited for his visit—was the symbol of fidelity and allure, despite her physical distance from or ignorance of the war. The self-interested woman obsessed with fashion, who spent time with the *embusqué*, and remained generally unconcerned with the war, was less admired by the *poilu*. But she still was never as despised as the male *embusqué*, and in some instances her naive ideas possessed an endearing quality.

The argument that soldiers saw an "enemy to the rear" raises another question about the motivation of troops in the trenches: what motivated *poilus* to continue fighting a long and devastating war for a homefront which appeared unconcerned with their sacrifices? Official propaganda and the *bourrage de crâne* published in national newspapers angered and further alienated soldiers. Rumors of civilian frivolity spread through the trenches, feeding *poilu* resentment. In order to reconcile this view of the homefront with questions of motivation, historical explanations of soldiers' continued willingness to fight ultimately steer away from analysis of the *poilu*'s daily experiences. Some historians have suggested that ideals such as patriotism, *devoir* (duty), dedication to one's fellow soldiers, and an irresistible "national feeling" created a psychological barrier in the soldier's mind that made it impossible for him to give up.[31] But this reliance on ideological influences shifts the discussion away from the war experience itself, towards the development of what must have been a tenacious national resolve across France in the pre-war period. There remains the issue of *how* soldiers from day to day reconciled a love of nation and countrymen with a resentment of the homefront and the civilian population over the devastating course of the war.

Although cartoons do not provide a complete answer to these questions, they do suggest at least one way in which soldiers made sense of the war experience and motivated themselves to continue their efforts. Cartoons, with their use of subversion and contradiction for comic effect, were a particularly effective medium for expressing and reconciling the complexities of *poilu* attitudes toward the homefront. The attempt to resolve the disdain for certain members of the homefront with the appeal of the comforts of home is most apparent in cartoons dealing with the *embusqué*. Though the most resented symbol of the homefront in trench cartoons, the *embusqué* led a life of ease that was, importantly, the life most *poilus* dreamt of for themselves. In the language of trench cartoons, civilization was not symbolized by tricolor flags, the French cock, and a female *Liberté*, but by cafes, bottles of wine, and well-dressed women. These mundane images were common symbols of the nation in the trenches, signposts of the "civilized" life behind the front that the war was meant to protect. A cartoon from *Face aux Boches Illustré* (no. 16, February 1917) (Figure 12) depicts this relation of civilization to the front nicely. The distance furthest from the trenches—that is, the place where the *embusqué* hid in a life of luxury—was not only the safest, but also the most attractive, fashionable, civilized. As one nears the front,

Figure 12. "From the rear of the front", from *Face aux Boches Illustré*, no. 16, February 1917.

one passes back through time, where mules and horses dragged wagons through mud roads. The line of trees on the city street is replaced with charred stumps 10 kilometers from the front. Just a kilometer from the fighting, the landscape is bare, beaten by shells. Does this cartoon simply sneer at the easy life of the city-dweller? A similar cartoon from *L'Echo des Marmites* (no. 18, 10 March 1917), called "The Return of the Warrior, or the joys of a day on leave" (Figure 13), suggests not. This cartoon presented a clear view of the *poilu* perception of a perfect day on leave: the beautiful family, a hot bath, good food and wine, conversation with friends, a soft bed, a night of love. These were symbols that appeared often in *poilu* fantasy cartoons. Yet all of these images were also used to describe the life of the *embusqué*. The important difference is that, in this cartoon, the main character is a *poilu*, and as a result the tone of the cartoon is positive. In this sense, the *embusqué*—who was almost always represented in cartoons as wealthy and comfortable—was as much a symbol of the pleasures of civilization as the fantasy woman of "*la perme*" with her canopy bed and perfume bottles. While many cartoons jeered the figure of the *embusqué* as cowardly and weak, his character also

Figure 13. "The Return of the Warrior", from *L'Echo des Marmites*, no. 18, 10 March 1917.

helped give shape to a *poilu* view of the war which revered the lifestyle enjoyed by those behind the trenches.

Trench cartoons, therefore, reveal two separate, and sometimes contradictory attitudes of the *poilu*. On the one hand, they provided moral values. Within this theme, French soldiers were the most virtuous of all. They were as incomparable to the buffoonery and butchery of the enemy as to the cowardice and comfort of the French civilian. The consumption of wine and cigars by the *embusqué* was an indication of his decadence in a time of national sacrifice. But cartoons also had a far more

Figure 14. "From the front to the rear", from *L'Echo des Marmites*, no. 23, 20 October 1917.

practical function: they served as simple reminders of what *poilus* were fighting for—the comforts of civilian life. Rather than draw on the symbolic language of duty, honor and *la patrie* found in national propaganda, trench cartoons drew on a repertoire of images closer to the average *poilu*'s own interests. Ironically, the comforts cherished by the *poilu* were veritably identical to the indulgences of the resented *embusqué*. Furniture, warm fires, coffee, liquor, a lover, trips to the cafe, a good smoke, such were the symbols of "civilization" which contrasted sharply with the deprivations of trench life.[32] The French *poilu*'s perception of the geography of the war, apparent in cartoons, was not founded on gross dichotomies, but on varying distances. The home front and the trenches were not separated by a No Man's Land, but rather a perceived space of complex moral values. Ultimately, as a cartoon in *L'Echo des Marmites* (no. 23, 20 October 1917) (Figure 14) shows, the front and the rear were connected as one nation engaged in war. The detail of this cartoon, moving from the cafe tables of the city to the explosions of the battlefield, reveals the *poilu*'s understanding of the varied terrain between themselves and the ideal homefront.

Trench cartoons perpetuated an image of moral pride for *poilus*, and continually reminded *poilus* of their role as defenders of France. This does not mean that cartoons were the sole motivating factor which kept men in the trenches of the Great War. Trench cartoons do suggest, however, that *poilus* found their own ways of encouraging and motivating themselves. *Poilus* might have withstood the detrimental experiences of the trenches, not simply with patriotism or a sense of *devoir*, but by joking together about the ignorance of the homefront, sharing *pinard*, jeering the *embusqué*, or by dreaming of the simple comforts of the home life they left behind. This helps explain the popularity of a number of cultural products created within the trench community, such as songs, newspapers, stories, and cartoons. Rather than simple distractions, these were means of expression which enabled soldiers to define and understand their roles and anxieties in an alien and dangerous environment where preexisting cultural references no longer worked. The trench cartoon, with humor, satire and ridicule at its base, was a perfect cultural medium to represent a range of contradictory *poilu* attitudes. By transforming tragedy into a harmless caricature, and emotional devastation into a quick laugh, the cartoon helped *poilus* make sense of the indescribable destruction of the war around them.

The First World War and the Public Sphere in Germany

Jeffrey R. Smith

———◆◆✦◆◆———

On 4 August 1914, just after Germany had entered the Great War, the Reichstag convened for perhaps the most famous session of its history, when, in the White Ballroom of his palace, Kaiser Wilhelm II ended his speech to the legislative body with the dramatic words "I no longer recognize parties, only Germans." Upon saying this the kaiser received a loud applause and shouts of "bravo" from his audience and concluded the session by stepping down to shake hands with leaders of the various political parties, an unprecedented gesture on the part of the monarch. Later that day, the public display of unity between the kaiser and the people seemed affirmed when the Social Democrats not only voted for war credits but stood for the first time in the history of the German parliament to hail the Kaiser, Fatherland, and *Volk*.[1] In many of the contemporary and historical accounts of the war, the dramatic Reichstag session as well as the outpouring of enthusiasm from the German public represented the new "spirit of 1914." All the old social and political divisions of Wilhelmine Germany were suddenly "set aside" in the Reichstag chamber, which led Chancellor Bethmann Hollweg to assert that 4 August 1914 would be remembered as one the greatest moments in German history, a time when all Germans, regardless of party or class affiliation, rallied to the national cause in August 1914.

Yet the experience of the First World War in Germany is actually a story of how the suspension of domestic conflict, or *Burgfrieden*, proclaimed in August 1914, completely unraveled during a four-year conflict that was not fought on German soil. In November 1918 the monarchical regime collapsed entirely from within, the result of a culmination of popular mistrust of authority that led to more and more public unrest. The war persistently revealed the extent to which the state failed to harness public opinion in support of its war policy. To help explain precisely how popular sentiment ultimately resulted in outright revolt, it is useful to consider the rapidly expanding role of the "public sphere" during the war and its increasing ability to constitute itself directly against the monarchical state. Vigilante crowds and rumors, which ranged from spy paranoia to stories of food hoarding and profiteering, were important vehicles for the public sphere to remain active and challenge official war policy. At the same time, the proliferation of war postcards, which easily eluded the military censor, disseminated images of the war to millions of Germans on the home front that the state could not influence.

Formulated most effectively by Jürgen Habermas, the "public sphere" can be most succinctly defined as when "private people come together as a public" and found it their duty "to compel public authority [i.e., the state] to legitimize itself before public opinion."[2] Habermas historically locates the public sphere with the growth of modern capitalism and the rise of cities, which provided a space for a "commerce and trafficking of news" among private citizens.[3] He argued that the public sphere found its ideal form in the flourishing salons and literary presses of the eighteenth century, when educated, bourgeois men of letters engaged in critical debates about the actions of the ruling authorities. In so doing, they questioned the absolutist state and its arbitrary monopoly on power. "As the bearer of public opinion," therefore, the public sphere serves as the crucial mediator "between society and state."[4]

Habermas's work has had considerable influence among historians, particularly of eighteenth-century France. Scholars such as Roger Chartier and Arlette Farge have associated the breakdown of the ancien regime with the rise of the public sphere. They have examined how the unregulated "popular opinions" of the lower classes, which the state constantly monitored, became a major source of frustration for the royal authorities. More generally, Chartier maintains that the "progress of critical modes of thinking" in eighteenth century France "undermined the absolute authority long associated with impenetrable and intimidating mysteries of state."[5] Yet for the historian of Wilhelmine Germany and the First World War in particular, the critical role of the public sphere in affecting the state's ability to successfully mobilize its citizens is only beginning to receive the attention it merits.

To delineate the public sphere in Wilhelmine Germany, the historian would not only focus on the concomitant expansion of literacy and the popular press, but also on the physical urban landscape composed of pubs, cafes, crowds, and the street in general, as Belinda Davis describes: "German officials and the broader public at the fin de siècle had no trouble envisioning . . . the street as important sites of the political public sphere . . . in which individuals could gather, in which a traffic of opinions might flow, and from which segments of 'the public' could exert considerable influence on other individuals and the state. The street in particular was considered contemporaneously as a foremost 'public site.'"[6] From the standpoint of the regime, the street formed a public arena where crowds could move, assemble, demonstrate, and even riot, thereby posing a threat to the authority of the state. The "street public [*Strassenöffentlichkeit*]," notes Thomas Lindenberger, created a special problem for German officials whose primary goal was "to maintain the state's monopoly on power in securing the existing socio-political order."[7]

Until the outbreak of war in 1914, the primary concern of the state in this regard were the Social Democrats and their working-class constituents, who repeatedly used the street to voice their oppositional agenda. In 1910, in the district of Berlin-Moabit, socialist demonstrations demanding suffrage reform led to several days of rioting and seemed to confirm anxieties that the authority of the state was in jeopardy. In fact, Berlin Police President Traugott von Jagow went so far as to immediately issue the following announcement: "I hereby proclaim the right to the streets. The streets exist for traffic. Resistance to the power of the state will lead to the use of weapons. I warn the curious."[8] As an embodiment of state authority, Jagow had literally attempted to "close" the street as a public site. The street as a "public sphere" thus becomes a valuable means through which the historian can view the political tensions of Wilhelmine Germany.

At first glance, "total war" seems an unlikely setting for the public realm to flourish, since the state, in harnessing its resources and mobilizing its citizens, in essence shuts this space down. The First World War in particular brought about considerable repression of public life and civil liberties in Germany. Invoking the Prussian Siege Law of 1851, Germany was divided into five military districts, each of which came under the leadership of a Deputy Commanding General, who subsequently instituted press censorship, a ban on political assembly, and a close monitoring of public spaces, including the street.[9] Wartime by definition seemed to render Habermas' conception of the public sphere ineffectual. Nevertheless, as will become evident, the state continued to feel the pressure of the public's demands throughout the war. "The state," Belinda Davis writes, "unwittingly played a role in forging the image of . . . patriotic commitment in the public sphere; and now, in consequence of this legitimation, officials were held responsible for responding to the demands of the population."[10] The historian can thus discern how the public sphere actually heightened its role during the war, frustrated the regime's attempts at managing the flow of information, and ultimately contributed to the collapse of the monarchy in 1918.

[5.1] The Street Public: Rumor and the Vigilante Crowd

At the same time the Reichstag was proclaiming the *Burgfrieden* in Berlin, anarchist writer Erich Mühsam wrote in his diary on 4 August 1914 that "the masses have been driven into genuine hysteria. Spies are witnessed everywhere. Wild, uncontrollable rumors are circulating. One can almost become superstitious in these times."[11] Mühsam's remarks accompanied a series of press reports in August 1914 depicting a hyperbolic, sensationalized urban landscape seized by rumors and mass paranoia. Rumors formed a key means by which the public sphere could remain active and played a fundamental role in the popular interpretation and construction of the war. The significance of rumors is that they represent a popular construction of reality completely separate from "authorized information." Rumors "challenge official reality by proposing other realities. They constitute an alternative source of information, a source that is perforce uncontrolled."[12] Most important, rumors are often indications that the population no longer trusts its leaders and that authority is breaking down, and they can especially flourish when there is extensive censorship of the press.[13] Rumors fill the void when official news is either withheld or tightly regulated as in wartime, thereby counteracting the state's attempts at information management.

The most prominent rumor involving the beginning of the war was the "spy scare" that gripped many cities and towns in August 1914, which, ironically was instigated by government itself. Right after the outbreak of the war, the governmental news agency, Wolff Telegraph Bureau (WTB), declared that "according to absolutely reliable reports, large numbers of Russian officers and agents are traveling through our country."[14] It thus became the "duty" of the population to keep a watchful eye and report "suspicious" individuals to the police and thereby contribute to the maintaining of public order. In putting forth such statements the regime hoped to rally the German population behind the war effort by suggesting that Germany was surrounded by enemies bent on destroying their nation, from within as well as from without. In essence, the spy scare was the government's first attempt to harness public opinion in wartime.

But the "hunt for spies" quickly assumed its own popular form, and stories soon appeared in newspapers throughout Germany depicting vigilante crowds spontaneously forming on the street, mistaking German citizens for spies, and violently persecuting them. In Munich, for example, a worker had apparently heard a rumor that two men disguised as nuns had just been arrested, and noticed that the face of a nun he saw on the street was covered and her gait seemed too large for a woman. He began to chase her and the nun began to walk faster, while a crowd of children shouted "A spy, a spy!" Although the nun fled into a nearby house and a policeman rushed to the scene, a local journalist reported that "in moments the street filled up with hundreds of people, the agitation kept growing, they wanted to break down the iron gate and in all circumstances lynch the spy, all the while shouting 'Get him out! Smash his skull in! Slit his throat!'"[15]

In the wake of such episodes the Munich police over several days published statements in the newspapers condemning the actions of the crowds and declaring that anyone engaging in such activity would be arrested immediately for disturbing public order. The police stated that such "street scenes" fostered by "wild rumors" were an "unpleasant contrast to the patriotic feeling of self-sacrifice that should exist in the fearful gravity of the situation."[16] They even admitted they had to fire blanks to drive back angry crowds. It seemed, moreover, that every major city experienced such occurrences; the press reported them in Dresden, Leipzig, Hamburg, Cologne, and Berlin. For the authorities, who hoped to galvanize morale and foster cooperation between citizens and police, the spy scare had the opposite consequences. At the local level, it contributed to a growing mistrust between the civilian population and the kaiser's police, and in a more general sense, the nature of the rumors and the actions of the crowd assumed a popular logic that the state was, in effect, unable to control its own borders and exposing the population to dangerous, subversive enemies. As a result, the "people" were forced to take matters into their own hands and were unable to look to their government for protection.

What is especially significant in these reports are the graphic, shocking, and sensationalized manner in which the press framed them. The popular Berlin newspaper *BZ am Mittag*, for example, described how on Potsdamer Platz a crowd had observed a Bavarian officer whom they thought was a Russian spy, supposedly due to his size. Upon doing so the "enraged crowd" actually captured the gentlemen and threatened to kill him. Four Prussian officers then "rescued" him by escorting him to police at a nearby train station, upon which "the crowd tried to push open the doors in order to lynch the 'spy.' [The police] then drew their sidearms and threatened to suppress the vulgar conduct of the raging mass with force."[17]

A similar scene took place at the Bremen train station, where in this instance the victim was a reservist called to active duty, and which the socialist *Bremer Bürger-Zeitung* vividly described:

> At the train station, one heard out of thickly crowded masses the cry: A spy, hold him! The masses who filled the station worked their way towards him; they grabbed him, hit him, and kicked him to the ground; hundreds of fists rained down upon his body, hundreds of boots tried to kick the life out of him. The police, who wanted to take him and lead him away, was powerless. And when the animal, raging mob finally released its victim, and when this victim, bleeding and barely still alive, brought himself to his feet, he did what he could have done at the beginning, if one had let him: he proves with his enlistment order that he is a German reservist on the way to join his division.[18]

Elsewhere in Berlin and in Leipzig Germans read stories of military figures mistaken for "spies."[19] More important than the incidents themselves, their widespread press coverage constituted the vigilante crowd as a new political subject and a popular "counter-authority" to the Wilhelmine state, whose representatives—officers, reservists, police— have suddenly become vulnerable to "popular justice."

Alongside these reports, therefore, the press began to release official and semi-official warnings and statements to the population attempting to put a stop to such activity, which further reinforced the authorities' frustration with these popular manifestations of the war. Not surprisingly, a key element of these phenomena was the distribution of newspaper extras that sustained the spy paranoia, and one self-proclaimed "patriot" thus appealed to the Munich police to put a stop to this activity. He complained that extras brought "unnecessary unrest in the street life and much unnecessary agitation in the population" and described the street scenes that resulted: "One behind the other runs about and calls out: Extra, the newest from the war, latest news, etc. People race to the window, race down the stairs . . . Such conduct is unworthy of the German nation in such grave times, . . ."[20] In the public sphere, the war was assuming a form that directly contrasted with the official "dignity" of Germany, traditional patriotism, and "grave times."

In some reports, moreover, isolated "street scenes" in the larger cities translated into crowds completely seizing entire towns. The *Rheinisch-Westfälische Zeitung* reported that in Bad Homburg a riot took place because the public somehow learned that the Viktoria Hotel had not yet fired its French cooks, and the mayor himself had to proceed to the scene to placate the crowd, who "withdrew satisfied singing patriotic songs" after the employees left the premise under police escort.[21] The same paper also reported that the entire town of Weimar had suddenly become gripped by mass hysteria: "the peaceful Weimar and its otherwise quiet citizens are no longer recognizable. From early on into the night the Marktplatz and especially the area in front of the city hall are occupied with dense crowds, who have conducted themselves in entirely scandalous ways . . . ."[22] The report finally stated the mayor had to introduce a "pacification measure" to help restore order to a town that the outbreak of war had influenced in such an "unpleasant manner."

By invoking exaggerated images of "dense crowds" "occupying" the center of town, rioting in front of hotels, and forcing the intervention of local leaders and "pacification measures," these reports illuminated the emerging popular choreography of the war. The press repeatedly legitimized the crowd, who "seized" the "otherwise peaceful Weimar" at the expense of a monarchist regime that appeared to lose control of entire urban areas gripped by rumors. As early as August 1914 the war was assigning a critical role to the public sphere and betraying the extent to which the state was vulnerable to the actions and demands of the German population that could no longer look to Wilhelm II for guidance or protection. In this sense, the seeds of 1918 had already been sown in 1914.

Such incidents and reports made clear that the regime's attempt to manipulate the fear of spies for its own purposes had failed. Throughout the spy craze, the

WTB was forced to issue statements in the press denying the validity of rumors and insuring the population that Germany's borders were secure, in essence a complete reversal of the initial warning that German citizens had to be on the lookout for spies.[23] And by the end of August, the government cracked down on the publication and dissemination of newspaper extras and began engaging in a rigorous press censorship. As a result, the spy scare finally subsided in the Autumn of 1914, but it was an early indication of the regime's increasing failure to mobilize public opinion during the First World War. By issuing denials and retractions and by censoring the press, the government conceded that its public information policy had backfired.

But the power of rumor and its interaction with urban crowds persisted throughout the war and challenged the authority of the state more and more directly. This is most evident in the food crisis that descended on Germany in the second year of the war, as outbursts against "spies" were now yielding to similar collective action against food distributors. Food riots became the new expression of the urban crowd, thereby revealing how the public sphere was mobilizing against the regime. In the public mind, the most important condition of the *Burgfrieden* was that the government would insure the sacrifices of war would be distributed equally and that the country's economic elite, privileged individuals within the Wilhelmine regime, would not profit at the expense of others. Nowhere was this sentiment echoed more fervently than with food.

As 1914 dragged on into 1915 and it became clear to the German people that any illusions of a short, decisive war had been shattered, the supply of food was emerging as the chief concern on the home front, especially since a British naval blockade of Germany's ports had isolated its economy from the rest of the world. The blockade intensified the sacrifice in consumer goods civilians would have to endure as the German economy was becoming more thoroughly militarized. By 1915, long, anxious food lines of women, children, and returning soldiers had replaced cheering crowds and carnivalesque celebrations of August 1914. Police reports out of Berlin and other cities repeatedly reflected popular concerns with growing food shortages, rising prices, and the demand that the state meet its moral obligations to its citizens by insuring fair prices and an adequate distribution of foodstuffs, and there were indications that the authorities were unable to accomplish this important task. In February 1915 thousands of women and children had gathered outside a municipal potato distribution center in Berlin "to obtain a couple of pounds of potatoes." What quickly ensued was literally a panicked stampede as the crowd stormed the food stand while children were trampled under foot. The report admitted that the police stationed in the area were "simply overwhelmed and powerless against the onslaught."[24]

The food crisis became especially pronounced in October 1915, when large scale riots occurred in Berlin-Lichtenberg, the same time, ironically, that the regime was celebrating the five-hundredth anniversary of the Hohenzollern dynasty. The target of the violence was the Assmann dairy on Niederbarnimstrasse, where a crowd of approximately one thousand people smashed the front windows of the establishment with rocks, while police rushed to the scene to prevent the crowd from completely plundering the shop. By the end of the evening, moreover, crowds had shattered the windows of two other Assmann branches, on Boxhagener Strasse and Gabriel-Maxstrasse.[25] The report concluded that the disturbances were "allegedly" caused by the "rude service" on the part of the saleswomen, but asserted that the validity of these "rumors" could not be ascertained.

Police President Jagow also reported such disturbances throughout the Lichtenberg area on 14-15 October, and in some instances violence erupted directly between the crowd and police, thereby foreshadowing the anti-regime sentiment that would continue to foster as the war dragged on. Jagow described how a crowd plundered an Assmann branch on Ebertystrasse, smashed windows, and stole some food while throwing butter, eggs, and cheese on the street. The greatest violence would then erupt that evening in front of the Göbel dairy on Landsbergerstrasse, where a crowd had gathered and began shattering windows with rocks. When the police attempted to intervene, a member of the crowd threw a rock at one officer, who received "considerable" head injuries, while another policeman actually lost his saber in the ensuing melee. Jagow concluded that "the danger persists that [food riots] will continue to recur and shall assume greater and greater scope," and the popular resentment became redirected from the retailers to officials, who were allowing a few individuals to profit from the misery of the general population.[26]

The Lichtenberg riots of October 1915 had introduced a new concern among the leaders of the Kaiserreich as to the situation emerging on the home front, and by the end of the year it had become commonplace to see angry crowds on the streets "angrily denouncing 'profiteering' of retailers, threatening to plunder the premises, demanding some sort of government action in the name of the beleaguered people."[27] Report after report spoke of the growing "discontent" of the population in the face of rising prices and irregular deliveries of foodstuffs, so that by the summer of 1916 the Berlin police conceded that "the mood can only be described as very bad."[28] More important, however, was Jagow's admission in March 1916 that "the popularity of His Majesty the Kaiser . . . has suffered heavy losses."[29] When the food crisis reached its low point in the "turnip winter" of 1916-17, therefore, the popular demand for food had yielded to a broader, more organized "demand for peace" that signified the twilight of the Wilhelmine regime. In the public imagination, the food crisis was an indication that the state was not living up to its responsibilities it had promised in the *Burgfrieden*; instead of ensuring equal and fair distribution of food, the regime was allowing Germany's economic elites to create shortages and drive up prices. The moral bond between kaiser and people was proving unable to withstand the war.

Moreover, it was becoming increasingly apparent to the population that the kaiser was living a life completely apart from his "subjects," and was essentially "cut off from political circles in Berlin and the common people."[30] Biographers of the kaiser also emphasize the failing health and depressed mood of a monarch out of control of the life of the nation. "Here was a man whose world had collapsed and who had some premonition of impending disaster," writes Michael Balfour. The kaiser "was soon rumoured to be found in tears in corners of churches."[31] One such episode took place in Cologne in 1916, in which the kaiser visited the cathedral dressed in a grey field uniform and it even took some time for the people in the area to even recognize him.[32] Wilhelm II was emerging more and more as a tragic figure, a victim of the war and escalating popular unrest. The language of Jagow's and other police reports of the incident further attest to the extent to which the state was finding it increasingly difficult to maintain its legitimacy. Like the August 1914 spy craze, the police seemed "overwhelmed" and out of step when confronted with an angry crowd, as revealed in the now commonplace expression "the police were powerless against the onslaught." Moreover, the disturbances in Lichtenberg invoked the familiar images of "popular justice," crowds attacking individuals and demolishing urban establishments; a policeman in 1915 had replaced the "spy" of 1914, a dairy shop in October had replaced a French restaurant in August.

As in the spy scare, the power of rumor continued to incite, drive, and sustain the popular agitation, and, more importantly, rumors had gone from representing popular disregard for public authority to outright hatred of the Wilhelmine state. As the police had admitted, the Lichtenberg violence had resulted from a "rumor" involving the behavior of the dairy shop personnel, but, as is the nature of rumor, the authorities could not "determine" its validity. Moreover, general rumors maintaining the existence of "food hoarding" and "profiteering" constantly spread among the population, thereby helping to galvanize popular opposition to the regime's war policy:

> Rumors were not only an outlet for the growing discontent, but also an expression of the mistrust of the official politics of information [*staatliche Informationspolitik*]. . . . An ideal rumor market [*Gerüchtebörse*] was the railroad compartment: here women on a hoarding trip met soldiers on leave. And here the most outrageous stories were told about . . . the debaucherous pleasures of the war profiteers and speculators.[33]

Like August 1914 the persistence of rumor was a fundamental element of the public's mistrust of authority and not only served to undermine the regime's efforts at harnessing public opinion but also indicated that the war had snapped the moral bond between the kaiser and his people as more and more ordinary men, women, and even children were mobilizing themselves against a regime that failed to meet the needs of the population.

[5.2] The Public Sphere and the Mail: The Picture Postcard

As rumors and vigilante crowds provided direct evidence of how the war fostered the expansion of the public sphere at the expense of the state, the proliferation of postcards in wartime, which translated and disseminated images of the conflict throughout Germany, were also evidence of regime's failure to direct the popular meaning of the war. Because they were the only means to keep in touch between the home front and the trenches and circulated in such large numbers, picture post-cards, many of which featured illustrations from popular magazines like *Jugend* and *Simplicissimus*, most effectively projected the image of the war.[34] Moreover, the regime, which issued its own patriotic postcards to soldiers at the front, ultimately failed to control this new, rapidly expanding popular medium.

As a relatively new mode of communication that emerged in the middle of the nineteenth century, the postcard industry experienced a rapid boom during the First World War in all of the belligerent countries.[35] In France, for example, the yearly production of postcards tripled during wartime, while in Germany it has been esti-mated that as many as nine million postcards were printed every month. Among the reasons behind this development were the need to maintain cheap, short forms of communication in a period of rather intense censorship of the mail and to help boost morale at the front. Moreover, according to one historian, postcards at the front could provide relief from the brutal, horrific routine of the war: "The picture post-card, . . . was a small gift for the recipient, a kind of surprise, and many postcards actually portray what one would have liked to send or receive: a girl emerging from a postal parcel or a banknote for 1,000 kisses payable to the receiver."[36]

Perhaps the most fundamental significance of the postcard, however, was that it provided simple means by which both soldier and civilian alike could put forth their own interpretations and feelings as to what the war meant for them: "Postcards al-lowed personal statements of patriotic feelings in a time of growing individualism. By signing on the back, one could identify oneself with the message on the front of a card. Because of this confessional character, postcards have rightly been called the campaign buttons or bumper stickers of World War I."[37] As a result, postcards emerged as the most important means by which the popular, vernacular images of the war were manufactured, distributed, and both privately and publicly archived. Moreover, as George Mosse has argued, the picture postcard came to have even more far-reaching implications, namely, the "trivialization" of the war, "cutting war down to size so that it would become commonplace instead of awesome and frightening," making conflict accessible to the public.[38]

Without a doubt, the regime attempted to take advantage of this proliferating popular market by manufacturing its own postcards to distribute among the soldiers at the front to bolster increasingly deteriorating morale. Not surprisingly, these so-called *Fürstenpostkarten* depicted virtuous and heroic images of the kaiser in different poses, like the helm of the *H.M.S Hohenzollern* leading the navy and the nation.[39] In so doing, the regime was continuously attempting to define the meaning of the conflict around loyal subjects fighting a just war for the Kaiser and Reich. The *Fürstenpostkarten* were evidence that the Imperial regime was persistently attempting to equate the images of the war with the monarchical state. A postcard depicting a strong and virtuous monarch in full military regalia signified the equation of "kaiser," "nation," and "war."[40]

Like many other aspects of the war, however, the monarchy failed to direct and define the rapidly expanding postcard market, and the millions of postcards that flowed back and forth between home and the front provided Germans with war images in which the kaiser was largely absent. In fact, by the end of the war postcards began undermining the popularity of the kaiser by equating the monarch with the brutality and tragedy of the war, such as one card depicting an aged, solemn Wilhelm II leaning on his cane over a grave, with the simple caption "I didn't want this."[41] Although the military leadership engaged in meticulous censorship of the mail, they conceded that it was impossible to maintain pace with the mass flow of material between soldiers and civilians.[42]

Although the content of the many war postcards varied considerably, an especially popular example of the type of illustration found on the picture postcard sufficiently attests to the manner in which the war experience was disseminated among the population. These were the "patriotic fantasy" illustrations of *Simplicissimus* artist B. Wennerberg, who depicted the war through idyllic, virtuous images centering around women, children, and the family on the home front.[43] Wennerberg's works frequently portrayed vibrant, smiling women and children greeting soldiers at train stations, waiting for them on the docks, or joyously chatting with soldiers on leave from the front. The magazine boasted in its advertisements that these "beautiful war postcards" could be easily purchased at any bookstore for sixty pfennigs and could be directly sent from the publisher, eliminating the need to even go to the post office.[44]

On the one hand, the Wennerberg postcards, with their soothing captions like "Abschied, [goodbye]" "Erfrischungsstation, [Refreshment Stand]" and "Daheim, [at home]" could provide both soldiers and civilians alike with relief from the harsh realities of war, much as Huss has argued. On the other hand, *Simplicissimus'* description of "war postcards" as "beautiful" underscores the extent to which such images tended to celebrate a distant, brutal war and make it accessible and virtuous to the millions of Germans at home. Postcards were an indication that the war was the "people's business." Through the dissemination of Wennerberg's sentimental drawings that easily filtered out the conflict's unpleasantness, the war had become a permanent, "beautiful" aspect of daily life in the German nation; in other words, however distorted, it had been popularized in a manner that fell completely outside the influence of the state.

Conclusion

In many fundamental respects, the events of November 1918 affirmed the critical role the public sphere attained as early as August 1914, for the rhetoric of socialist leaders like Philip Scheidemann as well as many bourgeois accounts of the revolution spoke in terms of the power of the *Volk* to dramatically affect the policies of the state and take hold of their own political destiny. Theodor Wolff, whose prestigious, liberal *Berliner Tageblatt* had so vividly captured so many images of the First World War, perhaps most effectively conveyed the significance of 9 November:

> The greatest of all revolutions has toppled the Imperial regime . . . like a storm wind suddenly unleashed.
> A few weeks ago there was a military and civilian administrative apparatus, so branched out, so entwined in one another, so deeply rooted, . . . the policemen stood on the squares like columns of power, a huge military organization seemed to encompass everything, . . . Yesterday morning it was all still there, yesterday afternoon nothing more of it existed.[45]

It seemed as if the German *Volk* literally swept away the monarchy "like a storm."

The most dramatic image of the November Revolution in Berlin, namely, Scheidemann's address to the crowds from the balcony of the Reichstag on Königsplatz, also spoke of the power of the *Volk* to shape their political destiny. Having learned the news of the kaiser's abdication, Scheidemann was immediately pulled out of the Reichstag cafeteria to proclaim the new republic to the throng of cheering masses. "Citizens, workers, comrades," he shouted, "The German *Volk* has won a complete victory. The old decadence has collapsed; militarism is ended. The Hohenzollerns have abdicated. Long live the German Republic."[46] The crowd below responded to Scheidemann's proclamation with a chorus of cheers, which, in the words of one observer, amounted to nothing less than "indescribable jubilation."

Other images of the revolution further reinforced the broad-based, popular appeal of an end to the old regime, such as the crowds of workers and soldiers marching and fraternizing in the streets, and socialist Otto Wels' calling for the kaiser's abdication at the *Alexanderkaserne*, where no member of the traditionally *kaisertreu* Naumberg Rifles Battalion intervened. This possessed special symbolic significance in that the barracks had been the site of Wilhelm II's infamous 1901 speech telling the soldiers they would have to be willing to shoot their own families to defend his authority.[47] Even the newspaper *Kreuz-Zeitung*, the traditional press organ of the old, aristocratic Prussian conservatives, recognized the new political climate when it changed its slogan on the title page from "for the King" to "for the German *Volk*."[48] The old order had been literally turned upside down.

In sum, war can easily be seen as a time when the ability of the public sphere to carry out its mediating duty between civil society and the state is either severely limited or undermined. Military dictatorships and rigorous control of public information would seem to render this function impossible. But, as the war experience in Germany has shown, the First World War actually had the opposite effect; its conditions allowed the public sphere to expand and for German citizens to mobilize themselves against an increasingly unpopular monarchy. From the outset, the Wilhelmine regime's attempts to control public opinion encountered repeated failures, as the spy scare fiasco demonstrated already in August 1914. Rumors of enemy subversion created alternative logics to the regime's intended policy and encouraged new forms of popular mobilization that became a direct counterweight to Wilhelmine authority, and popular stories of food hoarding and profiteering revealed the degree to which, in the public mind, the state had violated the implicit terms of the *Burgfrieden*.

In addition, millions of postcards flowed back and forth between home and the front that provided Germans with popular images of the war that the regime could not shape or influence, and the war was being defined in a manner in which the monarchy had become largely marginalized; the conflict had instead become exclusively the business of "the people." In this sense, the demise of the Kaiserreich began long before Germany's defeat and subsequent revolution in November 1918. The war had simply exposed the underlying tenuousness of the Wilhelmine regime's public legitimacy. For millions of Germans, the outbreak of the war was the ultimate test of that legitimacy, of whether the monarchy could forge a new consensus out of the deep social cleavages and discrimination that characterized Germany before 1914. In other words, could the monarchy rise above its rather narrow social and political base and truly come to embody the German nation at war? By early 1915, it was becoming clear that the answer was a resounding negative, as the regime was permanently burdened with popular suspicion, mistrust, and even hatred. Just as the public sphere has served as an effective explanation for the erosion of absolute monarchy in eighteenth-century France, so too can the expanding arena of rumors, vigilante crowds, newspaper extras, and postcards serve as a useful vehicle in examining the collapse of the Wilhelmine monarchy during the First World War.

The Paradox of Working Heroines

Conflict over the Changing Social Order in Wartime Britain, 1914-1918[1]

Janet Watson

———◆▸◢◣◂◆———

When Peggy Bate helped her recently married sister Trix set up her new flat in London, Peggy admitted to her sweetheart that though they had established relations "with laundry men butchers bakers etc." they had "absolutely failed to procure a maid—such things are unknown quantities since the war work for girls craze."[2] Bate herself served as a driver with the Women's Legion and considered her efforts to be important, but when working-class women became unavailable as servants, then war work in the middle-class perception became a "craze" rather than appropriate behavior. Women with experience of paid labor who did war work proved to be a distinct site for middle-class unease about changing ways of life in a time of crisis, when it seemed all the more important to preserve a specific hierarchical social order.

Peggy Bate was far from the only war worker who hypocritically condemned similar efforts by women accustomed to waged labor. As Eleanora Pemberton, a volunteer nurse, sympathetically asked her mother in 1916, "are all the servants making munitions?"[3] Contemporary estimates suggested that between 100,000 and 400,000 women left domestic service for new wartime jobs in 1914-1918.[4] The First World War was certainly not the beginning or the end of middle-class concern about the dearth and quality of servants, but was one point when debate crystallized around specific and seemingly-identifiable causes. Women were leaving posts in private homes for the opportunities newly open to them, whether in munitions, the army auxiliaries, on the land, or even taking tickets on the trams. The middle-class households which had increasing difficulties hiring the staff to which they were accustomed often viewed this exodus with little sympathy. Ethel Alec-Tweedie, a middle-class woman who seems to have considered social commentary a personal obligation, discussed at length what she saw as the insensitivity of wartime domestic servants, who remained selfishly unaware of the increasing financial restrictions on their employers. They also failed to grasp, according to Alec-Tweedie, that taking care of the household of a woman doing canteen or hospital work was their "bit of war work, and . . . a real help to the country."[5] Working-class women who left domestic service for war-related jobs were lauded as a group; as individuals, however, they were frequently condemned for "selfish" behavior in searching for higher wages, better conditions, or more interesting work when another parlourmaid could not easily be found.

Criticism of working women in wartime thus went well beyond concerns about the scarcity of servants and came not just from middle-class women. The war-related activities of working-class women were constantly called into question even as they were praised for their patriotic contribution. Soldiers by definition were patriots, whatever attitude they brought to their efforts; their actions were enough to demonstrate their commitment to the national cause. Working women, in contrast, whether in the factories, on the land, or in one of the official women's auxiliary military organizations, were cheapened by the very fact of their working for remuneration, whether or not it advanced the cause of the country in wartime. Allegations about their patriotism—or its lack—were thus often the center of debates over them. Class distinctions in these situations were highlighted as a means to emphasize concerns over gender. Financially and physically independent women, whatever their motivations, were fundamentally disturbing to wartime definitions of masculinity and femininity, images which represented the brotherhood of fighting men protecting the women of the nation and the social order they symbolized. This was particularly true for women in military uniforms, who seemed to be questioning by their very existence this critical wartime gender division in society. Such threats needed to be contained to preserve the society for which the soldiers were fighting and dying. Popular efforts to do so regularly employed a powerful language of class distinction and criticism, often focused on women's bodies and articulated through images of sexual danger.

The ongoing discussion about the so-called "servant problem" acted as a way to articulate the profound tension in wartime British society over the new-found independence of many working-class women. These women embodied a paradox which undermined the social order. Britons were fighting a war to preserve a vision of civilization which was highly gendered: men were risking their lives to support a world in which women were presented as remaining in the confines of the home. Yet a war of this massive scope could not be waged without the support of both the men and women of the nation, and significant propaganda efforts were focused on the necessary and substantive contributions required of women. Working women thus presented a particular kind of paradox in wartime. Whether in government-sponsored auxiliary military organizations, in agriculture, or employed in factories, these women were now outside the domestic control of the middle-class home, defying the very social order the war was allegedly being fought to preserve. Examination of women in each of these groups illustrates how middle-class representations of them were both critical and praising in ways that sought to contain the wartime threat to the social order which working-class women war workers embodied.

[6.1] Women in Military Uniform: Contradiction Embodied

Unofficial paramilitary efforts by women during the early days of the war met with almost universal indictment.[6] In contrast, when the War Office announced the creation of women's official auxiliary military organizations, these encountered a somewhat more positive welcome. By 1917, four years into the war, there was a general acknowledgment of the need for the work these women would be doing, and of course by doing it they would enable more men to move from support to combat positions. The praise of these women exhibited, however, a powerful ambivalence. Necessary as women in military uniform might be, much of the population continued to be distrustful of them, whether or not they were sanctioned by the government. Inherent in these reservations were specific concerns about the class position of the women members and their reliability in a time of national crisis. The very image of a woman as a soldier, or even a pseudo-soldier, undermined the fundamental conception of men fighting a war on behalf of women at home, whose task it was to preserve civilization as embodied in the conservative social order associated popularly with the pre-war years.

The Women's Army Auxiliary Corps (WAAC), Women's Royal Naval Service (WRNS), and Women's Royal Air Force (WRAF) sought "educated" women to act as pseudo-officers, and women of the working classes to fill the "ranks;" these women were paid, and found in the war an opportunity for new and often attractive work at wages usually higher than those to which they were accustomed. Use of the actual military rank titles was discussed and ultimately rejected as inappropriate for the women's services, maintaining a key level of distinction between the men serving in the military proper and women who belonged to the paramilitary counterparts: these women, though in uniform and under the command of the military, were not, in fact, really soldiers.[7] Dorothy Loveday, an educated woman who joined the ranks of the WAAC as a driver, wrote to her former teacher that "Having begun by calling them officers they are now trying to change it to 'Forewomen & Administrators.'" Her administrator "was at College and is attractive and interesting;" her roommate "has been a dressmaker."[8]

The majority of the women in the auxiliary services, like the majority of men in the army, came from the working classes. They had previous experience with waged labor, and cared that organizations like the WAAC gave them new work opportunities at higher wages than those available in traditional venues like domestic service. In the public eye, however, this work orientation counted against the women; only patriotism was a safe motivation for challenging pre-war mores, not personal benefit. Working-class women were legitimated by their official position within the military organization, but were not perceived to have what many considered to be sufficient restraints of "higher" motivations. They were thus considered by many to be dangerous to the social order. This danger was often expressed in sexual and behavioral terms, within a language of class difference. As a result, the "morality" of women in the military auxiliaries was constantly under question, both in the press and in popular discourse; sexual danger was a means of representing social threat.[9]

Improper behavior on the part of the "khaki girls" was thus one of the key criticisms of the WAACs, who were often compared negatively to other—less threatening—branches of women's war work. Peggy Bate, a member of the Women's Legion driving for the War Office in the later years of the war, hastened to make clear to her fiance, a POW, that she was not a WAAC. "Let me at once explain," she wrote to him, "that to ask one of my Squad if she is a Waac [sic] is rather like asking a Guardsman if he's in a labour corps!" She concluded, "We are the Women's Legion . . . and of course the most superior thing you could dream of."[10] Bate was defending her position as middle class in contrast to the predominantly working-class WAACs; she was making a distinction between war *service* and war *work*. While the WAACs were often associated with men in the ranks of the army, Bate thought of herself more as an officer, like her fiance. She even compared her salary and uniform and living expenses (unfavorably) to those of a "masculine subaltern," as if there were another, feminine, kind; this enabled her to distinguish herself from the working women of the WAAC.[11] Dorothy Loveday confirmed the tensions with the Women's Legion from the WAAC side. WAACs driving in London were asked either to join the Women's Legion if they wished to stay in London or to volunteer for overseas duty. Though Loveday herself chose the second option, she reported of the Women's Legion members that "the ones I have met . . . think themselves very above the Wacks [sic] and are furious at having such riff-raff put into their corps."[12]

The auxiliary military organizations were at times the subject of praise, but qualified in careful ways which were still about maintaining a social hierarchy. Ethel

Alec-Tweedie, echoing the government's patriotic tone, wrote of the WAAC and WRNS that "no praise can be too high for these bodies of women which grew up month by month."[13] Positive attention in the press, however, was often heavily class- and gender-weighted. One piece was told from the point of view of an American pilot, who could not say enough of how he appreciated the efforts of the WAACs. This approach was in keeping with the documented need to free men for active fighting. The women were described, however, as "the daughter of a theatrical manager" and "a young war widow who was counting the hours till she could reach her small son," rather than acknowledging that the majority of WAAC workers were single women who had left work in domestic service or the factories. Women workers associated with their families—and in particular with the male members—presented a less threatening version of independence. The last line of the article had the pilot adding "that *it's not only their work we admire, either!*"[14] WAACs could not be positively portrayed merely for the important work they were doing as army auxiliaries; instead they had to be described in socially acceptable and physically attractive terms. The emphasis here reassured the reader that the subjects of the article were above all *women*, and remained so despite their occupation as war workers. Critically, in this case that admiration also came from an outsider, an American, rather than from one of the WAAC's own countrymen, providing a certain distance to the representations.

There was, however, the obvious reverse side to this portrayal of attractiveness and admiration. "Immorality" continued to be the charge most often brought against the WAACs; clearly undermining any representation of them as effective or important. By the very fact of being women from the working classes, dressed in army-style uniforms and working in the traditionally male-identified war zone, even if behind the lines, they were socially dangerous. That danger was often described in terms of sexual misconduct, or its potential. Unfounded rumors were rampant, with perhaps the most popular concerning the number of pregnant WAACs alleged to have been sent home or to special maternity facilities.

Dorothy Loveday heard the rumors of large numbers of "war babies" among the WAACs and originally attributed them to inadequate supervision; she described a sub-depot "where four girls, under 20 and not of a reliable type, work together with four men, in charge of a sergeant. The place is very out of the way and isn't always visited by an officer . . . the door is kept shut." When Loveday entered the building, she "found the sergeant with a girl on either knee and we all had tea and another sergeant came in and a girl immediately sat on his knee."[15] Loveday discovered, though, that much of the scandal was in fact just speculation; in less than a month she reported that "the number of girls sent back from France has now dwindled from 200 (rumour) to 8 (official)."[16] Loveday resented the approaches of soldiers and suggested that they were hypocritical; she wrote to her former teacher that men in the army, whose advances she had rebuffed, had told her that they "respected women much less now than before the war and that they had made themselves cheap and had no pride." Loveday summed up the double bind faced by women in the WAAC by concluding bitterly that the women were caught in an unwinnable situation; the men "think that and yet they lead girls on and want to lark with them and despise them for it all the time."[17] Women's contributions were necessary to the propagation of the war effort, yet were simultaneously denigrated because they threatened the idea of a gender-stabilized Britain which the soldiers were told they were fighting for.

In an effort to redeem the reputation of the WAAC, both state and church offered official approval. The Minister of Labour spoke out in favor of the women's service, and the Archbishop of Canterbury also released a statement of support based on his encounters with them when visiting the British Expeditionary Force (BEF) in France. These voices of authority were not sufficient to smooth over the dangerous image of the military woman, however. Public feeling was sufficiently unsettled that a commission was appointed by the War Office to assess the work and behavior of the WAACs. This commission, which included both Violet Markham and the Independent Labour Party organizer Julia Varley as members, reported that they had found "a healthy, cheerful, self-respecting body of hard-working women, conscious of their position as links in the great chain of the Nation's purpose, and zealous in its service." The commission also found that the service women were resentful of the denigration of their characters.[18] Dorothy Pickford, a WAAC administrator (or "officer,") in France, wrote to her sister about the visit of the commission. Pickford confirmed that the overwhelming reaction of the women in her unit was that they were "furious that a word should be said against them." Pickford did not think very highly of the investigatory process, but also felt that the problem was not one of "good behavior" as an absolute, but of differing class-based expectations. The WAACs had their own moral code, she argued, which might be different from that of other English people, but they kept to it, and were not likely to consider it necessary to change. Pickford, a veteran of Girls' Club philanthropic work, concluded that based on her previous experiences, she felt that "the behaviour is exceedingly good."[19] This was not enough, however, for many members of the general public, who continued to question WAAC morality. As a racy cartoon in the *Sporting Times* asked, "Would you rather have a slap in the eye or a WAAC on the knee?"[20] Given popular perceptions of the war's corrosive effect on moral restraint, policing of differing codes of behavior became all the more important.

Pickford illustrated many of the class issues inherent in criticism of women in the ranks. Her difficulty lay in her newly acquired awareness of the personal lives of her workers, as she had not previously considered what her servants did in their off time. The war forced working-class lives into her conscious perception, as it did for the rest of middle-class society; she was unsure of how to react. Even in her philanthropic work, she was accustomed to the physical segregation of working-class recreation. She wrote to her sister that it "still strikes me as funny here to see all my household staff smoking about the place when they are off duty. I suppose one's own servants all do, but they are never seen, and here when they are not on duty they are as much at liberty to do as they please as anyone."[21] Even though the workers were her subordinates but not her employees, Pickford still thought of them as "my household staff," and it is clear that she had never given much, if any, thought to the private lives of her servants before. They were a distinct population to her, domestic workers rather than people, so that it was striking to a woman in her privileged socioeconomic position that these women should have the same liberties "as anyone." These freedoms represented a change in the social hierarchy, with which many people were uncomfortable, especially at a time of so much unsettling change. Pickford's letter also provides a clear explanation for women's motivations beyond patriotism in leaving domestic service and joining organizations like the WAAC. The work was clearly more attractive than that which many of them had left.

Helen Beale, who was responsible for organizing the WRNS in Dover when they were first founded, felt the effects of public attitudes toward the WAAC. She encountered difficulties finding women whom she considered appropriate for officer status in the WRNS, difficulties which were closely implicated with perceptions of class, gender, and appropriate war work. Much of the concern was connected with issues of female military uniforms, and was exacerbated by the widespread negative reaction to the WAAC, particularly expressed toward the working-class women who filled the "ranks." Beale thought much of the furor was ludicrous, though she and her organization suffered from its ramifications; as she argued in a letter to her sister Dorothy:

> The W.A.A.Cs have made a very bad impression here [in Dover]—though as far as I can make out it is largely caused by the inevitable want of imagination and power of change of thought and circumstance which people, as you say, show so much. They think it is dreadful to see girls in khaki walking out with a man—not realising a bit apparently, until you rub their noses into it, that things must change in the fourth year of a War like this and that a little wholesome walk out together is probably a mutual benefit to both the girl and the man. I don't hold any particular brief for the khaki young woman but I can't see why it should be considered quite all right for a little fluffy over-dressed female to walk out with a Tommy and not a girl who has deliberately given up the fluffiness.[22]

Despite her need for the important caveat that she held no "particular brief for the khaki young woman," Helen Beale was more ready than many members of her socioeconomic class both to give women who joined the auxiliary military organizations credit for the work they were doing and to acknowledge their position relative to their female "civilian" counterparts. Because this was a minority opinion, however, the WRNS were penalized, before they had even established themselves in Dover, through association by uniform with the WAACs.[23] Some of the civilian women already working for the Navy had to be fired, as they refused to join the WRNS "because they don't want to tie themselves [down], or to wear the uniform provided or for some similar reason."[24] Her own family was supportive of her (middle-class) military foray: Beale's cousin Sybil Field wrote requesting a photograph of her in her "swanky new togs,"[25] and her married sister Dorothy Brown jokingly worried that Beale would "become so imbued with the ways of high naval circles that you will feel the professional classes hardly suitable to know," focusing on her (desirable) status as an officer, and particularly one affiliated with the tradition-rich branch of the Royal Navy.[26] Beale, however, discovered that the general association with women in the military was more problematic, and reported that the WRNS were having difficulty finding women interested in being officers, as many women were already committed to other war work by 1918 and "all the superior and high class young women don't want to see themselves in [military] uniform."[27] The negative popular representations of working-class women in military uniform were spilling over onto the middle-class women who were supposed to command them; the officers' own class positions were not enough to overcome the social danger embodied by the woman in the ranks.

Generally, few people gave the WAACs the benefit of the doubt in social complications; Gwen Ware, a VAD, or volunteer amateur nurse, in Camiers, recorded in her diary relatively soon after the first WAACs had arrived overseas that there was "a riot at Etaples between MPs and men! It's really too awful! A man was shot by an MP or something, and a Khaki girl was mixed up in it all. It was an awful mistake, I think, sending those girls out here."[28] Women of the working classes were simply not considered reliable, especially under the exceptional conditions of military camp life in France. When the women's auxiliaries were first created, the need to get specific jobs done for the propagation of the war effort made them popularly acceptable, if not necessarily desirable. They always, however, simultaneously faced criticism, often from middle-class women who were perhaps protective of their own privileged social status, which focused on issues of morality rather than patriotism. Described using a language redolent of class divisions, women in military uniforms were the subject of discursive effort to control the threat they represented to existing conceptions of gender roles and the class-based social order. "Military woman" was an oxymoron in wartime.

[6.2] Women of the Land Army: Masculinity Romanticized

Of all the populations of women performing new work related to the war, those in farming were the farthest from the actual conflict. They did not wear military uniforms, or serve overseas, or support the troops with munitions, or make any contact with soldiers at all. This made recruitment challenging; conditions were difficult, and the romance of war was far distant. Their contributions were nonetheless necessary, in order to enable more men to go on active military service. Women working in agriculture were thus repeatedly appealed to, even more than were many other populations of women contributing to the war effort, as female "soldiers," giving to their country on an equivalent level to that of the men serving in the trenches. After all, they had joined the Women's Land Army, the first official organization to employ military terminology in its name. The President of the Board of Agriculture even averred late in 1916 that he was convinced that "the victory or defeat in this great War may be brought about on the cornfields and potato lands of Great Britain."[29] The language of service to the nation was thus employed to obscure the stolid work associations of heavy farm labor. This parity of representation was surely aimed as much at middle-class opinion as at working-class recruits, in an effort to overcome the perceived societal danger of women performing work traditionally associated with men - and in clothes which masked physical difference and permitted physical liberty. It was also a safe language to use for these women in ways that it would not be for the auxiliary military organizations: women working on the land were clearly not in the army, but members of the WAAC, WRNS, and WRAF had a more ambiguous status. The clothes were masculine, but not military; thus, for them, association with the army from a safe distance served to make their unwomanly work inherently less threatening to a social order at war.

The opening paragraph of the *Women's Land Army Handbook* explained to members that "You are now in the Women's Land Army; serving your Country just like the Soldiers and Sailors, though in a different way. You have to grow food for them and for the whole Country and your work is quite as important as theirs. You should always bear this in mind."[30] The work (for pay, though admittedly low) the women were to perform was transformed into service to the country through the language employed in the official handbook. This discourse of different-but-equal was very typical of the language used to describe much of women's war work across the class spectrum during the duration of the war itself, as it simultaneously sanctioned unusual work by women while reinforcing its temporary nature as a response to a time of crisis; its militarism was particularly safe when applied to women who were so clearly themselves not, in fact, soldiers. Such imagery continued to be employed in the *Handbook* well beyond the welcoming paragraph, and showed itself vividly in the "Land Army Songs" which actually preceded the text. Intended to be sung "to the tune of 'Come Lasses and Lads,'" the first song specifically invoked the idea of parallel service by women and men, because "If war shall fall / Then each and all / Must help to bring peace nigh;" both sexes respond to an equal call but for different yet comparable tasks:

> The men must take the swords,
> And we must take the ploughs,
> Our Front is where the wheat grows fair,
> Our Colours, orchard boughs.
> Our Front is where the wheat grows fair,
> Our Colours, orchard boughs.

The song then concluded, "We'll dig and sow and reap and mow, / And England shall be fed."[31] Not only is the physical location of the "Front," the location of combat invoked, but also the military tradition of regimental "Colours." The other "Land Army Song" included in the *Handbook* makes its comparison to men in the army only through its choice of melody: it was meant to be sung "to the tune of 'The British Grenadiers.'" The lyrics of the song carried a different gendered message, praising the women who "all are working" in different capacities, but all selflessly: "None ever dream of shirking / Or ask for fame or praise;" or even, perhaps, the glory of heroes; this depiction of the women agricultural workers also significantly glossed over any issues of remuneration for the predominantly working-class women members. And, of course, "none do work so grand . . . [as] our Women on the Land."[32] All these efforts made the women agricultural workers less threatening to the social hierarchy whose existence they challenged by their very presence.

The imagery invoked in the handbook also appeared in other published sources. In her essay, "Women in Agriculture," published in a collection on women's war work in 1917, Gladys Pott, a middle-class Land Army member, declared that:

> If that oft-repeated phrase be honestly spoken, 'To win the war is all that matters to us to-day,' then no considerations of personal advancement or future prospects will hinder those who can offer themselves: no sacrifice weigh too heavily in the scale against the nation's need. In response to the Empire's call our men have been required to lay aside all individual claims and family interests, and face indescribable hardships, suffering and death. . . . Are English women less prepared to shoulder their share of toil or endure petty hardships which are almost luxuries compared to the trials borne by our soldiers?[33]

All members of the Land Army were also given fancy certificates which read, "Every woman who helps in agriculture during the war is as truly serving her country as the man who is fighting in the trenches, on the sea, or in the air."[34] This equivalence to soldiers was useful as motivation for the women workers; it was also socially safe because of the very real distance between the land workers and the serving army.

This language of parallel service combined with the idea of hard but worthwhile work to make the effort more socially desirable and safe, and was also used in recruiting new members for the Land Army. Minister of Agriculture Prothero, speaking to "a great women's meeting" in London, emphasized the difficulties of the labor: "I do not pretend that work on the land is attractive to many women. It is hard work—fatiguing, backaching, monotonous, dirty work in all sorts of weather. It is poorly paid, the accommodation is rough, and those who undertake it have to face physical discomforts. In all respects it is comparable to the work your men-folk are doing in the trenches at the front. It is not a case of 'lilac sunbonnets.' There is no romance in it; it is prose."[35] Yet while Prothero was explicitly denying the romance of the labor, he was romantically invoking the image of work "comparable" to that of the soldiers—and not just soldiers in general, but specifically "your men-folk . . . in the trenches." This was a powerful emotional appeal on behalf of the Land Army, both to the women workers themselves and to the society at large.

Prothero's denial of the romance of his appeal is further undermined by the use of almost identical language in the explicitly romantic novel, *The Land Girl's Love Story*, published just after the end of the war. The recruiting officer might have been using Prothero as a model for the explanation offered to the heroine: "I have put before you the disadvantages of this life. Long hours. Hard work. Poor pay. . . . Very poor pay. But, girls—our boys at the Front are offering their lives for just that. Won't you offer your services for that—and for them?"[36] Here, wages were mentioned, but in such a way as to make their significance at best negligible. This imagery was not restricted to romance novels. F. I. Hildrick Smith, a middle-class land worker who published an account of her ongoing experiences in her school magazine, addressed her readers who might worry about ruining their hands with both practical and patriotic advice. "You haven't got to," she told them, "one good nail-brush, one cake of soap, a pair of nail scissors, and a pot of vaseline—I need not tell you how to use them—and the soldiers are sacrificing far more than their hands, aren't they?"[37] She was reassuring her readers about the ease with which a safe femininity could be preserved within the seemingly masculine environs of agricultural work.

Hildrick Smith's discussion of delicate skin reflected the debate which raged over whether work on the land was appropriate for women. The terms of this debate brought out clear concerns over gender and class threats, as represented through the female body, sexuality, and the necessity for its containment. Clothing was critical to this discussion; it was a particularly sensitive issue in land work, which by its nature necessitated recourse to attire which was repeatedly described as "masculine." The *Land Army Handbook* reminded members to save frills for days off duty and keep the uniform "workmanlike," but cautioned critically that though "you are doing a man's work and so you are dressed rather like a man . . . remember that just because you wear a smock and breeches you should take care to behave like an English girl who expects chivalry and respect from everyone she meets." Again, the values of a "traditional" English society were being emphasized in circumstances which threatened to undermine them. The ideal land worker, the *Handbook* continued, would make people "admire your independence and your modesty, your frankness and enthusiasm; [and] show them that an English girl who is working for her Country on the land is the best sort of girl."[38] She is not dangerous to the social order; in fact, she supports it. Hildrick Smith agreed. "You can have breeches," she explained, "but do wear a coat over them. Don't try to be a man if you are doing man's work. Please [stay] womanly."[39] Similarly, Gladys Pott suggested a "very short skirt or tunic" over "thick stockings and heavy boots, with gaiters or puttees, [and] knickerbockers."[40] The skirt was a necessary element, preserving the essential appearance of womanliness despite the circumstances, its very presence testifying to the true nature and preferences of its wearer. Ruck's fictionalized account found a different way to argue for the femininity of the wearer of such attire: though when "working as a man, you simply can't wear the clothes you wore when you were just sitting still as a girl," the recruiting officer wore "the Land Girl's uniform that sets off a woman's shape as no other costume has done yet!"[41] Active women, despite their gender-masking clothing and occupation, were still presented as ultimately feminine, as measured by their attractiveness and the shapeliness of their bodies. Since they were still fundamentally women, they did not represent undesired social change in a time of national crisis. Men were still men, and women were not.

Like gender, class also played a critical role in socially safe representations of women in the Land Army. Gladys Pott, for example, admitted that the difficult work on the land did not have the "glamour and attraction" of other war contributions, like "munition making, hospital nursing, [and] canteen management," which "all appear to be directly connected with Army organisation, and to be essential to the prosecution of the war." However, she considered this lack all the more reason that "the girl of good education be prepared to put aside all personal prejudice and natural desire for the comforts of life and take up for the sake of her country what may be a rough and uncongenial task."[42] Elaborating on the same theme, the wartime author Barbara McLaren made explicit why the patriotic self-sacrifice of educated women was so important:

> It is unnecessary to state the reasons which bring an educated woman voluntarily to take up such a hard and exacting life . . . only a deeply-rooted motive can be the compelling force, and there can be no finer form of patriotism than the unsensational performance of these strenuous tasks, far from the glamour and excitement of direct contact with the war. Not only in the fruits of her own labour, but by the force of her example, as one of the pioneers along a new road for women, [they each are] performing as fine a war service as any Englishwoman to-day.[43]

Repeating such socially-safe motivations was clearly not "unnecessary," since McLaren proceeded to do so despite her disclaimer. F. I. Hildrick Smith, the middle-class woman who wrote about her land work in her school magazine, embodied this image of the idealized land worker, serving the nation for the duration of the war through agriculture, but not, so to speak, upsetting the social apple-cart in the process.[44]

In its efforts to attract women to the difficult labor and comparatively low pay of land work, the Ministry of Agriculture used a gendered language of equality of service quite heavily, much more so than many other efforts which focused primarily on working-class populations. This was a safe form of legitimization, as the work itself was so far, as McLaren emphasized, from the actual fields of combat and from interaction with the army. The military parallels thus created bordered on the ridiculous: there was a Roll of Honour for deaths resulting from farm accidents (as there was for combat-related casualties), and a record of Distinguished Service in the Land Army structured like the official Mentioned in Dispatches.[45] In August 1918 land workers about to participate in the threshing season in Kent were prepared by official letter for the difficulty of the work and for potential problems with male threshers, but reminded that "it is up to you to show what the women of England can do when they are up against a stiff job. . . . [and to] always feel proud and thankful that you are one of the women chosen to serve their country in this most special way."[46] Members were later given a medal "to commemorate . . . service during the Threshing Season 1918-1919" by the War Agricultural Executive Committee of the County of Kent.[47] Similarly, the Food Production Department informed members of the Land Army that "British women, just like British men, know how to face difficulties" in their efforts to get current members to aid in recruiting additional land workers; they were exhorted to "remember that any Land Army girl who gets five new recruits receives a recruiting cockade to wear in her hat."[48] The more obviously women were not soldiers, the safer it was to describe them as such in the necessary task of soothing popular anxiety over violations of the established gender- and class-boundaries.

Results of the unofficial campaign to present Land Army workers in a positive social light were mixed, however. Walter Nevill, a naval officer, was amused but still approved of his friends Hilda and May going on the land; in contrast, Lt. Frank Ennor was glad his future wife Kathleen was prevented from doing the work because of an age limit (she then became a VAD), as he did not want her to become "somewhat muscular in the arms."[49] Again, disapproval was being expressed in terms of women's bodies; Ennor was not comfortable with the woman with whom he was romantically involved being in any way less feminine. Katharine Furse, though certainly not without an agenda of her own as the Commandant of the Voluntary Aid Detachments which placed workers in hospitals, also resisted the recruiting efforts to attract women onto the land, which she referred to denigratingly as "hoe[ing] turnips". Furse felt strongly that "it is a pity to tell our women that they are more needed on the land than in the hospitals."[50] Healing, in Furse's language, was more appropriate work for women in wartime than was farming; it was, of course, inherently feminine rather than dominantly masculine.

All of these propaganda efforts were an awkward mix of class-based language. While using the patriotic appeals and military parallels intended to appeal to upper- and middle-class women, who even in a small minority would lend the effort a greater degree of social approval with their orientation of patriotic national service, the tone remains condescendingly focused on the working-class recruits who were expected to respond in greater numbers. Popular portrayals like *The Land Girl's Love Story* emphasized a socially heterogeneous population, showing a typist, a socialite, a maid, a Somerville student, a factory hand, a music student, and "Vic the cockney" all laboring together.[51] In reality, however, women land workers, especially as the war progressed, were overwhelmingly women accustomed to paid manual labor. In this, land army work was similar to the munitions industry, which was subject to propaganda campaigns emphasizing the "lady munitionette." One socially-privileged land worker, Ina Scott, found an additional parallel; she wrote that the work was satisfying even though unpleasant because "one is doing what is really necessary." She explained that the "stimulating feeling is not easy to explain, only we felt that here we were really achieving something—something as tangible as making munitions, although we had to wait to see the result."[52]

[6.3] *"Munitionettes"*: Producing Dangerous Bodies

Scott's enthusiasm for the patriotic value of munitions work was not universal. Firmly grounded in the realm of industrial labor, factory work was not easily construed as uplifting service to the nation. Munitions was also distinct from many other types of war activities, as men and women were both doing effectively the same kinds of work.[53] Munitions production involved more women than any other sector of war work, yet men remained central to the factories and retained skilled jobs through their control of union activity. Women workers were praised for their heterogeneity, as munitions was portrayed repeatedly though inaccurately as the ultimate class melting pot. They were also lauded for their determination, putting up with strenuous work under difficult conditions in the name of the propagation of the war. Simultaneously, however, these women workers were condemned for earning wages which were seen as unreasonably high and spending the money on consumer luxuries like jewelry and fur coats; again, much of the criticism of war workers was articulated through a focus on women's bodies. In examining munitions, the role of gender in perceptions of contribution to the national cause is clear: for women, it was always construed as "war work," while for men, for whom the option of serving in the military was technically available (it could in reality have been difficult for a man skilled in a protected industry to leave his job), the language of patriotic contribution was muted. Women, after all, were portrayed as working only "for the duration," while men in the factories expected to remain there in peacetime. The temporality associated with women's efforts in industry permitted room to represent their work as patriotic effort without acknowledging explicitly that the vast majority had a history of paid labor and would continue to work for compensation, even if not in munitions, after the war. The language of "for the duration" helped defuse the threat these women represented by entering a relatively well-paid, traditionally male-dominated sphere, though those tensions continued just below the level of patriotic discourse and emerged regularly in criticism of the women workers, their behavior, and their attitudes.

Though not technically an "Army" as the women who worked in agriculture in the Land Army were, nor an official military organization as the WAAC, WRNS, and WRAF were, women munitions workers were also regularly imagined propagandistically as the female parallels to the men in the trenches, and given equivalent credit for their contribution to the war efforts. As with the women of the Land Army, this was a safe way to defuse the masculine associations of the work they were doing, since they were not, in fact, soldiers themselves. Barbara McLaren called for "public recognition [of] the great army of women munition workers," who "are working for the country as vitally as the soldiers."[54] David Lloyd George declared, after he became Prime Minister, that without the women "it would have been utterly impossible for us to have waged a successful war."[55] Similarly, his successor at the Ministry of Munitions, Sir Edwin Montagu, averred in 1916 that "it is not too much to say that our Armies have been saved and Victory assured largely by the women in the Munition Factories."[56] Ethel Alec-Tweedie's comparison of female munitions workers to men in the army was explicit, arguing that "surely if such a soldier-woman's labour ends in death, she deserves as honourable a military funeral as any fighting man in the field."[57]

Such representations were widespread. Ian Hay's Major Wagstaffe, in *Carrying On,* sequel to the best-seller *The First Hundred Thousand*, praised the efforts and attitude of the female munition workers.[58] Mary Ward, novelist, social reformer, and anti-suffrage leader, lauded the efforts of women munitions workers for responding to the call of the country in need; she even went so far as to argue that the work was healthy for them.[59] Though to some degree this language was widely available in wartime, when soldiers and casualties were forward in the minds of the majority of people, its explicit usage here goes beyond such a casual approach. The efforts of women in factories were equated with those of members of the military in combat for a double purpose. Women needed to be attracted into the necessary industrial work. At the same time, however, this approach minimized any threat they might seem to represent to a gendered social order by their presence in a "masculine" workplace through a language of patriotic sacrifice and service to the nation, which also emphasized the temporary nature of the work. As with agricultural workers, because women in factories were clearly not soldiers, it was safe to give them a military identification which was socially dangerous when applied to the auxiliary military organizations.

Class played an important role here: though one aspect of the public vision of women working in factories was of the mixing of members of all strata of society, when the workers were compared to the army it was always the working classes who were discussed. Women munitions workers were referred to as "Miss Tommy Atkins" or "Tommy's sisters," compared to the men serving in the ranks.[60] The propaganda writer Hall Caine used this language in his descriptions of women munitions workers, and made the class connection explicit; he referred to the "vast army of female soldiers," and went on to compare "Tommy's sister in the munition factories, like Tommy in the trenches."[61]

Though working-class women predominated, and class-based tensions certainly existed between the majority of workers and the minority of socially-elite women making munitions exclusively as a contribution to the war effort rather than as personal or familial support, the factory was almost inevitably represented as a class melting-pot. Women of all levels were portrayed working side by side for the greater good of the nation in its time of crisis, in an effort to defuse the social danger represented by women's widespread invasion into the masculine realm of arms production. L. K. Yates saw "the daughter of an earl, a shopkeeper's widow, a graduate from Girton, a domestic servant, and a young woman from a lonely farm in Rhodesia, whose husband had joined the colours."[62] The husband's military effort was often used in this way to justify the unusual work on the part of the wife, and the class balance represented by Yates's list, where only one woman of five came from the working classes, was clearly not proportionally representative. Yates also invoked the parallel to service in the army, though modifying the comparison with the language of the home, clearly an appropriate place for women to be: "social status, so stiff a barrier in this country in pre-war days, was forgotten in the factory, as in the trenches, and they were all working together as happily as the members of a united family."[63] The very acknowledgment of how unusual this social mix was served to emphasize its temporary nature: only for a cause as great as the nation's need were women of such diverse social positions uniting. Critically, as well, they functioned together as a "family," rather than a more dangerous unit of industrial organization like a union.

Explicit efforts were made to recruit middle- and upper-class women into the munitions factories. Because many of this targeted population would not commit the time and effort to full employment, Lady Moir and Lady Cowan formed the Women Relief Munition Workers' Organisation in 1915 to work weekends at the Vickers factory, replacing the regular staff on their off days.[64] Socioeconomically privileged women could work fewer hours than the regular workers, and still contribute to the operation of the factory at full capacity. Ideally, however, these women would join the regular factory shifts. The official rationale behind these efforts, which were not overwhelmingly successful, was that "educated" women would learn the new tasks more quickly than working-class novices. It was also critically true, however, that women who saw their time in the factories as service to the nation rather than as a new work opportunity would not resist being displaced from their jobs by returning soldiers at the war's end, as working-class women might.[65] Equally important, however, women who saw their work as temporary would not be interested in the labor unions. They were ultimately safe industrial laborers, not threatening at any level to the social order.

The historian Deborah Thom has pointed out that women workers were considered "substitutes" or "dilutees" even when they were in fact extra workers, necessitated by the increased demands of the war.[66] This language, of course, emphasized the temporary nature of their involvement with the factory; they were always by definition only filling the slots of the missing soldiers, who would one day return and take over their "own" jobs. Though the Ministry of Munitions ordered that women be paid the same rates for the same work, numerous evasions resulted in significant differentials in wage rates. The simplest way to avoid the restrictions from the Ministry was to reconstitute job descriptions; if a woman was not doing the identical combination of tasks that the man had previously performed, then the wage rate could be adjusted. Similarly, some jobs were redesigned to include a minimal amount of heavy physical labor to exclude women from equal pay. In April 1918, male workers in the national shell factories earned on average £4 6s. 6d. per week, while they earned £4 14s. 8d. per week in the national projectile factories. Comparable wage rates for women were £2 2s 4d and £2 16s 8d. respectively.[67]

Yet despite these differentials, the issue of women's wages in the munitions factories was at the center of negative perceptions of the workers. Certainly many women were earning more money than they had previously, particularly if they had been in domestic service but even if they had been in industrial work. These earnings were not seen in the light of wages for work, however, but as excessive money being spent in a reckless manner on the women worker's bodies, with fur coats, lavish underclothes, and jewelry often given as examples. One contemporary observer referred to an "orgy of silver bags and chiffons," and asserted that more money was being spent on "clothes, especially underclothes," in 1917 than 1915, primarily at "second, third, and fourth-class shops."[68] Not only were women workers being profligate; they also were not even buying quality goods, showing further their inability to be responsible for increased disposable income. The specter of the discourse of the prostitute, whose diseased body was always seen as a social danger, haunted these critical descriptions.

Several journalists attempted to deny the rumors of female munitions workers' extravagance, including one who pointed out the irony that "wealthy leisured women, who bought fur coats themselves, should complain about factory girls buying clothes with their hard-earned wages."[69] Some concerns were also expressed about elevated male wages, but not to the degree or with the virulence of the debate about women's. In combination with the new physical liberties that munitions work brought women workers, including freedom to travel, live away from home, and work fewer hours in less supervised circumstances than domestic service, the idea of young unmarried women (who were the culprits invoked in the popular representations, despite the number of married women and mothers who worked in the factories) seemed threatening to the social order, both to its gender and its class components. This was particularly the case in wartime, when the idealized soldier had given up freedom and comforts, along with any guarantee of safety, on behalf of the nation. Seeking out creature comforts while the men suffered in the trenches was thus portrayed as fundamentally unpatriotic.

This negative image was countered with efforts to demonstrate the patriotic commitment of women munitions workers. Monica Cosens, a middle-class munitions worker, argued that the women she knew who lived in the factory hostels were "home-birds" who missed their families. This allegation disproved "the idea that some people have that [Minister of Munitions] Lloyd George's girls only work for the sake of the wages. Of course, they could not afford to give their services, but they might find other work nearer home, less heavy and less irksome. They realize munitions are vital to the conclusion of the War, and they want to help by making them, no matter what discomforts they are called upon to bear."[70] By reassuring her readers that the working-class women were closely connected emotionally to their homes and families, Cosens was arguing that the workers, despite their new living circumstances and financial independence, were both patriotic and unthreatening to the existing social order. They were, in fact, good women and good citizens, not profligate spenders, excitement seekers, or prostitutes.

Middle-class munitions workers like Cosens and Naomi Loughlan, however, also argued that class differences in the factories illuminated fundamental distinctions in attitude toward the war. While Loughlan felt that her "stern sense of duty" was her "only weapon of defence" against sleep on long night shifts, "ordinary factory hands have little to help keep them awake [because] they lack interest in their work because of the undeveloped state of their imaginations . . . they do not definitely connect the work they are doing with the trenches."[71] Similarly, Cosens described a group of workers clustered around a current newspaper, and concluded that as "they look eager, excited, pleased . . . there [must have] been a great victory." When she joined the group, however, she discovered that the workers were discussing "the portrait of a new cinema star," and concluded that they were "queer, [because] their work is so vital to the war, and yet how that war is progressing is to them a second-ary thought."[72] This was, of course, not the right attitude toward the propagation of the war effort, and further evidence of how these women needed to be constrained from damaging the national cause.

To middle-class munitions workers, along with much of the public, motivation in doing the work was as important as the work itself. Workers had to understand *why*, in a patriotic sense, they were working, and not value the income they gained from it—a standard which revealed a deep class bias. To make this point clearly, Loughlan related, condescendingly, the story of a "girl, with a face growing sadder and paler as the days went by because no news came from France of her 'boy' who was missing, [who] when gently urged to work harder and not go to sleep so often, answered, with angry indignation: 'Why should I work any harder? My mother is satisfied with what I takes home of a Saturday.'"[73] This was not a unique criticism; women workers at Woolwich Arsenal were also alleged to work short weeks because they thought only of their pay. In their case, credit for expanding working hours for the majority was given in a popularly published account to Lillian Barker, Lady Su-perintendent of the factory, who explained to them how much the munitions they failed to make on their extra days off might mean "to Tommy in a tight corner."[74] Patriotism as a motivation would defuse the threat of their interest in their own so-cial welfare.

Belying the propagandistic picture of peaceful class mixing in factories which was central to so many popular representations, industry officials along with some writers clearly demonstrated the need to control the large numbers of working-class women in the factories by the placement of middle-class women above them, super-vising their "welfare." As Ethel Alec-Tweedie argued: "The best sort of fore-women—and they may have from 100 to 400 girls under them—are better-class ladies. The aristocrat who is accustomed to rule a large household has learnt to rule in a sympathetic way. Her girls respect her, love her, follow her. Like Tommy, they prefer not to follow their own class. The lady rubs the rough edges off the factory hand, and the factory hand teaches the lady a new side of life. Cleanliness, tidy hair, and more polite speech invariably follow the lady."[75] Again, criticism centered on workers' bodies: the "rough edges" consisted not just of poor manners but of unac-ceptable personal hygiene and insufficient attention to appearance. Because they re-sponded to their social superior, however, they were represented as firmly in their appropriate place in the social hierarchy.

The two-sided responsibility for both social control and improvement of condi-tions was explicit in a description of the Lady Superintendent (as the women chief welfare supervisors were called) at the munitions factory at Gretna. Mabel Cotterell's "wise administration" was credited not just with "a marked improvement . . . in health and physique, which good food, clean housing, and regular employment have brought the workers" but also with giving the women "a greater regard for truth, honesty, and duty."[76] To be sure, some of the reforms thus instituted led to safer working conditions and more pleasant amenities.[77] The language of their institution, however, was extremely paternalistic toward the working-class objects of the reforms. Lloyd George, then Minister of Munitions, declared that "the workers of today are the mothers of tomorrow." He continued, "in a war of workshops the women of Britain were needed to save Britain; it was for Britain to protect them."[78] Echoing the same sentiment, Alec-Tweedie argued for welfare improvements in the factories because they would boost productivity, and because the women workers "are the potential mothers of the race for which we are now fighting."[79] By invoking the image of the future maternal role of the women in the factories, this language worked to subvert the specter of the independent, masculinized female worker. The discourse further emphasized the idea of unusual work only "for the duration," after which the women would revert to the traditional responsibilities of motherhood. The middle-class "lady" supervisors were a critical part of this process of subversion, and a clear example of the need felt by figures of authority for social control over physically and financially independent working women. It also paralleled the traditional relationship between mistress and servant.

[6.4] Servants, Service, and the Social Order

These representational efforts to contain the perceived threat of working women in wartime were remarkably successful, as illustrated by middle-class expectations after the Armistice. Since the exodus of servants during the war years was only associated with the "the war work for girls craze," and not with the actual conditions of domestic service, many middle-class employers in fact expected a return to employment in private homes following the conclusion of the war. To facilitate the process, several training schemes were instigated by official agencies. Violet Markham led one effort which processed a large number of women; her Central Committee on Women's Training and Employment gave skills experience to almost 100,000 women, the majority for domestic service.[80] In another, as an offshoot of a program established by the Ministry of Labour to train "war brides" in the wifely arts they might not have learned while working in munitions factories, unmarried women were to be resettled into domestic service.[81] Woolwich Arsenal also organized a program to provide training in the domestic skills which might have been forgotten or never learned by its former women workers, with the intent of making them either better wives or better servants. This program was part of the general movement to return women to the household, whether their own or someone else's, and advertising for the venture described it as a new "call" to British women, "not to make shells or fill them so that a ruthless country can be destroyed but a call to help renew the homes of England, to sew and to mend, to cook and to clean and to rear babies in health and happiness. . . ."[82] The former munitions workers were being retrained in femininity and motherhood, revoking the masculinity of their independence in the war years.

Katharine Furse, who after her departure from the Voluntary Aid Detachments became the original Commandant of the Women's Royal Naval Service, also organized a scheme to aid in the placement of enlisted-level women as servants. This plan, however, met with lukewarm approval at best from the women themselves. What Furse was to discover was that the vast majority of former domestic servants, having experienced work which paid better, treated them with greater respect, and gave them more free time and less supervision, refused to return to the earlier conditions and demanded recognition of what they had accomplished.

This experience was not unique. During demobilization Helen Beale repeatedly received requests from people seeking to employ demobilized WRNS. Dorothy Brown had been employing a former WAAC irregularly, and her previous cook, who had left domestic service to work in a munitions factory, had written asking for a reference, "so they are some of them going back."[83] At first, Helen also believed that the Armistice would solve the wartime scarcity of servants; she wrote her sister Dorothy that "in a few months' time there will be quite a good supply of girls wanting employment and . . . you'll be able to get maids again pretty easily."[84] By May 1919, however, the supply had failed to materialize, and the same day that Mrs. Beale wrote to her daughter asking "have you got a kitchen maid for me amongst your staff,"[85] Helen reported to Maggie that their sister-in-law Daisy "wondered (as a large number of people do, we find) whether we happened to have any demobilized Wrens available for her house-hold! We haven't any . . . "[86] The situation was little better, from the hiring point of view, in September, when Helen was forced to tell her sister Amy that she was "very much afraid that [she couldn't] fit her out with any really nice demobilised Wrens suitable for her household.[87] The requests were not just from her family; Helen wrote home that "we are having to turn ourselves into a kind of Mrs. Hunt's Registry Office for demobilised Wrens and have calls from distracted and vague officers—evidently put up to it by their wives—anxious to get hold of maids."[88] Though Maggie told Helen she was sure that "the Devonport and Plymouth ladies will have deep reason to be grateful to the memory of the Wrens if you succeed in persuading your ratings to take up domestic service and if you fit them all out with good situations,"[89] the reality was that Helen "was afraid [she didn't] know of a single suitable Wren to offer" either the local ladies or her family members.[90] Helen did not generally complain of the character of the women working for her, so her inability to find someone "suitable" must have stemmed from general lack of interest in domestic service. Members of the middle classes may have been convinced that war work did not represent a new venue for working-class women, but the workers themselves clearly thought otherwise.

Resistance to a return to domestic service was costly for many women, as a job offer of any sort jeopardized their eligibility for the out-of-work benefit. Despite this, large numbers refused the work. Most of those who did return to household service attempted to set new conditions. Not only did they demand higher wage rates, but they much preferred to live out, and if required to live in insisted on more time off. The Labour Party became involved in the cause of domestic servants and proposed a Charter which would include a demand for a minimum wage, the right to work daily rather than live in when possible, autonomy over private bedroom space for those who did live in, and limitations on hours worked per day and week. One of the primary demands of the Domestic Servants' Union formed in Birmingham in 1920 was poignantly reflective of the powerless position of the prewar servant. The union members required that women in service be addressed by their own names, either first or last with appropriate title, rather than the long-standing custom of mistresses of households applying names which seemed convenient, pleasant, or simple.[91] Some of the middle-class fears of the effect of the war on working-class women were indeed realized. The prevalent language of "for the duration" meant that women's work which would not have been considered appropriate prior to 1914 was exceptional effort on behalf of the war needs—not a new long-term trend. However, this language ultimately failed to contain entirely the threat that such wartime working women had represented, as evidenced by the changes in their post-war behavior and demands.

Working-class women doing work on behalf of the war effort during the First World War were concerned with issues of pay and conditions as well as the needs of the country, and had to be socially controlled in order to protect the social order. They represented a double threat by their incursion into worlds of work usually explicitly associated with men, and through the increasing independence which their income gave them which seemed to undermine class positioning. Attempts at controlling such perceived dangers ranged from the institution of "leavening" middle-class workers in the factories and on the land who were appealed to on account of their patriotism to the insistence that auxiliary military "officers" be "educated women" to the institutionalized social supervision of "lady welfare superintendents." Their failures are visible through the widespread condemnation of women war workers' financial independence and allegedly questionable morals. This "crisis" over working women and servants shows the efforts which went into making work which was not traditionally considered appropriate for women acceptable for the duration of the war. To achieve this, popular discourse translated the language of work into that of service to the nation, but those representations could not contain entirely the threatening image of the independent working woman which lay just underneath the patriotic patina, and frequently broke through the surface. This is especially vivid in the ways the language of military equivalence was applied to working women: as a source of legitimization, it was safest to use for those who were most clearly not, in fact, soldiers.

The war served as a crucible of the tensions surrounding the position of the working classes in society, the position of women, and particularly working-class women. These concerns were heightened by the perception that the war was being fought to preserve a social order which itself had to violated in order to advance the national cause. Middle-class women were thus appealed to as "educated" elites, but the majority of positions, whether in auxiliary military organizations, on the land, or in munitions factories, were filled by women with experience with paid labor. Working-class women were condemned for not being sufficiently interested in the propagation of the war effort, and for caring too much about the money they required for personal and family support. In particular, they were condemned for the ways they were perceived to be spending their relative affluence, as the financially- and socially-independent working-class woman seemed a threat to the existing organization of society. Much of this criticism was focused on women's bodies and their sexuality, which became a suitable language for the expression of both gender and class concerns. This was an especially powerful discourse when it was contrasted to the risks and discomforts being faced by the soldiers in France, fighting—and dying—to preserve a certain kind of British hierarchical society.

Marketing Modernism in America During the Great War

The Case of Ezra Pound

Greg Barnhisel

In one of his best-known poems, the American poet Ezra Pound condemns the First World War as a conflict fought on behalf of "an old bitch gone in the teeth [. . .] a botched civilization [. . .] two gross of broken statues [and] a few thousand battered books." Bitterly, he refutes Horace:

> Died some, pro patria,
> non "dulce" non "et decor" . . .
> [. . .] disillusions as never told in the old days,
> hysterias, trench confessions,
> laughter out of dead bellies. ("Hugh Selwyn Mauberley")

Unlike World War I poets such as Siegfried Sassoon and Wilfred Owen, Pound did not express this acrimonious dismissal of the war's purposes and importance until years after the conflict ended. During its course, the war did not seem to affect Pound personally. When his friend and inspiration Henri Gaudier-Brzeska died in the trenches in 1915, Pound blithely wrote to his father that "Brzeska has been killed, which is pretty disgusting, though I suppose it is a marvel that it hasn't happened before."[1] In fact, his 1916 trouble with the English police for being an "Alien in a Prohibited Area" seems to have been the only kind of war-related hardship

Pound experienced. In fact, the period 1914-1918 was probably the most productive five years in Pound's literary life. During this period, Pound changed the course of his own writing and hit upon the ideas that would dominate his work for the rest of his life. Perhaps more importantly, though, he also helped change literary history by forging a symbiosis between modernist writers like Eliot, Joyce, and himself, and a new group of trade literary publishing houses, many of which still flourish today.

When the war began in 1914, Pound was best known as the irascible "foreign editor" of Harriet Monroe's *Poetry* magazine. Readers who knew his verse—and they were few—most likely saw him as a strange aesthete, equally influenced by medieval troubadour culture and the ornate Swinburnian verse that still dominated English poetry. With the exception of his friend W. B. Yeats, Pound's "Imagiste" circle—H. D., Richard Aldington, F. S. Flint, and Amy Lowell—were little known figures in the literary world, and when Alfred and Charles Boni published their anthology *Des Imagistes* in America in March of that year, the reaction was primarily profound derision. A few magazines eagerly received the nascent movement, but by this time Pound had already left the group and moved on to Vorticism and the Wyndham Lewis-edited magazine *Blast*. Compared to the brutality of the war that was just beginning, this literary movement's self-characterization as a violent attack against British society is ironic. After Vorticism, Pound's literary output increased dramatically, and by 1918 he had produced prefigurations of almost everything he wrote later, including early versions of the *Cantos*. In addition, by the war's end he had become a genuine literary celebrity on both sides of the Atlantic, both because of his own writings as well as his activities on behalf of other writers in his circle. But most importantly for the present argument, during this period Pound began to adopt the techniques of commercial promotion in his efforts on behalf of his own writing, of others' writing, and of what he would call later "the cause of literary cleanliness." For Pound, the period of the war was a sort of laboratory in which he developed his own vision of how commerce should be put to the service of art. His activities during this period prefigure the hidden symbiosis between anticommercial art and commercial culture that characterizes the modernist period.

Before 1914, most of Pound's work, and that of his colleagues, had been published by small publishers, private presses, and literary "little magazines." While many of the authors of the so-called "New Writing" craved a broader audience, before the war few of them had any access to one—their works simply did not sell. Limitation to the small presses and little magazines was not, at first, a problem for these writers; small publishers such as the Poetry Bookshop and journals such as *The Egoist* allowed the artists creative freedom without strictures on subject matter or saleability. By publishing in the small presses and magazines, these writers had a guaranteed audience of like-minded readers. As supportive as these readers and publishers were, though, there simply were not enough of them to provide a living to any of the modernist authors; Pound, for one, barely supported himself, obtaining five or six pounds wherever he could from gifts, contributions to magazines, lectures, prizes, and even parental assistance. Partly for this reason, Pound and many of the modernist writers looked back enviously to the period of artistic patronage. Pound cultivated a number of patrons during his years in London; Margaret Cravens and the New York lawyer John Quinn were among the most important. However, he was never able to fully support himself strictly through patronage, and his efforts to establish patronage funds for both Joyce and Eliot were only partially successful.

Pound brought a commercial approach to his use of the patronage system. The small sums that these magazines and presses provided Pound largely supported him through his London years. Unlike many of his colleagues who also found most of their income through these outlets, though, Pound became a driving force behind many of these magazines and presses. From the time he arrived in Europe in 1908, Pound approached writing and publishing as closely intertwined activities, and often took as much interest in publication as in composition. Pound also learned his way around the publishing world, and from the beginning felt as comfortable discussing marketing strategies as line breaks. He knew how to get his name in front of the literary public—as early as 1908, he was scheming how to get his self-published first book, *A Lume Spento*, into print in America: "The American reprint has got to be worked by kicking up such a hell of a row with genuine and faked reviews that Scribner or somebody can be brought to see the sense of making a reprint. I shall write a few myself and get some one to sign 'em."[2]

Pound, famously, also used his talents to promote the careers of other writers. He and T. S. Eliot orchestrated a campaign to promote each others' work: while Pound encouraged magazines such as *Poetry* and publishers such as Elkin Mathews and Horace Liveright to publish Eliot's work, Eliot wrote the short book *Ezra Pound His Metric and Poetry*, which Knopf published in 1917. Pound insisted that Eliot's essay be anonymous: "I want to boom Eliot," he said in a letter to John Quinn, "and one can't have too obvious a ping-pong match at that sort of thing."[3] All of these instances show us a Pound completely unlike the popular image of modernists as alienated drop-outs from the degraded world of commerce. Rather, Pound in this period (from about 1914 to 1925) is an aspiring operator: writing poetry, organizing movements, editing magazines, advising publishers, and even serving as an advertising consultant.[4] Pound was so well known for being a promoter, in fact, that D. H. Lawrence confided to Amy Lowell herself that Imagism was "just an advertising scheme." Ironically, Pound's talents at self-promotion were no match for Lowell's, and after the matronly Bostonian gained great public recognition for her place in Imagism, Pound left the movement, dismissing it as "Amygism."

In another use of commercial promotional strategies, Pound and small publishers such as the Cuala Press began to employ the limited availability of their books as a selling point in itself, emphasizing the commodity aspect of the work of art.[5] Contrary to the popular impression that the modernists were utterly uninterested in the economics of literature, and wanted only to create in an environment free of the taint of the market, many of the modernists engaged in such ploys as limiting the press runs of their books in order to increase their value. Numbered first editions (like Liveright's first run of Eliot's *The Waste Land* in 1922) and unannounced first printings intended for book collectors, the press, and influential critics (such as the first sixty copies of the Knopf edition of Pound's 1917 *Lustra*) emphasized the book-as-object over the book-as-literature. Pound, especially, encouraged his publishers to market his books as valuable financial investments. "Asked by Margaret Anderson in 1917 how best to announce his collaboration on *The Little Review*," Lawrence Rainey writes, "Pound . . . replied, 'IF it is any use for adv. purposes, you may state that a single copy of my first book has just fetched £8 (forty dollars).' " Rainey continues:

> Similarly, seven years later when William Bird was drafting the prospectus for the first edition of *A Draft of XVI. Cantos*, Pound would urge the same argument: "Yr. best ad is the quiet statement that at auction recently a copy of Mr. P's 'A Lume Spento' published in 1908 at $1.00 (one dollar) was sold for $52.50." These remarks, far from advancing assertions of intrinsic artistic value based on the presupposition of Art, offer straightforward claims about the performance record of investments within a commodity economy.[6]

Although the appeal to the "performance record of investments within a commodity economy" acknowledges the importance of the market system, in realistic terms selling such objects as rare editions or manuscripts also draws on the idea of patronage. Only the wealthy, of course, could afford to purchase these objects, and implicit in these arrangements was the understanding that the purchasers—Quinn is an excellent example—had a lasting interest in the works produced by particular artists, and would continue to purchase them, in effect becoming patrons to the artist. At this point, Pound was still unwilling to try his luck with the mass market, and sought to temper the uncertainty of the market with the assurances of patronage. In fact, he held a long resentment against Bennett Cerf, whom he felt "organized a sort of de luxe book monopoly" in the 1920s, "and excluded everything alive [i.e., anything experimental]." Pound's ire appears to have been raised by the fact that John Rodker and the Three Mountains Press were unable to export their fine-press editions of Pound's first two installments of *Cantos* in the United States.[7]

Pound's adoption of the tactics of the mass market in order to promote himself was the product of necessity. In his article "F. T. Marinetti and Ezra Pound," Rainey suggests that before the war, Pound had wished to emulate the Italian Futurist Filippo Marinetti's publicity strategies for his own artistic movement. The young poet, in pushing his "Imagiste" movement, adopted some of Marinetti's aggressive and theatrical techniques; unfortunately for Pound, the public found Imagism's quite non-confrontational character at odds with Pound's declamations and reacted mostly with bafflement. Pound then gave up on genteel Imagism and helped to create Vorticism, a movement which was quite near to Futurism in substance. Pound's main contribution to the movement were his contributions to *Blast*, the house organ. "Contrary to what later critics have suggested," Rainey explains, "contemporary critics were neither angered nor provoked by *Blast*. They were simply bored, and bored not because *Blast* was an incomprehensible novelty, but because it was all too familiar."[8] Rainey then goes on to state that this historical moment— the eve of the first world war—"force[d] intellectuals and artists to come to terms with the role of new institutions of mass culture and assess their bearings on the place of art in a cultural marketplace being radically transformed . . . [and] precipitate[d] a permanent collapse of the entire set of distinctions between art and commodity."[9] If Rainey states his case perhaps too categorically, the boundaries between experimental literature as art and avant-garde books as valuable commodities were blurring. Although they longed for the putative artistic "purity" that a system of patronage or of exclusively small-press publication would ensure for them, at the onset of the war writers like Pound began to look upon the institutions of mass culture as a potential, and necessary, outlet for their writing, and made their first efforts to break out of the small, insular world of the avant-garde and bring their work before the general public. Pound was the driving force behind this. He solicited large, established publishers for his own books; he brought Eliot to the attention of the literary magazines and, later, to book publishers; finally, with the assistance of John Quinn, he secured American magazine and book contracts for Joyce and helped find money to pay the Irish writer's living expenses. In England immediately before the war, Pound published his work primarily with Elkin Mathews, an established London publisher with literary credentials (he had published much of the Decadent literature of the 1890s), but Mathews was never able to widen Pound's appeal much beyond those readers who already knew the poet's work. As a result of Pound's efforts in America during the war, though, he and the other modernist writers gained a larger market than they ever could have reached through the little magazines and private press publishers alone, and made the first steps toward obtaining the wide popularity they would enjoy in the following decades.

The period of the war, also, saw the development of a new kind of literary publisher in America, a type of firm that saw no essential contradiction or disjunction in publishing works of serious or experimental literature and using modern, heavily commercial techniques of advertising and distribution to market those works. Established publishers like Ben Huebsch as well as new publishers such as Alfred A. Knopf, the Boni brothers, and Horace Liveright combined the mass-market outlook of the large publishing houses with a number of appeals also utilized by the smaller publishers: appeals using the object-value of the book; the "snob appeal" of owning experimental literature; and the growing feeling in American culture, identified by historians such as Joan Rubin and Jackson Lears, that the possession of good literature somehow performed a therapeutic or edifying function.[10] Five years before the war's inception, Charles W. Norton had introduced the "Five-Foot Shelf of Books" (also known as the Harvard Classics), the advertising for which emphasized both the practical value of reading and culture as well as the Classics' purported ability to be the "15 minutes a day" solution (the advertisement does not specify to what). This campaign, which encouraged consumers to "use books efficiently," played off the turn-of-the-century desire to maximize working and leisure time, as well as to enjoy the purportedly salutary effects of Great Books.[11] (Later, the Book-of-the-Month Club would utilize the same appeal with resounding success.)

Even though the bulk of their lists resembled that of the established mass-market publishers, this new group of American publishing houses became known as literary publishers, and obtained the prestige deriving therefrom, because of the presence of a Joyce or Pound on their rosters. Reciprocally, the enduring success of the publishers' innovative marketing techniques provided the modernist writers with a long-term income, and brought these often extremely difficult writers before the type of middle-class consumers who never read *Poetry* or the *Little Review*. While some critics such as John Quinn felt that the introduction of a commercial agenda threatened the integrity of art, many modernist writers—Pound especially—welcomed this cross-pollination, especially the greater cultural influence and financial rewards they hoped it would bring.

Although they all desired renown and influence in the larger culture, modernist writers were often quite hostile towards what Pound called "that many-eared monster with no sense, the reading public."[12] The geographical divide of Anglo-American culture underscores the tension between these two desires of the modernists. In London and Paris, where the movement began, modernism's main outlet continued to be the little magazines well into the 1920's. Although this was also initially the case in America, in about 1915 these new publishing houses began to bring high European modernism to the middle-class American public—and to market much of this difficult literature aggressively. American publishers were also forced to create their own designs and looks for much of the European literature they had been importing when, in 1917, the British government banned the exports of bound books and unbound sheets. This change in British export policy, therefore, led to a profound alteration in the way that literature was packaged, marketed, and "used" in America. The small-press appearance of the modernist books produced in Europe collided with the mass-production techniques that the larger publishers used, resulting in books barely distinct, at least on a shelf, from more popular literature. Knopf's and Huebsch's books physically resembled trade books while the fine-printing and private press books set themselves apart from books by their distinctive appearance (based on everything from gold-embossed bindings to unusual sizes and shapes). Knopf as well as the Modern Library, though, insisted to the public that their seemingly ordinary books were, in fact, refined objects. The Modern Library emphasized the bindings and quality look of their books in their early advertisements. Knopf's inclusion of a colophon in each book lovingly describing the paper, type, and binding of that book argued that the consumer had, in fact, purchased an item of enduring value. Giving difficult and often frankly anti-bourgeois works the comforting appearance of a typical consumer product, as these literary publishers did with the work of Pound, Eliot, and Joyce, encouraged the public to accept this new type of writing, or at least to grant it entry into the realm of the edifyingly "literary."

While these new publishers saw their first flush of success during the war years, the American publishing industry was still dominated by many of the names that had been prominent since the 1800's: Appleton, Doran, Dutton, Lippincott, Henry Holt, Harper Brothers, Houghton Mifflin, and Little, Brown. As in the period 1941-45, the American book market saw an upturn during the years of World War I. Even though the United States had no troops in Europe until the later stages of the war, Americans were fascinated by the war from its inception. Magazine advertisements and trade announcements were dominated by titles such as *A German Deserter's War Experience* (Huebsch), *How To Live at the Front* (Lippincott), and *Covered with Mud and Glory* (Small, Maynard & Co.). Although this increase in sales was driven primarily by war-related books, the sales of serious literature, as well, improved during the war. However, for the most part, the serious literature published by the established firms was quite conservative, with a few exceptions (Macmillan and Jack London, Doubleday and Joseph Conrad, for instance). The "New Writing," as the burgeoning modernist movement was then called, had very little success with the mainstream publishers until Liveright published Eliot's *The Waste Land* in 1922.

Pound was no exception to the rule of mainstream publishing ignoring experimental writing just before the war. After publishing a number of books with Boston's Small, Maynard and Company, Pound found that by late 1913 his books were no longer appearing in his home country. Quinn, his agent in America, shopped his manuscripts around, but got little interest from the old-school Boston and New York houses. Finally, in mid-1917, the fledgling publisher Alfred A. Knopf picked up the contract for an American edition of the controversial poetry collection *Lustra*. Through his brief affiliation with Knopf, Pound first made inroads to the American mainstream. Knopf, who founded his company in 1915, wanted his house to be more than a strictly literary publisher such as Pound's then-current British publisher, Mathews. Before his house's first anniversary, Knopf had already produced a list striking in its diversity. An early *Publishers' Weekly* advertisement featured W. H. Hudson's *Green Mansions*, a "big novel" that sold very well, along with blurbs for a cookbook, a doctor's memoirs, a "popular survey of Russia," a number of translated Eastern European novels, an "adventure tale," a dictionary, and an anthology of avant-garde poetry edited by Alfred Kreymbourg.[13] However, Knopf was by no means a strictly mass-market publisher. By 1920, his house was already known for its finely made books and its concern for every part of the production process. In addition to making sure that the main editions of his books used quality paper, good bindings, and attractive typefaces, Knopf also often printed limited runs of the same books, using even better materials. Pound's desire to see his work appear in limited editions that would become rare and valuable met with Knopf's desire to supplement his ordinary mass-market offerings with higher-quality printings, and for a short time both parties were satisfied.

Kreymbourg's collection, entitled *Others*, included six poems by Pound, and was one of a number of avant-garde anthologies published by large, mainstream American publishers at this time. It was also Pound's first appearance in a widely circulated anthology in the U.S. (Albert and Charles Boni had printed few copies of the book version of *Des Imagistes*).[14] Pound's appearance in *Others* signalled the start of Knopf's large investment in promoting Pound's career, and Knopf published four of Pound's books in the eighteen months between January 1917 and June 1918. In September 1917, Knopf published *Lustra*, portentously calling it "the first volume of his poems to appear in America for five years."[15] Mathews had already issued an English edition of this collection, but the Knopf edition included many poems that had been published in England since 1913 but were not yet available in the United States. Knopf distributed sixty advance copies to American fans of Pound's work and to important newspapers and magazines in an effort to broaden Pound's appeal, and followed this up with a second, much larger printing a month later. Before *Lustra*, Knopf had issued 350 copies of the British printing of Pound's essay on Japanese theatre, *"Noh" or Accomplishment*. The book barely earned back its initial investment, but Knopf apparently was trying to stir up interest in the forthcoming *Lustra*. In January 1918, Knopf published the short, hardbound *Ezra Pound His Metric And Poetry*, with its brief essay by T. S. Eliot and a bibliography of Pound's works, compiled by the poet himself. Finally, in June 1918 Knopf published Pound's *Pavannes and Divisions*, a compilation of literary critical essays.

The dustjacket for *Pavannes* epitomizes all of the most important differences between the small-press publishing philosophy and Knopf's desire to make Pound a popular writer. On the cover, in lieu of a picture, there are two paragraphs of jacket copy (later lifted verbatim for magazine advertisements), and on the inside flap Knopf gives a number of "blurbs" from the Cleveland *Plain Dealer*, the Philadelphia *Press*, and the *New York Times*—the fruit of his promotional efforts for *Lustra*. Knopf prefaces a 1918 quarter-page advertisement for *Pavannes* and Wyndham Lewis' *Tarr* with the motto *"FOR THE INTELLIGENTSIA,"* but the copy of these advertisements reads much like the publicity for any up-and-coming young writer, calling Pound's book "arresting and provoking, but too important to be overlooked by the lover of poetry." The language of Knopf's advertisement demonstrates his strategy for selling Pound: to position him not as a bombastic revolutionary, but as a respected figure, a poet whose works are important events. There is none of the self-satisfied, insular, self-congratulatory publicity we see in "little magazines" such as *The Egoist* or *Blast*. Knopf is careful to maintain Pound's avant- garde identity, but at the same time he reassures middle-class consumers that Pound's work will not be incomprehensible to them. By 1918, Pound produced another group of essays similar to his *Pavannes and Divisions* of the previous year. By 1919, he had a manuscript ready, which he called *Instigations*, and he submitted it to Knopf; however, the publisher backed out of his promise to publish it (most likely because of the disappointing sales of *Pavannes*). Pound was furious at what he felt to be Knopf's treachery, but when John Quinn, Pound's agent in New York, shopped the manuscript around, it was quickly picked up by Horace Liveright's brand-new firm, Boni & Liveright.

While Liveright had no prior publishing experience when his firm was founded, Albert and Charles Boni were already important figures in New York's avant-garde scene because of their Washington Square Bookshop and its Alfred Kreymbourg-edited "house magazine," *The Glebe* (which had published Pound's "Des Imagistes" collection in 1914).[16] Where Boni brought to the house his knowledge of and acquaintance with the avant-garde writers of the day, Liveright brought his enthusiasm for literature and his talent for innovative advertising and publicity campaigns. The house's first undertaking, in 1917, was the highly profitable Modern Library. As initially conceived and marketed by Albert Boni and Horace Liveright, the Modern Library's mission was to put out new and classic works at a low price. This objective in itself was not unique; what set the Modern Library apart was its enduring success, even as it passed from the hands of Liveright to Bennett Cerf (founder of what later became Random House). To American consumers, "the Modern Library was a kind of insurance policy guaranteeing that if a book was included in the series it *had* to be good," according to Liveright's biographer Tom Dardis.[17] In addition, the Modern Library was an early and remarkable success in what is called, in the marketing field, "branding." The brand identity that the Modern Library developed was so powerful that consumers would buy books simply because they were in the series, without knowing anything about the authors or books themselves. Modern Library volumes were originally bound "in exquisite limp Croft leather," as the dust jacket stated both on the spine and back cover, and also reminded readers that "People Are Judged By The Books They Read."[18] (The inital castor-oil-treated binding was quickly changed when consumers discovered that on hot days, the books smelled strongly of dead fish.) Eventually, this campaign accomplished its goal, as the possession of a shelf full of easily identifiable Modern Library books came to confer upon its owner a modicum of respect as a well-read, cultured person (or so the buyers hoped).[19]

Underwritten by the reliable income of the Modern Library, as well as the success of some of the other authors, Liveright's firm (Albert Boni had sold his share in the company in 1918) was able to provide new and risky authors with long-term contracts and yearly stipends. Almost immediately upon gaining full control over the company, Liveright began publishing members of Pound's circle, with Pound the first to benefit from Liveright's efforts. Liveright continued to publish Pound's work throughout most of the 1920's, but more importantly, he began to take Pound's advice on which of the Anglo-American authors were worth publishing in America. During his first visit to Europe, in 1922, Pound convinced Liveright to publish his works (and furnish him with a stipend), as well as to publish Joyce and Eliot. And while his agreement to publish Joyce's *Ulysses* fell through, Liveright did fulfill his contract to publish a long poem of Eliot's (which he had not read), and to provide the poet with a $150 advance. The poem was, of course, *The Waste Land*, and notwithstanding its difficulty, it sold very well for a work of poetry.[20] *The Waste Land*'s 1922 financial and critical success was modernism's first great victory in American publishing circles and signalled the beginning of modernism's domination of the American literary and critical world.

Although Pound failed to bring Liveright and Joyce to an agreement, he had already, during the war, done much for the Irish writer. At the start of the war, Joyce was essentially penniless; moreover, the houses that had shown some interest in publishing his *Dubliners* and *A Portrait of the Artist as a Young Man* had all finally declined to issue the works. Pound had read some of *Dubliners*, however, and in his admiration for Joyce's "hard, clear prose" resolved to secure money and a publishing contract for Joyce. In the period immediately preceding the declaration of war in 1914, Pound had been trying his hand in numerous American magazines, "little" and others. One magazine where he came to exercise some editorial influence was *The Smart Set*, a self-described "magazine of cleverness" popular on college campuses for its adventurous humor and original fiction. Through epistolary gladhanding and cajoling, Pound convinced *The Smart Set*'s editor, H. L. Mencken, to publish two of Joyce's stories, "The Boarding House" and "A Little Cloud," in May 1915. On the strength of these published works, Joyce found it easier to interest publishers in his books. In 1916, urged by Pound and John Quinn, the New York publisher Ben W. Huebsch picked up the American contracts for *Dubliners* and *A Portrait*. He also pursued *Ulysses*, but in 1920 decided against publishing the book because he was not willing to sink money into a doomed legal cause—the courts upheld the banning of serial publication of the book at the same time that Huebsch was considering publishing it.

Huebsch had a history of publishing risky works, and his house combined a left-wing and pro-labor outlook with an affinity for literature. He also sought out the type of avant-garde writing that brought with it not only a financial risk but a risk of prosecution. In 1917, he published D. H. Lawrence's *The Rainbow*, which was subsequently banned. His political and literary intrepidity endeared him to Pound: in a 1916 letter to Joyce, Harriet Shaw Weaver of *The Egoist* explains that Pound "considers Huebsch the best of the younger American publishers and by best he means the most imaginative honourable and resourceful."[21] Given Joyce's obscurity, Huebsch was remarkably generous with his publicity budget for *A Portrait*, placing advertisements in numerous magazines. These advertisements downplay the revolutionary nature of Joyce's technique, emphasizing the work's qualities as a realistic novel. "The psychological insight, fascinating simplicity of style and the extraordinary gift of vivid expression make it a promise of great things," read an advertisement in a *New Republic* of late 1916. By the next year, Huebsch was using blurbs by such literary celebrities as H. G. Wells and Francis Hackett. Like Knopf's and Liveright's copy for Pound, Huebsch's sales pitch for Joyce underscores the continuity of the literary tradition and reassures consumers that Joyce's books, although highbrow, are by no means aimed at a coterie audience. Ironically, these advertisements made their appeals directly to many of the same middle-class consumers that much of the literature advertised execrates.

Pound and Eliot, in their relations with publishers and the larger reading public, share one especially significant characteristic: their activities militate against the idea, now commonplace, that modernist writers hated the marketplace. The flowering of defiantly anti-capitalist little magazines and private presses in the period 1910–1930 is often seen as a result of the modernist writers' hostility towards the mainstream or corporate publishing houses. This is certainly true to some extent; modernist writers appreciated the freedom that magazines like *The Glebe* or *transition* offered them, and the spate of memoirs of the time (books such as Kreymbourg's *Troubadour*, Robert McAlmon and Kay Boyle's *Being Geniuses Together*, and Paris bartender Jimmie Charter's *This Must Be the Place*), with their now-famous stories of the editors and writers of the time drinking and living together, have caused critics and readers to associate the writing closely with the outlets. But Pound and Eliot both, for all of their pronouncements against the influence of the market on literature, sought not to separate themselves from the market but to try to work within the market's confines to transform it. Eliot's efforts were probably the more successful of the two. In 1925, he became "literary adviser" and a member of the board of directors of Faber & Faber; by the 1930's the house had become one of Britain's most important literary publishers. From his position at Faber, Eliot helped to shape and promote the careers of Pound, Cummings, Ted Hughes, Sylvia Plath, Philip Larkin, and many others. More importantly, by 1930 Eliot had become the most prominent literary voice in the English-speaking world, and had almost single-handedly transformed public and academic ideas of what was important and valuable in poetry. Ironically, given the despairing and pessimistic view of Western civilization expressed in his most famous poetry, he became one of the most eminent literary men in the world and his standards became the determining standards of what constituted high literature.

The intrusion of commodity culture upon the previously sacrosanct world of the avant-garde elicited a violent reaction from many of figures in modernism. John Quinn, for one, found himself at cross-purposes, needing for his own prestige to maintain the strict division of "high art" and "product," but also wanting to ensure sales and deserved respect for the artists he represented. Similarly, Pound saw this as a dilemma. Once he gained acceptance by the larger publishers, his profound desire to transform American tastes suddenly became a possibility; however, at this point he still feared the cheapening of his ideas which mass popularity would cause. Knopf and the other trade literary publishers brought Pound and Pound's group of modernist writers before the American public in a way that the literary magazines not only never could have accomplished, but (with the exception of *Poetry*) never wanted to accomplish.

But Pound's involvement with the new trade literary publishers changed this and, in the process, brought modernism to the mainstream. The literary tendency that, at the start of the war, proudly proclaimed its aloofness (as with Imagism) or its opposition to everything conventional (as with Vorticism) went into the 1920's taking full advantage of the very consumer culture it vocally abhorred. Modernism's ability to adapt to consumer culture ensured its enduring success. The John Quinns of the movement, skeptical of or outrightly hostile to glad-handing publishers, fade in importance in the 1920's, as the modernist writers and the mainstream publishers began to realize that their interests coincided. Responding to Quinn's vicious outbursts against Horace Liveright's "decadent" effect on literature, Pound simply said that Liveright was "the best of 'em. He is still young enough to think an author ought to be paid a living wage."[22] Later, Pound took the lessons he had learned from Huebsch, Liveright, and Knopf and tried to impart them to New Directions Books founder James Laughlin, who published Pound from 1938 on. Although his association with Laughlin is the most notable and enduring example of how Pound attempted to bridge the gap between publishers and writers and regain much of the autonomy and freedom of action he felt that writers had ceded to publishers, his work with other young publishers and magazines from *Contempo* to Kasper and Horton's Square Dollar Series also demonstrates this lasting desire of his. The relationship of the publishers and the authors was symbiotic, as well. Giving difficult and often frankly anti-bourgeois works the comforting appearance of a typical consumer product, as these literary publishers did with the work of Pound, Eliot, and Joyce, encouraged the public to accept this new type of writing, or at least to grant it entry into the realm of the edifyingly literary. The fact that Bennett Cerf turned *Ulysses* into probably the least-read best-seller in history testifies to publishers' ability to construct public tastes, and to the modernists' generally unacknowledged willingness to enter the realm of commercial culture.

Having spent the war years promoting his own and his friends' writings to American publishers, Pound was, by the end of the war, in a position to accept the role of "the most important young poetic force" in the Anglo-American world. He had fought his battles with publishers and critics, and for the most part, won. By 1918, it had become eminently clear that a new literary class had to emerge; after all, an entire generation of poets who might have become Pound's rivals had been slaughtered in the battlefields of Flanders. Dominating the avant-garde scene, with a strong foothold in the American mainstream literary market, and with no real rivals, at the end of the war Pound's revolutionary movement discovered that it was soon to become the literary establishment.

Dangerous Neutrality
Spain, the Great War, and Modern Catalan Nationalism

Geoffrey Jensen

From the initial invasions of Serbia and Belgium to the debates over Woodrow Wilson's Fourteen Points, the fate of small nations loomed large in the course and consequences of World War I. For many Allied supporters, the goal of a war provoked by imperialist, authoritarian aggression could be nothing less than the creation of a new world order based on the principles of democracy and self-determination. Correspondingly, representatives of oppressed nationalities from Czechs to Poles to the Irish perceived in the conflict a means to reach their long-held aspirations. And like many citizens of the belligerent states, these nationalists often related the war as much to notions of culture, civilization, modernity, and tradition as to pure geo-political power.

At the same time, even some established states that had taken care to remain outside the fray found themselves in the midst of war-related upheaval. In Italy, for example, the mere question of whether to take part in the war provoked substantial strife well before the official position of neutrality was abandoned and the first Italian troops actually saw action. Most notably, the editor of the Socialist party organ *Avanti!*—the young activist Benito Mussolini—lost his job shortly after the outbreak of war because of his openly interventionist stance. He responded by launching a new paper, *Il Popolo d'Italia* ("The Italian People"), where as editor he developed a new strategy of national revolution. It was in his position as editor—

and as a soldier for two years before he was injured—that he began to elaborate the intellectual foundations of the political program that in the end would affect his country at least as much as its actual participation in the war. In broader terms, some scholars have even argued that Mussolini's Fascism represented a rational response to the crisis of classical Marxism that came to a climax with the Great War.[1] In any case, the outbreak of the war did turn Mussolini away from the ideal of international proletarian solidarity and impress him with the power of popular nationalism. The failure of the so-called "Red Week" in June of 1914, moreover, convinced him and revolutionary syndicalists alike that the Italian working class and Socialist party were far from ready for revolution.[2]

These two ways in which the Great War profoundly shaped subsequent European history—by strengthening the claims of suppressed nationalities and by stimulating new political and cultural projects—come together in a fascinating but seldom studied way in Spain. Indeed, World War I had an impact on Spanish political leaders and intellectuals that was just as profound as that on Mussolini. Like Mussolini, many Spaniards responded to the events on the battlefield as well as to the social upheaval they unleashed by turning away from political, cultural, and social goals they had previously embraced. For some, the war represented a sort of holocaust of modernity, but it could also open their eyes to new methods and solutions for national regeneration.[3]

Prominent concerns of Spanish intellectuals during the war were nationalism and national identity, which—when not discussed explicitly—underlay discussions on topics as varied as social conditions, legal reform, cultural production, and parliamentary politics. This was particularly true in the case of the strongest form of nationalism in Spain: Catalan nationalism. Catalonia, a region in Spain with its own language, literature, customs, and historical traditions, can thus serve as an excellent case study of the important role the Great War could play even in neutral countries, especially with regard to questions of cultural crises, social transformations, and that most "modern" social phenomenon: mass nationalism.[4] The historian José Carlos Mainer has compared the Great War's impact on Spanish intellectuals to that of the Dreyfus Affair on their counterparts in France, describing the European war as a catalyst for passionate debate and soul-searching. But as the Catalan historian Josep Murgades points out, Mainer's statement is even more valid for the case of Catalonia.[5]

Catalan nationalism represents an obvious "problem" which, like its counterparts in northern Ireland, the Basque Country, the Balkans, and elsewhere, must be solved for the sake of a healthy European Union. Not surprisingly, then, it has attracted a fair amount of attention from scholars. As in many other cases, moreover, World War I, its aftermath, and the principles underlying Wilson's "Fourteen Points" contributed decisively to the character of the nationalist movement that emerged and has remained such a powerful force in Catalonia. But apart from some noteworthy studies published in Catalan, the profound influence of the Great War in shaping contemporary Catalan nationalism remains largely unnoticed and unexplored.[6]

This chapter attempts to make up for some of the scholarly neglect, offering an overview of the many ways in which the war colored politics, society, and culture in Catalonia. It emphasizes the war'ss role in strengthening the "modern" character of Catalan culture and nationalism—an ostensibly national trait that is routinely accepted and referred to in Spain by Catalans and non-Catalans alike. The war did not give birth to the notion of Catalanism as a vehicle of modernity; this idea had existed as early as the late nineteenth century. But Catalan regionalism then was overwhelmingly traditionalist and anti-liberal, and its corresponding cultural manifestation—the *Renaixença*, or literary "rebirth"—looked to a rural, romanticized medieval past for inspiration. As the twentieth century progressed, leading groups of Catalan nationalists did sometimes try to portray their movement as pluralist and inclusive, and some Catalanists did employ European-style modernist rhetoric.[7] But in practice socially conservative elements continued to dominate the movement until World War I finally guaranteed their definitive decline.[8] Furthermore, as this article will suggest, wartime conditions not only fostered a radicalization of Catalan nationalism, but they also may have helped set the stage for subsequent modern, radical right-wing nationalist thought in Spain as a whole.

Probably the most obvious effect of the European conflict on Catalonia was economic: the war precipitated a regional economic boom with social ramifications lasting into the 1920s. After the outbreak of the war orders from the French army as well as reduced competition from other European countries in the Spanish and Latin-American markets created a trade situation extremely favorable to Catalan industry. At the same time, however, workers' wages fell well behind inflation, and from 1916 onwards Catalonia experienced severe labor unrest. In that year the socialist and anarchist labor organizations rather uncharacteristically decided to work together and sign a joint-action agreement. The following year marked the beginning of the so-called "Bolshevik triennium," a period characterized by frequent political assassinations by *pistoleros*—paid gunmen who sold their services to either working-class organizations or to industrialists (or in some cases, to both). At least some responsibility for this climate of terror may have lay with German agents who wanted to disrupt the production of industrial goods destined for allied countries, as Spanish and foreign observers noted at the time.[9] In any case, the social unrest in Catalonia first unleashed by the war contributed decisively to the destabilization of Spain's parliamentary regime and thus helped pave the way for General Miguel Primo de Rivera's subsequent dictatorship.[10]

The Great War also coincided with some of the most important political developments in modern Catalan history. The Mancomunitat, a commonwealth of the four Catalan provinces, was set up on April 6, 1914. As a prominent Catalan historian has written, "Although the Mancomunitat was a purely administrative creation, its very existence marked for the first time recognition of the distinct personality of Catalonia."[11] The Mancomunitat attempted to rectify the infrastructural deficiencies and administrative incompetence of officials from elsewhere in Spain who, in the eyes of many, were both ignorant of and prejudiced toward Catalans. But cultural projects were at least as important to many members of the Mancomunitat, and it is in these endeavors that the background of the Great War becomes clear. For example, the Mancomunitat sponsored the standardization of the rules of written Catalan, thus helping transform it from a means of purely poetic expression into a truly modern language of practical use in the worlds of commerce, technology, and elsewhere. At the same time, the body promoted the publication of works in Catalan. The Mancomunitat also established post-secondary and vocational schools as rivals to the official state schools, and it attempted to foster the Catalan publishing industry. In addition, the Mancomunitat emphasized the study and preservation of the historical, artistic, and archaeological heritage of Catalonia.[12]

Why were these matters so important to the Mancomunitat? First, because culture and politics in modern Catalonia have always been very closely linked. But more concretely, many Catalan leaders believed—even before Wilson became a prominent figure in Europe—that the war was about freedom and self-determination. In his multi-volume *History of Nationalist Movements*, published during 1913 and 1914, the nationalist republican Antoni Rovira i Virgili had even speculated on the role Catalonia would play in a future world war.[13] After such a war actually broke out, some Catalanists began to reason that if they could prove their status as a modern, culturally and politically well-developed people capable of self-rule, the Entente powers would support their freedom from what they perceived as the oppressive, backwards monarchical Spanish state under which they suffered. In their eyes, the clear superiority of Catalans over Castilians in the basic elements of the modern state—bureaucracy and administration—dramatically demonstrated the strong regenerative potential of Catalonia. And such a demonstration would help them reach the next logical step in Catalonia's political evolution: a statute of autonomy. Such thinking came to a climax in late 1918 in the rhetoric of Francesc Cambó, the main defender of the statute before the Spanish parliament in Madrid. For him the Great War served as a lesson in how the reorganization of states might take place. Just as the militarily defeated "belligerent" states were now subject to the decisions of "paternalist" and "directing" (*dirigista*) outside forces, he argued, the Spanish state might also suffer some sort of forced reorganization. A way to avoid such outside intervention, he implied, would be to grant Catalonia the autonomy statute it deserved and thereby provide it—as the most advanced part of Spain—with the opportunity to direct the regeneration of the entire Spanish state.[14]

Cambó's program thus reflected the reaction of more affluent sectors of Catalan society to wartime social turmoil and Wilsonian nationalism—an attempt to simultaneously satisfy popular nationalist sentiments, preserve the bourgeois status quo, and reshape the Spanish state to the benefit of Catalan economic interests. Such a solution was by no means out of the question. As even the Spanish king Alfonso XIII had admitted in a wartime conversation with the British ambassador about Irish, Catalan, and Basque nationalism, a "federalist," less centralized Spanish state might be in order.[15] Had severe labor unrest beginning in 1917 not hindered Cambó=s attempts to push through this sort of federalist devolution, Catalan nationalism might have become integrated into the political system, thereby strengthening the monarchy rather than fostering instability in an already tottering regime.[16]

Thanks to the war and subsequent upheaval, however, the radical elements of Catalan nationalism had strengthened enough to make even this solution unpalatable to many Catalans. Hence the war served as a crucial agent in the definitive decline of conservative Catalanism, which had been embodied by the political coalition of the Lliga Regionalista. From this point on the Lliga, which had counted even the ultra-conservative Carlists among its ranks, lost all hope of retaining indefinitely the hegemony it had once enjoyed in the Catalan political scene—even though it did attempt to transform itself at least somewhat to meet the demands of changing Catalan society. Correspondingly, its relatively conservative cultural program, lost its appeal to the growing number of Catalan intellectuals who now followed the earlier example of their compatriot Eugenio d'Ors and turned to more radical ideas and thinkers outside Spain for inspiration.[17] The ongoing "modernization" of Catalan nationalism, it seems, had received a great impetus from World War I in the political as well as cultural spheres. Hence while conservative Catalanists were doing their best to promote the idea of Catalonia's suitability to lead Spain into the modern world, figures from the Catalan cultural scene were turning to futurism and other projects of a decidedly modernist flavor. In the end, d'Ors himself would even go as far as to make the fomenting of right-wing *Spanish*—not Catalan—nationalism his goal.[18]

To understand these developments fully, however, we must first look beyond the status quo associated with the Lliga and consider as well the context of wartime leftist Catalanism, more closely associated with the interests of the petit bourgeoisie. On the most basic level, the mere issue of which side to favor in the war provoked a far different response from the Catalanist left than the right. Whereas more conservative Catalan leaders like Cambó and Mancomunitat president Enric Prat de la Riba—even when known to be Germanophile—remained prudently silent on the issue in public, their more idealistic counterparts of left-wing Catalan nationalism openly interpreted the European conflict in terms of the values of the lower middle classes. For them it was the war to end all wars, standing for democracy, progress, and the rights of small nations in the face of monarchical and militarist oppression. It concerned, they believed, the very ideological foundations on which the French Third Republic had been built.[19] The Entente represented democratic and national unity, and its enemies imperialism and authoritarianism. An Entente victory, they argued, would bring with it the fall of monarchies all over Europe and the freeing of oppressed nationalities. The Catalan nationalist Eugeni Xammar even went as far as to differentiate the British empire, which he rather curiously labeled a "federation of democracies," from the aggressive imperialism of the German Reich.[20] Along the same lines, Rovira i Virgili excused English colonialism in India and Egypt because of the benefits he believed British rule had brought with it,[21] and he was anything but an unconditional supporter of the violent Irish nationalist rising of 1916.

Ironically, Rovira criticized the "German intrigue" that he suspected was lurking behind the Irish movement for home rule not long before reports surfaced that Britain was providing financial support to people its diplomats called the "Spanish Sinn Feiners" in Catalonia. According to reports by the British ambassador, the Germans were spreading these rumors about the role of "English gold" in the regionalist disorder with the hope of turning the Spanish government and conservative public opinion against England. As the ambassador's reports make clear, the British were well aware of the similar nature of the threats the Irish nationalists and the "Catalan Home Rulers" posed to their respective central monarchies.[22] The idealistic Catalan left, however, did not let even such obvious political realities prevent them from linking Allied success on the battlefield—even that of the same British armies that oppressed other nationalities within the empire—to their own nationalist aspirations. In contrast, the most traditionally conservative backers of Catalanism, the Carlists—who had emerged in the nineteenth century to oppose the "liberal" Spanish monarchy—continued to regard the British as inherent enemies of national and regional sovereignty. These self-proclaimed defenders of religion, family rights, and traditional regionalism vehemently supported the Irish actions, even organizing a funeral mass and subscription drive for the victims of British repression."[23]

A more pragmatic response to the Great War by the left-nationalists was their use of the myth of the "Catalan Volunteers," who, at the outbreak of the war, joined the French Foreign Legion and fought in France and the Balkans. Catalanist propaganda portrayed them as a group of 12,000 volunteers who had enlisted for political reasons. Actually, they numbered less than 1,000, and nationalism probably had little to do with most of the enlistees' decisions. Nevertheless, Catalan nationalists generated an amazing amount of propaganda about the volunteers. Auxiliary and fund-raising associations were created to raise money for the men, and the Spanish socialist leader Luis Araquistain liked the idea so much that he created a Castilian (Spanish) campaign along the same lines. He even organized an art exhibit meant to raise money for the "Spanish Volunteers." In Catalonia, the end of the war saw the appropriation of the Catalan Volunteers, once the object of radical Catalanist attention, by the Lliga, which now realized their potential as propaganda in the struggle for international recognition.[24] Even long after the war, nationalist historians continued to make widely exaggerated claims about their numbers, feats, and motives.[25]

The origins and long life of the myth of the Catalan Volunteers demonstrate how the radicalization of Catalan nationalism during the Great War brought with it a militarization of the movement in some respects, with a growing interest in spiritual vitalism and a concurrent need for a more martial nationalist model. The notion of bloody struggle was nothing new to Catalan nationalism, as the medieval combat described in the traditional nationalist hymn "Els Segadors" attests. But the Catalan Volunteers can also be viewed in the modern context of militarist, revolutionary nationalism. Just as Mussolini and some Italian syndicalist leaders saw intervention in the war as a means of fostering national unity, leading Catalanists portrayed the volunteers as the embodiment of the same sort of nationalist belligerence and self-sacrifice. This was not just a matter of helping Catalonia find a place in the peace negotiations after an allied victory, but it was also about vitalism and Darwinist strength through struggle. Not surprisingly, then, the pro-allied Catalan press portrayed Mussolini's nationalist form of "socialism" positively. And later radical Catalan nationalists would turn to this image of armed struggle—"*la fúria catalana*"—for ideological support. The leading post-war radical Catalan nationalist, Francesc Macià, would go as far as to consider the establishment of combat decorations called "Creu dels Ardits" for Catalan soldiers, clearly modeled on the Italian Fascist example.[26]

Not surprisingly, in the end the Catalan Volunteers made little impression on general public opinion in Catalonia or on the peacemakers at Versailles. The Entente powers saw the Spanish crown as anything but an enemy, realizing that it in fact shared economic interests with France in North Africa. Indeed, during the latter part of the war the Allies associated Catalan claims for home rule with Germanophilia.[27] But the war and its aftermath did affect subsequent Catalan nationalism in other important ways. Politically, the once-moderate republican nationalist Rovira would found Acció Catalana, a "modernist and radical" party[28] whose roots lay in the wartime Junta d'Afirmació Catalana.[29] And in the increasingly radicalized Catalan political atmosphere Macià's populist Catalan separatist movement of the 1920s, Estat Català, established what many considered a fascist youth wing: the paramilitary "escamots," or "squads." At the same time, intellectuals closely associated with Acció, such as Josep Carbonell and J. F. Foix, looked to the likes of Action Française founder Charles Maurras and Italian futurist F. T. Marinetti for inspiration. Indeed, as editor of the journal *Acció Catalana* in 1922, Foix was willing to write positively of Mussolini and Italian Fascism, even if he also made fine distinctions between the Italian case and his own ideas of nationalism and cultural revolution. As Enric Ucelay da Cal pointed out in an important but too-often overlooked article, the relationship in general between Catalanism and Spanish fascism was far greater than usually assumed, and the leading exponent of Spanish fascism, Ernesto Giménez Caballero, appropriated aspects of radical Catalanist thought.[30] The nationalist sentiment directed at Macià—whom Giménez Caballero called "our caudillo" and "our Duce"—could in the eyes of some intellectuals represent that "attractive Catalan combination of cultural vanguard and political populism," as Ucelay da Cal writes.[31] Although Giménez Caballero, as a quasi-official representative of the Franco dictatorship during the Civil War and thereafter, soon associated himself more with traditionalist, Castile-based nationalism, initially he perceived a leading role for Catalonia in the modern, national revolution he envisaged for Spain. With Giménez Caballero, it seems, Cambó's vision of Catalonia regenerating Spain through liberal, democratic principles of Wilsonian optimism took a fascist turn: Catalonia was now to lead all of Spain not merely in its modernization, but in the sort of national revolution typically promoted by the radical right.

Of course, much remains to be learned about the fascinating relationship between the Great War, Catalan nationalism, and the modern radical right in Europe. Yet even this brief look at the Catalan case has demonstrate how profound a political, cultural, and social impact World War I could have on countries that never took part in the conflict directly—even if many aspects of that impact still need further research. Spain may have lacked that basic social problem often linked to the rise of the European radical right: large numbers of restless, disenchanted veterans of "the war to end all wars." But the country did experience upheaval as a consequence of the war that could have highly significant ramifications. And although the nationalist aspirations in Catalonia so stimulated by the war may have failed ultimately to find satisfaction in the new world order that emerged, they did take new forms and directions that have characterized Catalan nationalism ever since. Above all, the Great War and its aftermath greatly strengthened the "modern" character of Catalanism, and in some cases this transformation may have helped set the stage for Spanish versions of the fascist-type organizations arising elsewhere in Europe. The Great War's role in shaping the modern world was simply too great to remain confined within the borders of the belligerent states.

Regaining the "Lost Provinces"

Textual Battles for Alsace-Lorraine and the First World War

Douglas Mackaman

Like so many other writers, a young man named Marius LeBlond visited Alsace-Lorraine during the era when the provinces were administered as a *Reichsland* of the German Empire. Touring through the Vosges Mountains and seeing in turn Strasbourg and Metz, LeBlond was struck enough by the people and places in his path to subject all of his time beyond the French frontier to a textual revisitation. His humble travel guide to Alsace and Lorraine, amounting to barely over one hundred pages and written in the second year of the Great War, had as its goal an artistic and literary glorification of the territory France had lost in the wake of its 1870 conflict with Germany.[1] Telling his readers that Alsace had left him shaken and haunted, LeBlond waxed eloquent about an "admirable countryside with majestic forests, lush green fields and a gentle, filtered sunlight everywhere," only to dispatch quickly with his landscape rhapsody and focus instead on the so-called "problem of Alsace-Lorraine."[2] The author then rebutted all those who in the epoch after 1870 had seen in Alsace and Lorraine not images of "Marianne" but instead either "Germania" or some ghastly amalgamation of the two by reminding his audience that since the eighteenth century Alsace's destiny had been a French one.[3] "The good people of these lands," the author lamented, who "live as we do and think as we think," had a history and a future at total odds with their unfortunate present.[4] Stating the matter succinctly, LeBlond assured the architects and supporters of the

125

"Germanization" of Alsace and Lorraine that their nefarious project was doomed: "She has nothing in common with you. The motherland for her is and always will be France. The stranger, for her, is you . . . Germany."[5]

Guidebooks and travel accounts written for German consumption, of course, begged to differ with the opinions offered by LeBlond and so many other French writers.[6] And the German position on Alsace-Lorraine, which held that the territory had a deep association with Teutonic traditions, the economy of the Rhine and the German language, was by no means a terrifically difficult one to hold or endorse. Not when travel writers, from Germany or elsewhere, could so effortlessly invoke an everyman's anthropology with regard to lineage and family names, writing as one did about a wartime visit to the city of Colmar, that: "the originally Germanic character of the people of Alsace is plainly shown by the family names. Passing down Rufacherstrasse, I noted these names on the doorplates and signs: Lang, Heilgendorf, Scherrer, Schultz, Weil. . . ." Travel writers who saw Alsace and Lorraine as German or at least rightly "Germanizable" easily adopted a language of realpolitik with respect to how France had gained the contested territory in the first place, telling readers that "melancholy is the tale of our (French) neighbors appropriating Lorraine first and then Alsace."[7] Taking Alsace and Lorraine back in 1870, therefore, was from the German perspective a question of restoration rather than conquest.

Textual battles like these, contained in books so miniscule that many of them were easily carried in a tourist's pocket, have never received the scholarly scrutiny that more traditionally political and "high" cultural texts from the war era have enjoyed. But these miniature books and their nationalist agendas expose an important discursive realm whose authors and audiences were conscious parties to a debate of no mean geo-political importance. With internationally heralded collections such as the Baedekker and Joanne series being joined in the years before 1914 by Michelin's offerings, tourists books were bought and sold almost everywhere in the second half of the nineteenth century, just as the decreased costs of taking trips and increases in literacy saw such books become not just needed but ubiquitously possessed. Belonging, then, to the revolution in print and the expansion of the public sphere assessed above in the essays of Regina Sweeney, James Daughton and Jeffrey Smith, travel books and tourist guides from the era of the war and before it are optics onto why the war was fought and how books were used to argue for different war aims.

What I seek to view through these lenses are the terms according to which travel and guidebook writers constructed their narratives and framed a vision of landscape such that international readers would find a compellingly French "story" and "mood" in their textual meetings with the lost provinces.[8] Together with official pronouncements on French war aims, general notions of the 1914 war as a *revanchiste* struggle and sundry tracts by bellicose nationalists in, it is my contention that these books formulated powerful French claims over Alsace and Lorraine and secured at least a textual precedent for the arguments that Clemenceau would go on to raise and at least partly win, when peace was made at Versailles.

[9.1] Constructing Myths of Community: Narrative Immediacy and the Rhetoric of Place

Travel guides of the late nineteenth and early twentieth century were not innovative in their genre by seeking to establish narrative intimacy with readers. Almost by design, works of this sort had historically featured an intensely close communion between writer and reader.[9] How could it be otherwise, when one tourist had to admit something tantamount to ignorance, by privileging the touristically acquired expertise of a fellow traveler?[10] But if eighteenth-century writers like Smolette offered their readers a portrait of worlds both large and small, nineteenth-century guidebooks would seek to invite the interested reader into the stories and landscapes under review, even if expertise and perspective often changed hands—from writer to reader—through some measure of condescension.[11] Thus in one guide from the early 1870s, after the author has promised his readers a description that will make the alpine foothills around Aix-les-Bains seem so real as to become familiar, the writer goes on to tell his followers "the exact paths to walk on and the precise places to stop and take in the stunning views."[12]

Guidebooks to the "lost provinces" were persistently oriented toward the related quests for immediacy and authenticity, which had characterized the partly Romanticist and partly Realist form of the best nineteenth-century guidebooks.[13] Crafting descriptions and issuing invitations to really "see" and "feel" the world under textual revisitation, authors took pains to explicitly frame for there readers what might be called the "touristic eye."[14] One standard technique for helping a book to become transparent before its readers depended upon the introduction of a local expert, whose vision of the land in question was supposed to set the sights of readers. Thus in George Edward's *Alsace-Lorraine* of 1918, the first of the book's descriptive episodes was staged around the charming stories of a hired, Alsatian driver. In a rickety car, the two story tellers—guide book author and local expert—pass toward the French frontier. Readers are tipped off early in this pleasant ride that something perhaps poignant or more is supposed to be felt when one leaves France to enter the *Reichsland*. The driver notes solemnly that just a bit up the road there will be a marker worth viewing. Worth viewing, indeed, as the travelers come to a halt before a landscape that sweeps to the edge of viewability, all around them. The driver tells his passengers to notice that the cock on top of the monument, where the letters of the republic—RF—are inscribed, faces hopefully back toward France. And then the temporary narrator climbs from the car to take us all closer, so that the monument's inscription can be read aloud: "To the soldiers of France who died for their country." Quietly as his guests reflect on the boundary between France and the lost territories, our story-teller once removed closes this first episode in a very personal way, by telling us that "there fell my father in 1870. Always there are wreaths of fresh flowers on the mounds hereabouts."[15]

The touristic eye was often appealed to even more directly in these guides. In the midst of some miniature episode on the culture and history of Alsace, for example, writers would try to offer Flaubert's attention to detail, while seeking to portray the moods and *mentalité* of a local population whose burden, readers learn, was to live as French people outside of France. Simple and lovely, locals were cast in these books to become people around whom the signifiers of nature could function with perfect ease.[16] Thus when one book turned its observational powers toward a far horizon, farmers at work seemed to merge so fully with the natural world as to make land over into landscape. What readers were given, therefore, were the "figures of ploughman, rising and falling with the rolling of the land, turning the fertile sod for the new crop," while in the foreground, the scene framed for readers was that of a welcoming femininity.[17] Detailing a village view where the heads of children popped in and out of windows, while children wondered who has come to see a small town in Alsace or Lorraine, the writer invited readers to look closely at "the flower framed face of a woman, glancing out at us as we passed," just as they were asked to feel the warmth of her welcoming cries: "V'la les touristes—they have come!"[18]

The community tourists found in such books was a mythically historicized and medieval one, where sober and solid citizens were positioned by the writer to stand in stark if unstated contrast to the dislocuted moderns known elsewhere in one's life. A quiet world of people who seemed to be human signatures of stability, the towns of the provinces were characterized as peaceful places where "little life was visible at the curtained windows, save occasionally the wrinkled face of an old velvet-capped woman.[19] From descriptions of so many old churches, which authors described as being "withdrawn immeasurably into the dim past, sunk in the forgotten memories of ancient Gaul," travel readers were asked to turn their focus toward "chanting circles of children, dancing a kind of ring around the rosy" and otherwise showing a calm and well mannered comportment as befitted the scene.[20] Stability and happiness, worn on the faces of the region's townspeople, were made tantamount to Frenchness in travel writing: "The people of Altkirch are very French in their manner. All those whom we encountered . . . were smiling and good humored, and the little old man in the stiff blue blouse at the inn, who was draining the lettuce in a wire cage, which he swung about his head, each pursued his activities with cheerful acceptance of the conditions attached to their several occupations."[21] If much of the modern age seems to have been erased in such accounts of humble and happily classless locales, this fabrication of community was very much a project by design. Readers learned that each of these content citizens "was apparently conscious of his established walk in life and gloried in it."[22] Thus the "really admirable fitting of each member of the community into the fabric of everyday existence" could be touted by guide writers as proof of the provinces' enduring fidelity to both France and its history of "community and good manners."[23]

Readers of these guides, in effect, became textual tourists as they were invited to both join the tour and take the voyeur's highly privileged views.[24] As one guide described the ruins of the Abbey of Murbach, readers were taken into the text by the author's friendly usage of an inclusive pronoun: "We dip into a little valley which opens into the Florival near the village; we skirt a great dried-up pool; a brook babbles under the trees; we pass under a large gateway, and suddenly we discover before us the two towers of a great church in Vosgian red sandstone, rising in the midst of the forest."[25] Told by the writer/tour leader that "we cannot forget the sudden vision of this grand mass rising, all glowing, among the clumps of wood which dot the hillside," readers/tourists assumed the traveler's responsibility to see and remember.[26]

The objectifying vistas that visitors to Paris could enjoy high atop the Eiffel Tower were in Alsace the rewards of a mountain hike or a cathedral ascent. Writers asked patience of their readers/tourists, as they began together a visit to some scopic height by first passing much time—while the drama was built—in the obfuscating density of a medieval town or forested path. But the reward was always hinted at, as writers invited their followers to "come along with me on this winding road and I will show you first a world of dark, undulating rock ground and clad in green herbage and decked with heather bells," all the while preparing the sojourners for the vision that was to come on high.[27] At the top of the mountain, pilgrim shrine or cathedral, the view toward forever was a savored narration that saw the tourist's eye gaze in awe and then with proprietary intent over the "endless rows of trees, silhouetted against the horizon, through the meadows, bright with poppies and cornflowers . . . and the summer haze to the faintly visible ghosts of mountains."[28] To look out from Strasbourg's cathedral and see the "blue slopes of the Vosges, running North and South," or to stand among the ruins of an old monastery, atop a mountain, and feel the optical expansion the guide books promised—so that one could "view the immense green and golden plains of cultivated fields . . . and even the distant silvery ribbon of the Rhine, where rises the mistily seen towers of Strasbourg's Notre Dame, or the snow-capped mountains of Switzerland"—was to transcend at least partially the traumas and banalities of everyday life, by reading these natural and cultural signatures of the Romantic eternal.[29]

Alsace and Lorraine offered writers, readers and tourists alike a peculiarly emotional story to interpret, explore and aesthetically memorialize.[30] Indeed, guidebook writers had an unmastered and recent past to contend with that was different from what a writer found when the subject at hand was Normandy, the Loire and so forth.

If guides to those other places had great cathedrals, pilgrimage sites, medicinal air or the lure of the sea to make their stories interesting and compelling, Alsace and Lorraine were unique in the period 1870 to 1914 for their hold over the French imagination. Travel to the territory was not something for the casual tourist to embark upon, as many guides noted, because the terms of visitation were more complicated and emotional than one found when traveling elsewhere.[31] Books about Bayeux, Nice or Vichy, for example, were unlikely to adopt the tone of this description of urban Alsace, as the author explained how in the territory "there are towns which at first sight impart to the passerby the secret of their destiny. The aspect of their streets, of their houses, of their monuments . . . tell clearly the lives, the customs and the souls of the men who built them."[32]

In case readers might have failed to see that visiting Alsace and Lorraine meant a pilgrimage of sorts, writers explicitly described pilgrim behavior in their works, just as they sought to show how community and the power of the church lived on in Alsatian pilgrimage. Softening what might otherwise have been an overtly didactic description of a pilgrim procession, one writer introduced the theme of pilgrimage as though he has come upon the devotional marchers by chance, noting that "in exploring the valley one day, we found the road thronged with pilgrims on their way to or from a shrine."[33] Readers are meant to see these souls as representatives both of a simple life and of an intact, almost medieval community, as the author reveals that: "the greater number were on foot, in scattered parties, but later on we met with the procession marching in two files. The children came first, generally clad in white and carrying banners and emblems. Those who followed seemed to march in the order of their age. Between the files were the priests, in full regalia."[34] What readers and the book's story of tourism are supposed to see and feel in such an account as this one, of course, is the enduring religiosity of communal life in Alsace and Lorraine. But at least as much as this, descriptions of piety, religiosity and pilgrimage were recitations of the devotive iconography that stood, too, for nationalism in France. So it was that in relating to readers how "a crucifix was borne in advance of the whole train, and an ornate painted and embroidered banner at the head of each file," writers were reminding their audience that higher causes and deeper commitments were never eroded quickly or without a fight.[35] Alsatian pilgrims, caught by writers in the act of "singing hymns or reciting prayers," became in these guides a solid stand against the ultimate encroachment of germanization. Fusing together references to a Romanticist natural world with appeals to the place of communal beauty in the nationalist figuring of the sublime, these descriptions of pilgrim behavior challenged readers to seek an exaltation in the tourist's literary pilgrimage: "We were told that these processions at night were most beautiful and impressive, and that the most attractive sight of all the poetic scenes which the festival presented was when the pilgrims, lighted by the glare of torches, embarked in large barges and floated down the river with their banners and sacred symbols all displayed, making the night resound with the sweet voices of the women and children and the deep responses of the chanting priests and choristers."[36]

Foreshadowing the rush to the form of pilgrimage that would come when tourism began to the atrociously scarred landscapes of the western front whose history is detailed below by Modris Eksteins, writers on Alsace and Lorraine paid homage to the war of 1870 in their prose, exploring in immediate narrative terms why textual and touristic revisitations to the history of France were vitally important if emotionally difficult to do.[37] As the most extensive French guide to the provinces would record, "it is a pious duty for every French person who comes to Metz to visit the graves of the soldiers who died during the siege."[38] In a detailed description of the cemetery and the history that had laid so many young men there, the writer sets very precisely the strict terms of comportment and sensitivity required of those who would visit this place.[39] Past the lone guard who watches over the military commentary, readers are lead to view the "fallen soldiers of France and Germany alike, who rest forever side by side, under an arch of billowing trees; seeing the graves, of course one can say nothing at all."[40]

Other guides would prefigure different if equally horrendous and sad visions of France's post-1918 modernity in the treatment they gave to the history of Alsace and Lorraine in the first years after 1870. Following the Treaty of Frankfurt, which had ceded Alsace and Lorraine to Germany and given citizens of the territory the right to remain French and emigrate from the new *Reichsland* to enjoy that privilege, the citizens of Alsace and Lorraine spent the summer and early autumn of 1871 deciding whether to stay French or become defacto Germans. Given until the first of October to decide, the period was necessarily sad, tense and full of drama. Guides and travel books to the territory almost all include an episodic treatment of the horrible epoch when deciding for Frenchness meant abandoning one's home, land and sometimes even family.

"As the fateful day approached," one book recounted, "the agitation of the people increased, as they confronted the bitter choice."[41] Sadly, this author continued, "many postponed the decision until the final moment and the trains going westward were, during the last few days, crowded with those who had chosen to expatriate themselves."[42] To French readers, the retelling of this story, even in a guide book's synopsis, was a call if not for renewed *revanchisme* at least for a reconsideration of the nation's importance. How could it have been anything less, as a guide reminded its readers of how "pathetic and heartbreaking were the signs of distress and sorrow."[43] While for American or English readers, many of whom knew the history of Alsace and Lorraine far less well, the events around the citizenship issue—which one guide would characterize as "unprecendented in the enlightened and human nineteenth century"—produced much sympathy for the French position that the provinces had to be regained.[44]

[9.2] The Romanticist Eye and the Cultural Politics of Seeing

If 1871 served in most guides to the territory as an opening episode of sadness under German occupation, the narration of this mood often continued through a discussion of linguistic "Germanization." Such accounts inform the reader not that France had been aggressively seeking to force much of the territory to learn French in the decades preceding the Franco-Prussian War—as France would continue to do in her rural and less "Frenchified" departments to the Great War—but that Germany after 1871 had imposed the German language on the people of the lost provinces.[45] Guides explained that French signs disappeared everywhere and that meetings—public, private and administrative—were all to be conducted in German. Even if many authors were willing to concede that barely one third of the people of the territory chose to speak French as a first language, writers stressed that "even the most ignorant of the peasantry are conversant in French."[46] Other writers sought to show that citizens of the provinces were equally at home in either of the two languages, citing anecdotal evidence, for example, of a bus passenger in Strasbourg, reading "Le Petit Journal" and then easily giving directions to a questioner in fluent German.[47] Whatever the linguistic capabilities and inclinations of the people in Alsace and Lorraine might have been, guide book writers with French sympathies wished their readers to imagine—in an era when language had come to be so centrally figured in definitions of nationalism—how it must have felt to be forced to witness one's children be taught a language in school that ran counter to a family's national identity.[48]

Standard for inclusion in these guides, on the matter of language and patriotism, were stories about how the embattled French of the territories was made to sneak into public view. One travel writer applauded French resourcefulness, after having explained that the tricolor could not be displayed just as shopkeepers were unable to advertise their wares in French, by telling his readers what he had seen in a grocery store window in Strasbourg. White candles, conspicuously placed together with red and blue ones produced a sign of living Frenchness such that, in the writer's words, "it was indeed a dull man who did not see at once the French flag."[49]

The pre-war and wartime guides to Alsace and Lorraine sought to construct Frenchness through a Romanticist description of landscape and cultural artifacts, whose lush and compelling contours served to bind the territory's impossible present and uncertain future in a masterable and useable—if mythical—French past.[50] In this spirit, guidebook writers tried to show that something eternal and of the sublime was the stuff of the territory's civic communion with nature's setting. Thus guides from the 1870–1914 period portray an evocative natural world, where the most perfect of all landscapes must feature historical artifacts—signs of culture—wedged deeply and rightly into the natural context of their production. For one writer, therefore, Alsace's charm peaks upon sighting a "beautiful church of red sandstone, the irregular gables of a little town, vines straggling up the hill, and, on the highest summit, the feudal ruin."[51]

Churches and ruins—the spirited religiosity inspired by these artifacts and their slow settling into ever more perfect rapport with nature—had captured the imagination of European tourists since eighteenth-century sensibilities had fostered Romanticism's first writers and travelers. In guides to Alsace and Lorraine, churches, ruins—and stories of religious pilgrimage—appear as signifiers of the devotional Frenchness which writers claimed was so much in evidence among the people of the lost provinces.[52] Similarly, cultural artifacts and their natural settings conspire to suggest precisely the long sweep of history that writers felt could contextualize the modern era of the German administration. History in this landscape was everywhere, and in its omnipresence it mitigated against the present's noxious everyday. "Written all over the plains, hills and valleys of Alsace-Lorraine in ancient ruins, prehistoric monuments and stone piles," as one guide book writer would reveal, "is the epic of a land already old when Caesar came."[53] Just as the castles and chateaux of the territory had come in the nineteenth century to be so many noble ruins, "where great courts are carpeted now with green moss and the walls are curtained with ivy," so would the sweep of time continue such that the pained press of the Germanic present would pass away. What was the *Kaiserreich*, after all, but modernity's addition to a storehouse of cultural relics that history had catalogued in Alsace? Germany and Germanization, the guides indicate, would take their place where "the remains of Druid temples still stand even today, beside the crumbling stones marking the walls built by Romans."[54]

In these fanciful and touristic renderings of artifacts and the out-of-doors, travel writers showed their readers what one guide book author would call "the holy places of Alsace . . . where the trees, the rocks and the streams are legendary and sacred."[55] Such sites, writers insisted, were veritable touchstones to the thorny matter of a national and cultural identity. If religion generally and Catholicism more particularly appear in many guides as crucial matrices of culture and nature, other writers chose to isolate the natural world of Alsace and Lorraine and see in it an identity that no Germanic invasion—not the present one nor earlier incantations of it—would ever obliterate. The lovely woods of the territory, as one writer would rhapsodize, were signifiers of the eternal. To the French who sought a timely reassurance that the *Reichsland* would be a fleeting administrative designation, his guide asked them only to search "under the mosses of the forest to discover the great stones of the wall behind which our ancestors sheltered their gods and their children when the barbarians last burst into the plain."[56]

To whatever extent Frenchness was formulated in the bellicose *revanchisme* that Barrès, Maurras, Déroulède and so many others would write during the forty-eight years when Alsace and Lorraine were a German territory, these textual articulations of nationalism were by no means alone in framing arguments for what France was and why Alsace and Lorraine were together with her in a shared destiny. Political, literary and toursitic, the guides we have considered in this essay constitute a significant set of utterances in support of a political and international position that would not form fully until after the bloodletting of the first war would end. If French war aims had explicitly cast the return of the provinces as a major justification for what the Marne and Verdun had cost, the latter months of war and the first season of peace would witness much talk about plebiscites, buffer states, independence and the like for Alsace and Lorraine. If nationalist writers would be joined by moderate politicians and a broad popular consensus on the fate of the provinces—which held that they had to be delivered back to France—then clearly the ground for this shared belief had been set as far back as the early 1870s. What we have tentatively suggested here is that tourist books and literary tourism were part and parcel of how and why a viable measure of *revanchisme* was maintained over the decades when Alsace and Lorraine were becoming ever more comfortably situated in Germany's sphere.

The privileging I have given to an assessment of narrative deserves a last reprise. The episodic fabrication of guide narratives to Alsace and Lorraine invariably had as certain an ending as it did a beginning. Tears, metaphorical or real, were easily let down to mark the end of a literary visit to the territory. Lest France or any of the great powers forget why the provinces had been worth fighting for, writers had only to appeal one last time—as George Edwards does in his work of 1918—to a "local expert" for a satisfyingly emotional drive toward the book's denouement: "Yes Monsieur and Madame," as you say, you have now seen and known Alsace-Lorraine, as tourists, of course, it is well understood, but, nevertheless, one can see that you have penetrated somewhat beneath the surface. Have you understood that since the annexation of our beloved territory, our land of tears is also a house of the dead? We are in mourning, Monsieur and Madame! In mourning for nearly fifty years, the people of Alsace-Lorraine cannot utter the word 'patrie' with dry eyes."[57] If the touristic eye was made to moisten over this discourse, it was not unintended. Just as the authors of these works would have been glad to hear that the small world under their scrutiny had come to seem like the most cloyingly romantic place on earth. Alsace and Lorraine, which the peacemakers of Versailles would return to France, seemed so beautifully and sensitively French a place, that authors like Edwards could make the land itself weep to be freed from the Reich: "Our last day it rained. Autumn drew her scarlet and gold draperies, and the stage was set for winter. Enormous storms of hail and sleet rolled down the mountains and spread themselves over the valleys, while on the peaks above the black clouds split themselves in fury. In the midst of one of these storms we left Alsace-Lorraine."[58]

The Iniquities of the Fathers
Ted Hughes and the Great War

Dwight Eddins

———◆◆✖◆◆———

> Visiting the iniquities of the fathers upon the children, and upon the
> children's children.
> —Exodus, 34:7

Ted Hughes's status as a second-generation modernist is closely bound up with his
status as a second-generation "survivor" of World War I. The vision of ubiquitous, un-
relenting carnage that Hughes inherited from his father, an *actual* survivor of Gallipoli, opens directly into the quest that he inherited from Joseph Conrad and D. H.
Lawrence: to explore the dark psychic energies, the quasi-demonic vectors, at the root
of natural process, both as they manifest themselves in the non-human cosmos and as
they surface with often explosive results in the human unconscious. Hughes locates in
this elemental vortex both positive and negative manifestations. In the nature poems
for which he is best known, the demonic is identified with the desire, instinct, and energy that fuel existence—what William Blake means by "Hell" in *The Marriage of
Heaven and Hell*. But in its negative, destructive aspect, with which we are concerned
here, it undermines the will to live and produces only desolation. Hughes's transac-
tions with this negative modality in his war poems exemplify what Northrop Frye describes as the *ironic* mode of literature in the "late phase in which it returns to myth"
and seizes upon "demonic" imagery to describe the world as "nightmare," as a wasteland of ruins, pain, confusion, and predatory creatures.[1]

The Lancashire Fusiliers, William Hughes's regiment, would have had no trouble recognizing Gallipoli in this description. A hundred yards out from W Beach, one of the two most fiercely-defended landing sites, they came under a murderous fusillade from the Turkish artillery, machine guns, and rifles massed on the cliffs above. As one medic put it, "Men had lost arms and legs, brains oozed out of shattered skulls, and lungs protruded from riven chests; many had lost their faces and were, I think, unrecognizable to their friends."[2] More of the same followed in the succeeding weeks as the Fusiliers tried to storm the heights above in suicidal charges. But the peculiar horrors of this disastrous eight-month campaign took other forms as well. Geoffrey Moorhouse's account gives the notion of a demonic wasteland a terrifying specificity: "as the thousands of corpses lay in the sun with their guts and their shattered limbs and their stove-in heads disgustingly exposed, the stench of death sickened the living for miles around. Someone said of Helles at the time that it looked like a midden and smelled like an open cemetery. So much raw meat was scattered around this part of the peninsula in the mounting heat of summer that the flies multiplied with Biblical abundance."[3] In a sort of metastasizing nightmare, these clouds of flies then spread dysentery through the vast majority of the troops, leaving them fouled and debilitated. "It is impossible," said one observer, "to describe how these men were living. Tall men slouched, thin, round-shouldered, bandaged over their septic sores, dirty, unshaven, unwashed. Men were living like swine, or worse than swine. Above these crowded trenches there hung the smells of latrines and the dead. Flies and lice tormented men who had hardly enough strength left to scratch or fan the flies off for a few seconds."[4]

Trapped in this crucible of putrid horrors, Ted Hughes's father was one of only seventeen members of his battalion to survive—and this after the battalion had been brought up to full strength *three* times during the conflict.[5] He emerged, in his son's phrase, "killed but alive,"[6] so scarred by it all that he spent much of the day sitting absolutely silent in his chair, occasionally breaking into jarring laughter, and spent the night shouting aloud as he dreamed of the trenches. Ironically, he was unwilling to talk to his son about his war experiences, which the boy had to learn about from relatives. Thus, it was the silences themselves that embodied for the younger Hughes a traumatic eloquence, and that forced him—together with the incoherent night-shouts—to apprehend a demonic darkness beyond the pale of words.

The pattern of tensions at work here is basic to Ted Hughes's poetic enterprise as a whole, and is almost certainly one of the dynamics that engendered it. The everyday consciousness is challenged by a vortex of elemental infra-human forces, of violent instinctual energies so incommensurable with that consciousness that they resist conceptualization. This resistance may be expressed in silence or disjointed utterances if the challenge is immediate and traumatic enough, but at a remove it generates the demonic mythopoeia anatomized by Frye.

136

The parallel with Conrad's *Heart of Darkness* is instructive. It is Kurtz whose psyche is actually invaded and ravished by the "implacable" forces of a savagery beyond comprehension and Marlow—like the younger Hughes—who experiences this vicariously. The former is ultimately reduced to wild fantasizing and incoherent utterance, while the latter weaves an elaborate demonic narrative that moves from the "Inferno" of the Outer Station to the "Mephistopheles" of the Central Station, and finally to a memory of the "infernal" river up which the nightmarish voyage took place.[7]

In light of these observations, the most striking thing about the three Great War poems in Hughes's first volume, *The Hawk in the Rain*, is that they do *not* involve the infra-human vortex or its demonic mythopoeia. Instead, the poet turns to the ironic modes closely identified with the original World War I poets, especially Wilfred Owen and Siegfried Sassoon. These modes are so strongly enshrined as definitive poetic responses to the cataclysm that they have acquired mythic status in themselves, and thus provide Hughes with artistic distance—in a sense, a double distance—from the horrific immediacies of his father's trauma.

Hughes himself, reviewing an anthology of World War I poetry, speaks of "patterns" that are "familiar" and "stereotyped" because these poems have made them so:

> After the first flush, the pattern settles to variations of the contrast between the battlefield in France and the rural beauties of England. Owen, Sassoon, Graves, and Thomas all use this in some of their best pieces. This simple strategy sharpens to something more serious later on, a bitter contrast between the landscape of dead bodies and the English-in-England complacency. . . . We know that . . . [Owen] intended his poems—as he intended those photographs of the trenches, emergency operations, and the like, which he wanted to magnify and display in London—to drive the actuality of the front-line sufferings into the faces of those safe in England.[8]

Both stages of this "pattern" are reflected in Hughes's earliest war poetry, along with other techniques in Owen's arsenal of irony. "Griefs for Dead Soldiers" imputes a much greater emotional authenticity to the unique brotherhood of combat—in this case, a "burial party weighing its grief ounce by ounce"—than can be found in "crowds" at the official "unveiling" of a "cenotaph" or even in the grieving widows.[9] One thinks here of Owen's "Apologia Pro Poemate Meo," with its closed communion of initiates, or his "Anthem for Doomed Youth," where the only funeral bell "for those who die as cattle" is "the monstrous anger of the guns."[10] Hughes's "Bayonet Charge" turns on the same mordant irony as Owen's "Dulce et Decorum Est," the gap between the traumatic actualities of combat and the deceptive euphoria of patriotic slogans: "He plunged past with his bayonet toward the green hedge. / King, honour, human dignity, etcetera / Dropped like luxuries in a yelling alarm." The details of the attack itself are strikingly similar to those of Owen's "Spring Offensive," where the soldiers charge beneath a sky burning "With fury against them" toward a "green slope / Chasmed and steepened sheer to infinite space."

Hughes's most subtle and complex embodiment of the Owen mythos is "Six Young Men." This poem relies basically on consecutive juxtapositions of peace-time idylls with war-time carnage even as it echoes the bitterly ironic "photograph" motif of the last poem Owen ever wrote, "Smile, Smile, Smile." Owen's allusion, of course, is to the Great War song in which the soldier is told to "pack up" his troubles in his "old kit bag" and to avoid wondering "if it's all worth while." In the poem itself, Owen describes smiling pictures of dead soldiers appearing regularly in a London newspaper amid patriotic rhetoric and promises of cheap homes for the returnees, even as he mocks the murderous hypocrisy and willed blindness of the Home Front. His ironic masterstroke is to suggest that the essence of the English "Nation" has been removed from the island to the battlefields: "England one by one had fled to France, / Not many elsewhere now, save under France."

In Hughes's poem, young men dressed in their "Sunday best" look out from a photograph taken six months before every one of them had died in battle. The beauty and peacefulness of the rural Yorkshire backdrop set up a poignant contrast with their fates: "This one was shot in an attack and lay / Calling in the wire, then this one, his best friend, / Went out to bring him in, and was shot too." For both Hughes and Owen, the photograph functions as a consolatory icon that conceals a dynamic of pain and desolation:

> Here see a man's photograph,
> The locket of a smile turned overnight
> Into the hospital of his mangled last
> Agony and hours; see bundled in it
> His mightier-than-a-man dead bulk and weight.

The difference—already suggestive of Hughes's role as belated survivor—is that the essence drained away is not so much that of a complacent England as it is that of a complacent present still threatened by the unassimilable tragedy of the past:

> To regard this photograph might well dement,
> Such contradictory permanent horrors here
> Smile from the single exposure and shoulder out
> One's own body from its instant and heat.

This notion of the war as unassimilable horror is crucial to understanding Hughes's development as a war poet. His appropriation of the Owen mythos represents an attempt to achieve this assimilation, but it appears retrograde and mannered beside those nature poems, in the same volume, where he is already exploring the possibilities of the infrahuman vortex and its role in a demonic mythopoeia. The disjuncture is significant. The demonic strain revealed in "The Jaguar" and "Macaw and Little Miss" is the *affirmative*, Blakean one mentioned earlier. Hughes, in fact,

138

refers to the two jaguar poems he wrote as "invocations" of the Goddess Isis, whom he identifies with "Nature" as the "devil" rejected by Jehovah, and also "invocations of a jaguar-like body of elemental force, demonic force."[11]

The jaguar in the zoo, "hurrying enraged / Through prison darkness after the drills of his eyes" and the caged macaw who "hangs in clear flames, / Like a torturer's iron instrument" represent a primal vitality beyond the ken of their human observers, who are in thrall to the realm of reason and restraint that Blake characterizes as "Heaven." When Hughes describes the bird as staring at "his furnace / With eyes red-raw," he invokes Blake's awe before the demonic fury of the tiger: "In what furnace was thy brain?".[12] Hughes's development into the major poet that he is has centered upon the question raised by Blake in its wider applications, and in the course of time he has—as we shall see—learned to deal with the demonic in its negative, destructive aspect. In his first volume, however, he is unable to reconcile the hell loosed by the Great War with the Blakean Hell of a necessary eros. Thus the incongruity between a derivative poetry of war and a highly original poetry of the animal mind.

By the time of his next volume, *Lupercal*, three years later, Hughes is seeking ways to close the gap. "Mayday on Holderness" attempts to assimilate the devouring maw of the Great War into a larger vision of natural process as endless appetency. A pond filled with decomposing leaves becomes a "furnace door whirling with larvae," a metaphor that recollects the brains of Blake's tiger and Hughes's macaw, but this time in an ominously expanded application.[13] Omnivorous, the North Sea swallows the unspeakable effluents of "tributary / Graves, dunghills, kitchens, hospitals." Organically inseparable from this voracity, the poet himself is an "incinerator"—another incarnation of the bestial furnace—and, in an elemental sense, nothing more than "a length of gut . . . growing and breathing."

Hughes makes it clear—in a stark line set off by itself—that this seemingly monstrous nexus of predation and digestion is not some animalistic aberration from the norm; rather, it *is* the norm, the very ground of existence as sanctified by the irremediable order of things: "The stars make pietas. The owl announces its sanity." It follows that new life, whether it springs from the "eye-guarded eggs of birds" or the courtship of couples "laughing in the lanes," is merely fodder for weasels in the first instance, or cannons in the second: "The North Sea lies soundless. Beneath it / Smoulder the wars: to heartbeats, bomb, bayonet./ 'Mother, Mother!' cries the pierced helmet." In this context, "the wars" are themselves fiery organisms that devour the son of man, giving the pietas of the mothers and the stars an awful immediacy.

It is significant that the poem climaxes this carnivorous frenzy by turning to the Great War in particular and linking it not only to the extremes of infra-human predation but to Hughes's filial heritage:

Cordite oozings of Gallipoli,
Curded to beastings, broached my palate,
The expressionless gaze of the leopard,
The coils of the sleeping anaconda,
The nightlong frenzy of shrews.

The choice of the obscure term "beastings" here is a brilliant stroke on Hughes's part. On the surface, it suggests the bestializing to which Gallipoli subjected its participants and—by extension—their heirs. But it refers literally to a substance secreted by the mammary glands of a cow just after calving to supply essential nutrients to the young animal and aid in the establishment of the intestinal function. The young Hughes "ingested" the effluvium of his father's brutal initiation as the paternal equivalent of mother's milk and it aided in forming the bestial innerness that he shares with the leopard, the anaconda, and the shrew. Grouping those who have internalized Gallipoli's carnage with predators that, however vicious and ruthless, are only performing their natural functions represents Hughes's most extreme attempt to normalize the seemingly abnormal; but the compound is inherently unstable. Hughes is imagining the animals in their wild natural environment, but the experience of the soldiers belongs to the "unnatural" demonic waste land, with its "cities of destruction," described by Frye: "Images of perverted work belong here too: engines of torture, weapons of war, armor, and images of a dead mechanism which, because it does not humanize nature, is unnatural as well as inhuman."[14] The denaturing and dehumanizing dynamic of war militates against the *normality* of the "beasts of prey"—including the tiger and the serpent—that Frye identifies as denizens of the demonic realm, where they are associated with monstrosity and evil rather than the amoral vitality of the life force.

Even within *Lupercal*, Hughes is already registering this incongruity between the savagery of the human animal and that of other species. The poem "Wilfred Owen's Photographs" takes Owen's reaction to the war not as its subject but as a referential mythos that also illuminates other forms of human violence. Owen had hoped, as Hughes's review has shown us, to use these war photographs as shock therapy to awaken a complacent home front to the pain and horror that it routinely countenanced. In the poem, the atrocity at issue is the continued use of the cat-o-nine-tails to enforce discipline in the British Navy. The M.P.'s agitating to abolish it are from Ireland, a country long familiar with the British lash. Those opposed represent the hidebound British establishment, who consider the "cat" a "monument" rather than a "shame" and identify it explicitly with "the old school tie."

Hughes relates the roots of this opposition directly to the war in the review where he alludes to Owen's photographs. He asserts there that the war represents the "fantasy dimension," the slippage into "nightmare gear," of the "oppressions and corruptions" of entrenched authority.[15] This analysis reflects in turn his earlier indictment—in a review of Owen's poetry entitled "The Crimes of Fools Exposed"—of the "politicians, financiers, businessmen, all who found themselves too old, or too importantly placed, or too deeply embedded in business, or too much of the wrong sex, fastened like a lid over the men who were rubbished with such incredible abandon into the trenches."[16]

This lid of civilized repression was involved not only, in Hughes's view, in perpetuating the war, but in causing it. The explosion of 1914 is the most dramatic example of what the poet calls in an interview with Ekbert Faas "the explosion against civilization itself, the oppressive deadness of civilization, the spiritless materialism of it, the stupidity of it."[17] Because we have denied the demonic energies of the cosmos in the name of mechanism and Mammon, they periodically resurface in cataclysmic forms. Jung, a thinker in whose works Hughes early steeped himself,[18] dramatically outlines the dynamic of this peculiarly human repression and explosion: "Dionysus is the abyss of impassioned dissolution, where all human distinctions are merged in the primordial psyche—a blissful and terrible experience. Humanity, huddling behind the walls of its culture, believes it has escaped this experience until it succeeds in letting loose another orgy of bloodshed."[19] The fatal mistake of this culture, according to Jung, was to abolish just those rituals of Dionysian intoxication that served to "exorcise the danger that threatened from Hades. Our solution, however, has been to throw the gates of hell wide open."[20]

It is in light of this unsapient quirk of *homo sapiens* that Hughes invokes the specter of the Great War in "Wilfred Owen's Photographs" and characterizes the opposition to the humanitarian motion as being—ironically—"Neither Irish nor English nor of that / Decade, but of the *species*" [my italics]. It is—as Nietzsche would put it—human, all-too-human, to hide from the truth of our animal natures behind bulwarks of tradition and custom, and to be traumatized when this nature suddenly emerges with an unnatural ferocity and indiscriminacy. The demonic, it seems, has its own norms and equilibria, which we alone are capable of violating. The resultant *breaching* of our barriers is, in this poem, quite a literal one. Exposed to the actual sight of a "cat" in all its gruesome potentiality, the "gentry" sits "fingering its stained tails" and passes the motion unanimously.

By the time of his next volume, *Wodwo*, Hughes is ready to discriminate between the demonic as the life-affirming instinctuality of eros and as the life-negating pathology of thanatos. The vehicle for both manifestations is a newly-aggressive, wide-ranging mythopoeia that conjures not only the larger significance of natural phenomena but the vortex of demonic energies that invest them. It is this technique and the surrealistic, dream-scape quality associated with it that brings Hughes's nightmare vision of the Great War into congruence with the archetype of the demonic wasteland described by Frye.

"Ghost Crabs" is an unsettling phantasmagoria that deftly exploits the ontological ambiguity of these spectral creatures, which are figments of our unquiet dreams on the one hand and embodiments of "the powers of the world" on the other. It is Jung once again who outlines the relevant psychodynamic, with his theory—according to Hughes—that "the psyche during sleep regresses to a genetic reinstatement of aboriginal chaos."[21] The demonic realm to which these monstrous fauna belong thus appears as an alternative shadow reality that haunts our everyday existence and periodically drains it of its substance, reducing our "cluttered countries" to "empty battleground."

Connections with the archetype abound. Frye identifies the water of the wasteland as "the water of death," which appears most often as the sea in its most alien and life-denying aspects.[22] He also mentions "the imagery of cannibalism," which includes "not only images of torture and mutilation, but of . . . *sparagmos*, or the tearing apart of the sacrificial body."[23] Finally, there are the "remote, invisible gods, whose freedom and pleasure are ironic because they exclude man" and who induce in man a sense of "futility."[24] In keeping with this pattern, Hughes's crabs emerge from the thickening "depth darkness" of "submarine badlands" to "stalk each other" and "tear each other to pieces" in their capacity as "God's only toys."[25] Since these "toys" have the effect of making us "jerk awake . . . With a gasp, in a sweat burst, brains jamming blind," it is clear that we are the ones ultimately being toyed with by sadistic powers. The situation is closely akin to that portrayed in an earlier demonic wasteland, when Shakespeare's blinded Gloucester laments: "As flies to wanton boys, are we to the gods, / They kill us for their sport."[26]

The most striking thing about Hughes's intruding of Great War imagery into this archetype is that it does not constitute an intrusion. On the contrary, this imagery is absorbed quite naturally into the demonic plexus established by the ghostly crabs, who appear "under flat skulls, staring inland / Like a packed trench of helmets," and whose attack explicitly recalls the suicidal charges across no man's land: "They spill inland, into . . . smoking purple . . . a bristling surge / Of tall and staggering spectres." It is the ontological incongruity that makes the easy absorption significant and truly ominous. The Great War, after all, was an actual and sustained physical occurrence in the waking, daylight world and the crabs are monstrous phantasms from the dream realm of psychic phenomena. It is as though, in the case of the war, the nightmare was made flesh and dwelt among us, proving that no substantial barriers exist between the worst we can imagine and the worst that can happen. Far from being the war to end all wars, it is the war that has never ended and never will, apotheosized into the eternal crabs that embody, in Hughes's words, "the turmoil of history, the convulsion / In the roots of the blood, in the cycles of concurrence."

The other war poem in *Wodwo*, entitled "Out," is perhaps Hughes's greatest triumph in the genre. Focused directly upon the carnage and the traumatic aftermath of the Great War, it extends the technique of demonic mythopoeia into new and fertile dimensions. It is here that the poet's father appears as the avatar of the war's psychic damage and as the legator of this awful heritage to his son. A quest that moved through the distancing mythos of Owen to the generalized demonic has circled back to find its mythopoeic origins in the immediate and the all-too-personal. But this epiphany, too, fits into the demonic progress described by Frye. "Tragedy and tragic irony," he points out, "take us into a hell of narrowing circles and culminate in . . . [a] vision of the source of all evil in a personal form."[27] It is hardly Hughes's intention, of course, to suggest that his father is "evil"; rather, we are to understand that the father is forced, as a scapegoat, to bear the mental burden of the war's satanic atrocities, and to be the inadvertent infector of those around him.

This last outpost of the demonic wasteland thus becomes, ironically, the psychic landscape of Hughes's early childhood. It is a place, says Frye, where human life is represented "in terms of largely unrelieved bondage. . . . and it differs from a pure inferno mainly in the fact that in human experience suffering has an end in death . . . . The human figures in this phase are, of course, *desdichado* figures of misery or madness. . . . Sinister parental figures naturally abound."[28] The "unrelieved bondage" in "Out" is suffered by both father and son. The former has been buried for the two decades since the war "under / The mortised four-year strata of dead Englishmen He belonged with," though he is slowly being dragged out by domestic immediacies. But the poet, "small and four," is trapped in the role of his father's "luckless double":

> His memory's buried, immovable anchor,
> Among jawbones and blown-off boots, tree-stumps,
> shell-cases and craters,
> Under rain that goes on drumming its rods and
>   thickening
> Its kingdom, which the sun has abandoned, and where
>   nobody
> Can ever move again from shelter.

Echoes of T.S. Eliot's wastelands abound here, and for a purpose. The demonic "kingdom" of the rain, with its incessant haunting of memory, and the scattered "jawbones" of once-intact men recall "death's dream kingdom" and "This broken jaw of our lost kingdoms" in "The Hollow Men."[29] Eliot's poem *The Waste Land* is also recapitulated, but with a life-negating rain systematically substituted for the life-negating drought. Eliot's "Son of man," like the son of William Hughes, inherits only: "A heap of broken images, where the sun beats / And the dead tree gives no shelter . . . / And the dry stone no sound of water.[30] Hughes as mythopoeic practitioner here appropriates a poem that is itself a compendious appropriation of myths, thus ensconcing the Great War in the classical succession of demonic archetypes. The hallucinatory memories stored by both father and son in turn acquire something of the mythical resonance associated with the harrowing visions of the seer Tiresias, who unites Eliot's poem—according to the poet's own note—through what he in some sense beholds.

In a brilliant rhetorical move, Hughes frames this rich melange of myth with an affirmative creation myth, to which it then lends its demonic coloration. "The Dream Time," the title of the first section of "Out," is the name given by Australian aborigines to the period in which supernatural beings first shaped human beings and other living creatures into their present form and laid down the rules by which we are to order our existence: "The mythological era . . . is regarded as setting a precedent for all human behavior from that time on. It was the period when patterns of living were established, and laws laid down for human beings to follow."[31] The disclosure of this sacred history to the new initiate sometimes takes, according to Mircea Eliade, "many years. Step by step, the individual becomes aware of the greatness of the mythical past. He learns how to relive the Dream Time," and perpetually reenacts "the stupendous events of the beginning."[32]

There is a richly mordant irony in applying this myth of humanity's shaping by the gods to the war's demonic shaping of Hughes's childhood. This "Dream Time" was, in fact, a nightmare time, and the greatest horror of all is that it sets an immutable precedent, a pattern of ghastly revelation and trauma that is definitive and inescapable in its awful repetitions and the psychic damage it leaves behind:

> My father sat in his chair recovering
> From the four-year mastication by gunfire and mud,
> Body buffeted wordless, estranged by long soaking
> In the colors of mutilation.

"Fair seed-time had my soul," exclaims Wordsworth, looking back on a childhood blessed by a benevolent, nurturing landscape.[33] Hughes, however, brought up in ironic proximity to the English Lake District, endured a seed-time shaped by Gallipoli, twenty years and half a world away. His nurturing landscape is the monstrous realm of "Ghost Crabs," with its mastication, mutilation, and mythical *sparagmos*.

The rest of the poem expands this notion of a demonic seed-time through the basic "wasteland" technique by which fertility symbols are perverted into their opposites. In the second section, the regeneration represented by birth is ironically conflated with the degeneration of a dead soldier: "The dead man in his cave beginning to sweat; / The melting bronze visor of flesh / Of the mother in the baby-furnace." After the moments of intense anguish represented by both birth pains and decimating combat wounds, the participants experience a deceptive moment of trivial routine:

144

And it's just another baby.
As after being blasted to bits
The reassembled infantryman
Tentatively totters out, gazing about with the eyes
Of an exhausted clerk.

This last image takes us back to the wounded father of the first stanza, "His outer perforations . . . valiantly healed" but his spirit stunned and depleted, and to the infant Hughes as his grotesquely premature replica.

The last section of the poem, entitled "Remembrance Day," is centered upon the artificial poppies worn annually to commemorate the British dead of the Great War. Here we might recall the "hyacinth garden" scene of Eliot's poem *The Waste Land*, in which that flower, an ancient Greek symbol of fertility and renewal, presides over a scene of sterility and emotional deadness.[34] The red poppy supposedly symbolizes the new life springing from the spilt blood of the soldiers, and thus the vital fruition of their sacrifice in the rich garden of national memory. But in Hughes's demonic waste land it is a decadent and fabricated parody of this, "A canvas-beauty puppet on a wire / Today whoring everywhere." Like the conflated corpse and new-born of section II, it suggests the "mouth / Of the grave, maybe of the womb searching" for their hapless occupant. Its power to resurrect the dead and make them one with the living is preempted by a more sinister dynamic of demonic bondage:

The shrapnel that shattered my father's paybook

Gripped me, and all his dead
Gripped him to a time

He no more than they could outgrow, but, cast into one,
    like iron,
Hung deeper than refreshing of ploughs

In the woe-dark under my mother's eye.

This notion of shrapnel as the symbol of the wasteland's mutilating forces clearly haunts Hughes. In the Faas interview, he traces the origins of T.S. Eliot's *The Waste Land* to the spiritual lacerations inflicted by "the disintegration of Western civilization," and suggests that "His sickness told him the cause. . . . He cleaned his wounds and found the shrapnel."[35] The landscape of the mutilated psyche, like the French fields rendered untillable by the shredded metal of explosives, remains impervious to "the refreshing of ploughs." This being the case, the only resurrection Remembrance Day effects is that of spectral figures ravaged by a predatory war under the auspices of patriotic sacrifice. It is this meditation that leads to Hughes's concluding line: "Let England close. Let the green sea-anemone close." In his poem *Milton*,

William Blake had lamented the demonic metamorphosis of "England's green & pleasant land"[36] into a waste land of "dark, Satanic Mills." For Hughes, that metamorphosis produced a green invertebrate carnivore that devoured its own in the name of nationalism. By refusing the sustenance of commemoration, the poet undertakes to "close" the tentacles of the cannibalistic motherland.

It is one thing to refuse to honor a memory, however; quite another to heal the psychic wound of the memory's persistence. The Great War as cultural trauma exhibits a pernicious tenacity in the Yorkshire valley that was home to William Hughes and others of the Lancashire Fusiliers and is the setting of his son's volume *Remains of Elmet*, published eight years after *Wodwo*. In this book, Hughes is beginning to examine more seriously the usefulness of various Oriental philosophies, especially the Tao, in harmonizing the sense of dissonance that arises from the encounter of the human ego with the demonic energies of nature. As Leonard Scigaj, the most assiduous scholar of Oriental influences on Hughes, describes it: "In Taoism, one achieves the Great Serenity by participating in the Allness of nature and penetrating beyond sense objects to glimpse a higher reality (the Tao) orchestrating the panoply of change in the phenomenal world."[37] It seems to me that Scigaj overestimates the degree to which the Taoist view prevails in *Remains of Elmet*, and that the demonic mythopoeia of the earlier poems continues to appear in alternation with its Taoist counterpart. At times one ends up with an almost Manichaean dialectic between the two. Even so, Scigaj emphasizes, quite rightly, the anti-Taoist nature of the rigid "Protestant ethic" and the "mechanistic science" that covered the Calder valley with the spirit-stifling mills of the Industrial Revolution and contributed substantially to the demonic eruption of 1914.[38] The Great War is, on a grand scale, precisely the sort of event that Alan Watts describes as incompatible with the Tao principle of harmonizing, an event that forces those involved "into conformity with some arbitrary, artificial, and abstract order."[39]

The poem "Hardcastle Crags" opens with a Taoist proverb, "Think often of the silent valley, for the God lives there."[40] The notion here is of a silence betokening a divinely-ordained equilibrium between natural destruction and natural renewal as the fallen leaves turn into rich loam and the ants carry on a "warfare" that is ultimately in the interest of their species. This beatific silence is opposed, however, by the more sinister silence of the now-defunct mills and the post-Armistice guns—an all-too-present absence now inseparable from the *genius loci* of the Calder valley, where "the beech-tree solemnities / Muffle much cordite." Even the waters of the valley reflect the conflict. According to the Taoist philosopher Lao-tzu, "The highest good is like water, / for the good of water is that it nourishes everything without striving. . . . It is thus that Tao in the world is like a / river going down the valley to the ocean."[41] But the demonic wasteland superimposed upon the harmonious valley also has—as we have seen—its "water of death." The Calder so polluted by the mills is now a "dilapidated river," its voice mystified by "Name lists" from the cenotaphs commemorating the dead soldiers. Even the picnickers on its shore are subject to this haunting as they "paddle in the fringes of fear." The last stanza returns us to the Taoist water of "happiness," which is "broken water at the bottom of a precipice" in a place where nature benevolently repairs its own damages and the "air-stir" is identical with the "love-murmurs" of young men who once courted here. But even this idyll is disrupted by the description of the lovers as "a generation of slaves / Whose bones melted in Asia Minor." It is a desolating and desecrating image in which two demonic waste lands, that of the dark, Satanic mills and that of Gallipoli, merge to suggest that some ravagings, at least in the short run, lie beyond the pale of cosmic healing.

Two other poems in the volume also rely upon this nexus of technological oppression and battlefield carnage—the malaise of the spirit in grotesquely intimate connection with the destruction of the body—and upon the same notion of silence perverted into the silence of death. In one of them, "First, Mills," the title is one of the premises in a brutally compressed enthymeme: "First Mills and steep stone cobbles / Then cenotaphs." The despoiling of the valley into a charnel midden is presented in battle terminology: the railway station as a "bottomless wound . . . That bled this valley to death," the hills "commandeered / For gravemounds," the "sacked" towns. And, to remind us which war is providing this figuration: "Over this trench / A sky like an empty helmet / With a hole in it." The "two minutes" of "silence / In the childhood of earth" that follow this litany of ruin mock the very notion of commemoration in the face of impersonal cosmic process.

In the other poem, "The Sheep Went On Being Dead," the sheep's crumbling skeleton becomes an insidiously powerful and tenacious *momento mori* that expands to include the men who experienced a living death in the now-closed mills and who were themselves reduced to skeletal remains by the Great War. In this waste land of "crucified oaks" and "slovenly bracken," the "shouting above looms" blends with other vanished sounds among the decaying remains:

> The throb of mills and the crying of lambs
> Like shouting in Flanders
> Muffled away
> In white curls
> And memorial knuckles
> Under hikers' heels.

Hughes brilliantly brings together in these lines the exploitation of the innocents deplored by Blake and the slaughter of the innocents deplored by Owen. The chimney sweep who cries in *Songs of Innocence* because "his head, / That curled like a

147

lamb's back, was shaved"[42] is a victim of the same dark forces that co-opt the subject of Owen's "Arms and the Boy." The child-soldier is mechanically transformed into both predator and prey even though "God will grow no talons at his heels, / Nor antlers through the thickness of his curls."[43]

These three poems in *Remains of Elmet* quite literally bring the war home for Hughes, illustrating Frye's notion, discussed above, of the "hell of narrowing circles" into which the waste-land journey leads us. And at the end of this journey, anticipated by the poem "Out," is William Hughes, who embodies the demonic ravagings "in a personal form." In the volume *Wolfwatching*, published in 1989, this personalization of mythic horror is fleshed out in extensive detail in no fewer than five poems—a tribute to Hughes's continuing obsession with the war and its effects. The domestic realm, depicted here with painstaking realism, is so intensely and thoroughly penetrated by the demonic that both its ontological status and its chronological status as familiar quotidian reality are destabilized. It is precisely because the Great War was so radically disorientating and so violently destructive of previous human norms that its awful phantasmagoria is able to infiltrate and subvert the seemingly solid structures of the nurturing home environment and supportive family relations. It is exactly these structures, in fact, that serve as intensifying foils for the spectral terrors, an ironic technique anticipated by W.H. Auden when he describes the wasteland invoked by wildly selfish fantasy:

> The glacier knocks in the cupboard,
>   The desert sighs in the bed,
> And the crack in the tea-cup opens
>   A lane to the land of the dead.[44]

In "Dust as We Are," Hughes recalls his "post-war father" sitting silent in his chair, listening to sounds not literally present, but which the young son imagines to be the noise of machine guns raking the trenches and filling them with bloody, mangled corpses. The reassuring solidity of the domestic sanctum is violated by phantasmal carnage so that even the most innocent, playful gestures are transformed into demonic visions. The father's attempt, for instance to take up "his pre-war *joie de vivre*" by flexing his muscles produces instead a "bleached montage":

>   lit landscapes:
> Swampquakes of the slime of puddled soldiers
> Where bones and bits of equipment
> Showered from every shell-burst.
>   Naked men
> Slithered staring where their mothers and sisters
> Would never have to meet their eyes, or see
> Exactly how they sprawled and were trodden.

148

Alternatively, his father's muscles are the "marble-white" muscles of a corpse that has been somehow resurrected—"killed but alive"—like the walking dead of Eliot's waste land, who elicit the exclamation "so many, / I had not thought death had undone so many."[45] The forbidden "knowledge" that produced this death-in-life is passed on to the hapless son as the "mother's milk" of the soul, which is deformed into a grotesque denizen of the demonic wasteland: "So the soul grew. / A strange thing with rickets—a hyena. / No singing—that kind of laughter." There is no "pre-war" or "post-war" in such a spiritual heritage, there is only a spectral carnage that renews itself endlessly.

It is significant to find, as I mentioned earlier, that Hughes gleaned the specifics of his fatal knowledge not from the father but from others who knew of the father's wartime experiences. In "For the Duration," we learn not only that William Hughes was blasted into a trench by an exploding shell as he carried the wounded to safety—an action for which he won the D.C.M.—but also that he was wounded over the heart by shrapnel and in the ankle, as he went over the top, by a traversing machine gun. For the vulnerable son, the very talk of war was like "a creeping barrage" in their own house, menacing a still-vulnerable father, whose silence seemed to suggest that his experience had been too terrible for words. Articulate description, no matter how horrendous, would have dragged that experience into the daylight realm of a delimited and ultimately assimilable past rather than leaving it to fester in the realm of ineffable nightmare. But it is precisely in the father's nightmares that it surfaces, in shouts that resurrect the purgatorial vistas of his memory in the very precincts of familial security:

> I could hear you from my bedroom—
> The whole hopelessness still going on,
> No man's land still crying and burning
> Inside our house, and you climbing again
> Out of the trench, and wading back into the glare
>
> As if you might still not manage to reach us
> And carry us to safety.

In the last poem I will examine, "Walt," we find that Hughes's father is not the family's only carrier of the demonic infection, which now comes to seem so epidemic as to preclude any hope of escape. During a country walk, the poet's maternal uncle passes on to his young nephew his own harrowing experience of the Great War. The memory, encroaching on the present pastoral, involves a German prisoner whose eye, the uncle believes, cursed him as he passed and brought on his subsequent wounding in the groin. Rolling into a shell-hole, he was clipped by yet another bullet, and burrowed "deeper down" while the sniper's shots dug at the crater. Lying there bleeding and frightened, he sought escape in memories of long walks through the familiar, beloved countryside of the present excursion.

Using the corn field where he and his nephew are standing to illustrate the episode, Uncle Walt ends up conflating the peaceful present with the violent past and the Yorkshire landscape with the killing fields of Flanders: " 'Here,' he hazarded, 'Somewhere just about here. / This is where he stopped me. I got this far.' " The identity is not entirely metaphorical; both uncle and nephew suffer the sense of dis-orientation that marks the encroachment of the demonic on the quotidian. Hughes's description of his uncle's imaginary walk is skillfully phrased to capture the eerie breakdown of the temporal and spatial orderings that keep the traumatic past at bay: "all day / He walked about that valley, as he lay / Under High Wood in the shell-hole." There is an awful sense here in which the present day is *that* day, in which the present walk is that desperate *imagined* walk, and in which the shell-hole has reappeared in rural Yorkshire. Nor does the dissolution of basic identities stop there :

> We stood in the young March corn
> Of a perfect field. His fortune made.
> His life's hope over. Me beside him
> Just the age he'd been when that German
> Took aim with his eye and hit him so hard
> It brought him and his wife down together,
> With all his children one after the other.

The triumph of the demonic haunting over time and space could hardly be more complete. It assumes Biblical proportions, as the curse of the spectral German is magnified into the curse of life itself upon those involved, however haplessly, in the iniquitous carnage, and upon their wives and blood-relations. Nature's revenge for the wastelands of Gallipoli and Flanders is a wasteland of the spirit that persists in the face of generational renewal and gives the darker ironies of modernism an un-natural life span.

War, Memory, and the Modern
Pilgrimage and Tourism
to the Western Front

Modris Eksteins

———◆◆▶◀◆◆———

"In the dusk the stranger hurries away," It's not an inspired final line to a serious novel—in fact it has the ring of cheap romance—but perhaps it s an appropriate line in an age where the traditional boundaries between high and low culture have blurred.[1] The line comes from the 1920s, from R. H. Mottram's from a final section entitled "The Stranger" which Mottram appended to his trilogy when the three war novels, set in Flanders, were published as one in 1927. The stranger is an ex-serviceman who has journeyed back to the wet Flanders' plain to revisit a world he once knew intimately. But the experience of that visit is like lost love. Nothing connects. Everything hurts. And "in the dusk the stranger hurries away."

The stranger, the outsider, the traveler is a central figure of not only twentieth-century fiction but twentieth-century culture as a whole; the stranger is emblematic of modernism—as a mode and a mood; and the journey, a journey away from home, either literally or figuratively, is perhaps the central experience of that stranger. Henry de Montherlant's first play was called *L'Exil;* James Joyce wrote a play entitled *The Exiles*, and his greatest work is about the most renowned of all travelers, Ulysses.

The words "stranger" and "journey" figure in so many twentieth-century titles: there is W. H. Auden's *Look, Stranger!*, and of course Albert Camus' *L'etranger*. There is Edward Upward's *Journey to the Border*, Graham Greene's *Journey Without*

Maps, Eugene O'Neill's *Long Day's Journey Into Night*, and Louis-Ferdinand Celine's *Voyage au bout de la nuit*. And there is Charlie Chaplin, the vagabond, who abandons everything and goes in search of fortune.

So much of modernism is about disconnectedness, expressed in terms of a journey into the unknown, to a new frontier, or into darkness. And so much of modernity, if that is the social and economic counterpart to cultural modernism, is expressed, too, by the travel industry, which is expected to become the world's leading industry by the end of this century. My suggestion in this paper is that in the tourist, and specifically the tourist to the battlefields of this century, we may find a figure of considerable symbolic interest.[2]

War and travel have naturally gone hand in hand throughout history, whether this was in the Crusades of the Middle Ages or in the imperial adventures of the nineteenth century. But never has this dual vision attracted or affected as many human beings as in this century. In 1914 many British and Empire soldiers were excited initially by the prospect of going not just to a war but to see France. In Australia, recruiting posters offered "a free world tour to Great Britain and Europe: the chance of a lifetime."[3] Those images did not disappear, but, as the war bogged down and as a different mood set in, new images surfaced.

Less than a year into the war, in June 1915, a young British officer, Douglas Gillespie, whose brother had already been killed, wrote from the front line in northern France:

> These fields are sacred in a sense, and I wish that when the peace comes, our Government might combine with the French Government to make one long avenue between the lines from the Vosges to the sea, or if that is too much, at any rate from La Bassee to Ypres. . . . I would make a fine broad road in the No Man's Land between the lines, with paths for pilgrims on foot, and plant trees for shade, and fruit trees, so that the soil should not be altogether waste. Some of the shattered farms and houses might be left as evidence, and the regiments might put up their records beside the trenches which they held all through the winter. Then I would like to send every man, woman, and child in Western Europe on pilgrimage along that Via Sacra, so that they might think and learn what war means from the silent witnesses on either side. . . .[4]

Within three months Gillespie, like his brother, was a silent witness. He was dead. But his vision was not. It was eagerly discussed in the press in Britain and was spawning all kinds of images in the minds of soldiers. J. W. Gamble, viewing the ruins of Ypres in late 1915, noted: "It is really a wonderful sight—weird, grotesque, and desolate of course—but most interesting. I expect the place will be flooded with sight-seers and tourists after the war, and they will be amazed by what they see. The ancient ruins of Pompeii and such places will be simply out of it."[5] A postwar guide on Ypres, without mentioning Pompeii, described the city in much the same terms as Gamble: "One finds in history few examples of a similar grandeur followed by a destruction more rapid and more complete. Ypres is nothing but a memory."[6] In January 1919, Winston Churchill, who had served in Flanders during the war, told the Imperial War Graves Commission: "I should like us to acquire the whole of the ruins of Ypres. . . . A more sacred place for the British race does not exist in the world."[7] And for a time in the Britain of 1919, the idea of preserving the old Ypres as a ruin and building a new Ypres some miles away was discussed. The ruins of Ypres had become not just a symbol of disaster and tragedy but an evocation.

When, in 1918, the Germans evacuated the town of Peronne leaving it in ruins, they left a large placard on the Hotel de Ville with the inscription: *Nicht drfzern-nur wundern* ("Don't be angry, only amazed").[8] Though presumably mischievous in intent, that message nevertheless overlapped with the mood of Gamble, Churchill, and many others. The Germans might have left similar messages on the library at Louvain, on the cathedrals at Rheims, Soissons, Albert, and on the 14th-century Cloth Hall in Ypres. "Beautiful in its tragic ruin," remarked Olive Edis, a photographer, of the Cloth Hall in March 1919, "a monument to be left for ever. . . ."[9]

The sight of a civilization in ruin produces, here, an interesting mix of piety and titillation, of rumination and excitement. Destruction and death seem able to produce energy and even exuberance. *Nicht drfzern, nur wundern.*

Michelin, the French tire company, sensed, early on, the potential, not only for piety and patriotism but also for prestige and profit. It began producing, for motorists, as early as 1917, tour guides of the Western Front. The Michelin guides to the war zones, most of which were turned out within eighteen months of the end of the war, were perhaps the most concentrated effort at travel writing ever. They were begun with patriotic fervour and with imminent victory in mind, but also with a vision of thousands of motorized tourists coming to view the destruction of France and Belgium. The itineraries suggested were to be unique tours of devastation, of villages that were no more, of churches reduced to rubble, of nature despoiled and unrecognizable, of primitive crosses, everywhere, crowded and confused. It was a bizarre landscape of nightmare and horror, and the guides made every effort to point that out. But at the same time they said to the traveller, come and see certainly not to enjoy, not necessarily even to learn, but to experience. That was a very modern invitation: the invitation to live life as experience rather than moral endeavour.[10]

Tourism, at that time, was still a new phenomenon in France. Only in 1878 had the Academie Francaise sanctioned the word touriste. Before the advent of the automobile, the French did not tour; foreigners toured. The idea of tourism, in French eyes a somewhat vulgar pursuit suggestive of transience and superficiality, was associated especially with the materialistic and soulless British, that nation of shopkeepers. The French prided themselves on holidays with intellectual and spiritual content, at the seaside, in the mountains, or at a spa. In this context the Michelin idea of motor tours to the battle areas of the Great War was novel in the extreme.[11]

The London travel firm of Pickfords quickly picked up the Michelin idea. In the winter of 1918–19 it was busy planning tours to the battlefields which were scheduled to start on 30 March and run through to 16 October. A ten-day, luxury tour would cost 36 pounds. "REMEMBER," the Pickfords' brochure stated, "that on the first sign of fine weather Hundreds of Thousands of men will set to work to clean up the ravages of War. France must grow Food. She cannot afford to import. Trenches and shell holes will disappear and neatly tilled fields will take their place. Therefore BOOK EARLY if you want to see anything of the chaos and debris of War . . . . YOU MUST COME NOW if you want to see anything of the chaos of a modern Battlefield."[12]

It is impossible to establish how many tourists actually used the Michelin guides in the early years. The guides were certainly intended for use; they included lists not only of hotels but of garages and mechanics. Given the state of the roads in the areas to be traversed, the latter were essential. Flat tires and mechanical breakdowns were a constant feature of early motoring even in the best of conditions, let alone in the desolation of the Western Front. Not only were there physical barriers to touring in the first months after the war—shell-holes, mud, derelict vehicles blocking roads—but some areas were closed for security reasons. Special "white" passes were required to travel through many areas, and cameras were forbidden. Gasoline was rationed. Unexploded bombs still lay everywhere, and the Pickfords' brochure had a full-page warning about the dangers.[13]

In view of this, it is likely that most of the Michelin volumes were purchased for their detailed accounts of the major battles of the war and as mementos rather than as actual guides. Many, in the immediate aftermath of the war, craved details about the battles; others simply wanted to pay homage.[14]

Those who did come in the early days were few and felt as if they had journeyed to another planet. Phyllis Goodliff, a secretary with the British Red Cross based in Boulogne, travelled to Ypres in January 1919. "There was scarcely a soul about," she wrote home to her family, "and the mid-day sun gave light and heat and energy to nothing but a few poor blades of grass. . . . As we stood in the square a party of American Sisters passed through on a bus. They might have accidentally taken the wrong turning from Picadilly Circus into the Land-that-never-could-be-in-a-civilized world, they looked so out of place. . . ." She went on to describe the surreal landscape around Ypres: "There was not a bird or an animal anywhere. It seemed as if the land were lying exhausted. . . ."[15] By March little had changed. Olive Edis, a photographer, was sent out to Flanders and France by the Imperial War Museum to take pictures. "The desolation of the villages," she noted of Belgium, "struck us very much—no fowls, no dogs, no cats, no people. We heard that all the cats had been eaten, and I only saw one in the course of the whole trip in Belgium."[16]

Those first travellers certainly got their fill of experience. Motoring from Brussels to Ypres on 6 March, a distance of about 120 kilometres, Edis and her companions had three flat tires. Alison Mullineaux, an irrepressibly energetic and vivacious nurse from Montreal who worked for the American Red Cross was in the vicinity of Rheims in April 1919: "Scattered about were . . . human bones, vertebrae, a skull (this was taken by an American soldier as a souvenir, to the horror and disdain of the French soldiers working nearby)—and clusters of unexploded hand grenades lay around. . . . Village after village lay inert and empty." A month later she was in Ypres with a group of nurses where she met an American lieutenant with the A.E.F. who was touring the Flanders area on foot. "Lieut. D.," she wrote in her diary, "was going to trek across country to St. Julien—sleeping out—and then on to Armentieres—taking about six days, and asked us to Join him. I wanted to, terribly, but the others were too tired. . . ." During the entire visit to Ypres and surrounding area, "we had seen no one," she wrote, "but military and a few French women in deep mourning, searching for their men's graves." By 31 July, 1919, she, aged 28, was home, staying on a lake north of Montreal where her family had a summer cottage. After all the excitement of the war and the travel, the quiet of Lake Manitou was unbearable. Her diary ends with the words: "Long, long days and longer nights! I feel terribly nothing!"[17]

Others found the old front line equally exhilarating. The Canadian artist David Milne was sent to France in May, 1919, to paint. "For four months," he wrote later, "I saw and painted battlefields and trenches, tanks and wreckage and wire and obliterated villages, still just as the war had left them. I never could quite decide whether I was the last soldier or the first tourist, but it was thrilling. Everything!"[18]

However, tourism to the Western Front never reached the proportions that were initially expected. One enthusiastic promoter of tourism, Pierre Chabert, who had been active in the French alpine and hotel business and had spent some time in North America, predicted during the war: "Our glorious battlefields will bring the American masses [*la grande foule americaine*] to France." He estimated that up to 700,000 Americans would visit France in the first year after the war. "We have an immense fortune in our ruins," he went on to say, ". . . provided that we don't rebuild too quickly and that everything is well organized." We must promote "a cult of memory."

Chabert's vision became increasingly ambitious as he thought further: everything should be organized, he wrote, "so that the first American party can leave New York in the very same week that hostilities cease and then the next ones would follow week by week." Aware of a lack of appropriate accommodation, he foresaw using train sleeper cars to ferry American visitors overnight from the Channel ports to

Belfort, near the Swiss border, whence they would be taken to the American battle sites near Chateau-Thierry and St. Mihiel during the day and then put back on the trains in the evening. He insisted also that special post offices be created at the major battle points to deal with the enormous quantity of postcards that Americans, in his experience, send—these cards should be postmarked boldly so that the recipients could see that they were receiving mail from a famous battle area. In short, tourism, if properly organized, would help France not only recuperate but prosper in the postwar age.[19]

The Touring-Club of France predicted a million and a half tourists from abroad in the first year after the war; as the year advanced that figure was reduced to a third of the original prediction; and even that proved to be too optimistic. Leon Auscher, vice-president of the Touring-Club, ever hopeful, despite the slow start, predicted in 1920 a total of three million tourists for the first three postwar years; enough, he thought, to turn the French economy from crisis to recovery.[20] Those predictions, needless to say, did not materialize.

The Touring-Club did erect 118 granite demarcation stones in the battle areas, from Dixmude in Flanders to the Swiss frontier, to assist travellers, but apart from that kind of gesture and Michelin's efforts, not a great deal was done to promote tourism to the war zones. These areas, the Marne, Champagne, the Somme, the Chemin des Dames, Verdun, and the Vosges, were often mentioned but did not figure prominently in tourist literature and advertisements of the 1920s, and apart from pilgrims—veterans and the bereaved—there does not seem to have been much interest in resurrecting the war, for most of the decade. In 1927, the American travel writer Frank Schoonmaker, rather than encouraging his readers to visit the battlefields, advised against such a trip. In suggesting excursions from Brussels, he wrote: "Be content with Belgium the beautiful and let the mutilated cities of Western Flanders bury their dead."[21]

In the early twenties the cemeteries were prepared. Between 1920 and 1923 shipments of headstones from Britain to France, to replace the makeshift crosses, reached 4,000 a week. Memorials were built, some small, some vast. Some of the larger monuments would not be completed until near the outbreak of another war. The Vimy memorial, commemorating Canada's effort on that deadly ridge, was not unveiled until July 1936, four months after Hitler had remilitarized the Rhineland. The Australian memorial at Villers-Bretonneux was completed only in 1938. But in the meantime, towns had been rebuilt, Rheims, Peronne, Lens, Albert, Ypres, usually with considerable attention to historical detail. The scars on the landscape were gradually removed: fields were plowed, trees planted. With the exception of the national parks at Vimy, Beaumont Hamel, Verdun, and a few famous battle sites like Hartmannswillerkopf in the Vosges, the undulating cratered ground of No Man's Land disappeared. As early as 1924 a reporter for the *Dundee Courier* who accompanied a Scottish pilgrimage to Ypres could write: "Passing through the late battle-fields one could scarcely credit that they had been the scene of so much bloodshed and tragedy. On every side of the road of the cemeteries were fields of waving corn with rebuilt homes scattered about or gathered in little hamlets."[22]

By the late twenties the tour of the Western Front had become an experience entirely different from that ten years earlier. The cemeteries, instead of the actual battlefields, had become the primary attractions and reminders of the war. If vicarious experience was a strong urge behind early postwar tourism, commemoration marked the second phase—commemoration on a massive scale. Royalty, politicians, mothers and fathers flocked to the memorial sites. In this phase, as nature and reconstruction gradually hid the physical scars, the psychological wounds were covered by a carapace of piety. Edmund Blunden pointed out that no previous war had been followed "by anything like this fulfilment of piety towards those who gave their lives."[23]

As it moved from visible reality to commemoration and imagination, the war was changed. Inspired by their serene order and glorious flowers, Blunden called the British and Empire cemeteries "the poetry of that high action" that was the war; "the dead speak yet through achievement of beauty."[24] Rudyard Kipling, who lost his son in the war, called the cemeteries "the silent cities."[25] An aura of ceremonious tradition surrounded the cemeteries and monuments, of all states. In tradition, it was hoped, the former sense of purpose would be fortified and solace found. But many now found the tradition wanting.

The pilgrimages reached their high point in 1928–29, before the onset of the Great Depression. The British Legion organized a huge pilgrimage to Ypres, with close to 15,000 participants, in the summer of 1928. The visitors' books at the Menin Gate memorial to the missing contained over 8,000 signatures for the month of July and almost 15,000 for the month of August.[26] By 1928–29 the Germans, initially prohibited, then discouraged, had started coming too. It is hard to assess the response of those pilgrims; the visitors' books at the memorials and in the cemeteries have not been kept. Official allied speeches all reiterated the moral purpose of the war: to preserve liberty and dignity through duty and sacrifice. While disillusionment and disenchantment were to surface with a vengeance in 1929–30 in literature and film, in the so-called "war boom," it is nevertheless hard to imagine all too many entries in the cemetery visitors' books expressing the sentiment "in vain." Economic difficulties and then the heightened nationalism of the 1930s reduced tourism and pilgrimage considerably. German travelling, for instance, was severely curtailed by Hitler's regime. From a high point of nearly two million foreign tourists to France in 1929, the figure plummeted to 390,000 in 1935.[27]

As the landscape recovered, as travel became easier, and as the cemeteries came to dominate the visit to the Western Front, many ex-servicemen felt that they were losing their war. "Was the War, after all, only the hideous nightmare it seemed?" asked H. A. Taylor, formerly a captain with the Royal Fusiliers, in 1928.[28] The war was being corrupted not only by time, but also by sentimentality, vulgarity, and ignorance. Gerhard Schinke, a German, journeyed to Flanders in 1927. He was surprised by how the countryside had revived but even more upset at how Ypres had commercialized the war. In addition to a profusion of manufactured souvenirs for sale in shops, children on the street offered to sell him rusted weapons, helmets, grenades, and tunic buttons. Schinke was appalled by the hucksterism.[29] The lack of piety disturbed many. "Surely, the Cloth Hall of Ypres must rank close to Niagara as one of the world's most-photographed sights," remarked H. A. Taylor.[30] Christopher Isherwood visited Ypres on 11 November 1935 to pay his respects to his father who had been killed in the salient in 1915. Isherwood, too, was taken aback by the vulgarity: "The town is certainly 'for ever England, ' " he wrote in his diary — "the England of sordid little teashops, faked souvenirs and touts."[31]

R. H. Mottram kept being drawn to the old front line but found each visit increasingly discomforting. On a trip in the mid-1930s his Flemish taxi driver asked him at one point whether he had seen the monument to the Egyptians. Mottram was flummoxed. A monument to the Egyptians in Flanders? When they arrived it turned out to be a memorial to the Gloucestershire Regiment whose crest was the sphinx. "That mistake of my driver's, " wrote Mottram, "seems to epitomise something which is happening. . . . Our War . . . is being turned by time and change into something fabulous, misunderstood and made romantic by distance, as it recedes into the Past. For half of the people alive to-day it might almost as well be something that happened to the Ancient Egyptians, so little can they, who did not experience it, conceive what it was like."[32] Ypres Mottram found frighteningly peaceful. He missed the ruins. He felt himself confirmed as the stranger he had depicted in his *Spanish Farm Trilogy* ten years earlier.[33]

The Second World War of course brought tourism to a halt in Europe, though, paradoxically, the war produced the greatest movement of peoples that the world has ever seen—with its slave labour, mass expulsions, refugees, and genocide. In some cases armies moved over the same ground that they had covered in the First War. The Germans destroyed some allied memorials and deleted some inscriptions that they found offensive but for the most part left cemeteries and commemorative sites untouched. Ironically, the Americans badly damaged their own memorial at Montsec in the St. Mihiel salient when they were advancing against the Germans in 1944. After World War II tourism recovered rapidly. As early as 1948 France had as good a year as her best year between the wars, 1929, when almost two million foreign tourists visited. From 1948 the numbers continued to climb, almost irreversibly, to the present day.

Who tours the Western Front these days? It's difficult to produce any kind of systematic analysis. Statistics indicate that the number of visitors to the battle sites is increasing, in keeping with the general growth of tourism.[34] The proportion of pilgrims, people with a family connection to the War, is still high. Time and time again, in the visitors' books at cemeteries,[35] one encounters the moving comment, often from Australians, New Zealanders, South Africans, Canadians: "Found at last granddad." Tour groups are plentiful: in some cases the groups are on a specialized battlefield tour (the British seem particularly good at organizing these), and in others a visit to a World War I cemetery is simply part of a general tour. Visits by school groups are frequent and increasing. The military are also sent to visit. For locals the cemeteries and memorials are like parks and gardens.

The commentary in the visitors' books is intriguing, and it is a shame that even a sampling of these books from various decades does not seem to be available.[36] Much of the commentary is of course repetitive: "R.I.P." once started can go on for pages; lines from Rupert Brooke, Rudyard Kipling, John McCrae are cited endlessly. Many comments are platitudinous or sentimental: "Well done lads," or "Duty done," or "I wish them soft pillows and sweet music." Political, nationalistic, and ideological comments are frequent: "Thanks for freedom," "Proud to be a Canadian," "We owe our way of life to these brave men," "Europder vereinigt Euch!!" But there are also many highly personal and emotional entries: "At last we meet"; "Grandad rest in peace"; "The Father I never knew"; and a wonderfully straightforward Australian entry in the New Irish Farm cemetery visitors' book: "Glad to have visited here. Life's ambition."

The Dutch, the Belgians, and the Scandinavians are most likely to express pacifist sentiments; the British to cite poetry—"some corner of a foreign field / That is forever England" from Rupert Brooke's poem "The Soldier" are the lines most frequently cited; the Americans are most likely to be colloquial. At Dochy Farm cemetery a Californian writes: "WOW! Thanks. Awesome."

But little, in the context of current Western European affluence—the good hotels, the splendid food, the fine roads, the fertile fields—connects to the horror that was once. In this context of prosperity it is difficult to comprehend this war. As a result a constant motif in the visitors' books is "In vain," "What a waste," "Angry at the loss of so many lives." At Poelkapelle cemetery a woman from London writes: "At last I've got to see my grandfather's memorial. A pity that England wasn't worth saving." At Delville Wood, where the South Africans were decimated, an entry reads: "What a good job the South Africans cannot see the country they died for now." In the same visitors' book, a Londoner asks: "Oh why oh why oh why?!!!" and three firemen from Kent put a rhetorical question: "For a better world?" In the visitors' book of Bard Cottage cemetery near Ypres, one couple, he English, she German, writes: "Our grandparents fought each other. It seems so very strange now. So distant." An Ulsterman, from strife-torn Derry, refers to the soldiers of the Great War as "a generation that will haunt the world forever."

What is very striking about the visitors' books is the inadequacy of language. Many visitors want to say something but don't know how to say it. In the middle of a page full of cliches produced by others, a man from Devon confronts his quandary: "I cannot find the words without breaking into cliches. "Beyond words" is a frequent entry. In the column under "Remarks" in the visitors' book at Bernafay cemetery a man from Kent writes "None needed." A strong theme in modernism, from Franz Kafka to John Cage, has been the language of silence.

The comments by youth may be the most disconnected from, and hence, in an absurd, utterly modern way, the most telling about, the tragedy and the horror. A young girl from Ypres, who has obviously been sent to Ypres Reservoir Cemetery on a school assignment, writes: "All we need is love. All we get is more work." The boys write obscenities, "Let's fuck." The girls respond: "All the nice boys are dead." Two young female punsters write in the Menin Gate visitors' book: "Dead good!" What could be more modern, more succinct, more appropriate than that comment—with its Juvenile silliness, and yet at the same time its ability to capture irony, paradox, and confusion? Dead good.

What makes the First World War cemeteries so indescribably sad is more than the numbers buried there; more than the loss of life; it is the loss of connections. The early visitors to the Western Front found a vision of hell that seemed disconnected from its moral framework, and some were genuinely intrigued by that atmosphere. The traveller today finds an extraordinary beauty that doesn't connect either, certainly not to the horror though perhaps for a few to the cause. One is indeed a stranger in these silent cities. And in the dusk you hurry away.

Notes

Preface

Epigraphs:

A.A. Milne, "Gold Braid," in Martin Stephen, ed., Poems of the First World War: 'Never Such Innocence' (London: Everyman, Dent, 1993), pp. 126-27; Ford Maddox Ford, "Arms and the Mind," Esquire (December 1980): 80.

1. On the names of trenches, see James Morris, Farewell the Trumpets: An Imperial Retreat (New York and London: Harcourt Brace Jovanovich, 1978), p. 193; for Rutter's poem, see Stephen, pp. 92-93 (from "The Song of Tiadatha"); for the "saturated" landscape, see Eric M. Leed, No Man's Land: Combat & Identity in World War I (London & New York: Cambridge University Press, 1979), p. 20.

2. "Trenches rise up": quoted in Leed, p. 21; "Sodom and Gomorrah . . . . ," see Owen, January 19, 1917, Collected Letters, ed. Harold Owen and John Bell (Oxford and New York: Oxford University Press, 1967); Kipling and Gamble, see Eksteins in this volume; Mackaman and Mays, see introduction to this volume.

3. See Frye, Anatomy of Criticism: Four Essays (Atheneum: New York, 1970), p. 150.

4. "Reflections Upon War and Death," in Freud, Character and Culture, ed. Philip Rieff (New York: Collier, 1963), pp. 109, 113, 124; "MCMXIV," in Larkin, Collected Poems, ed. Anthony Thwaite (New York: Noonday, 1997), pp. 127-28.

5. "The Painter of Modern Life," in The Painter of Modern Life and Other Essays by Charles Baudelaire, tr. and ed. Jonathan Mayne (London: Phaidon Press, 1964), pp. 9, 11, 13.

6. See Stephen, p. 107, "Canadian Song," by "Anonymous," a poem that's worth quoting in its entirety:

> There's a little wet home in the trench,
> That the rain storms continually drench,
> A dead cow close by, with her hooves in the sky,
> And she gives off a beautiful stench.

161

Underneath us, in place of a floor
Is a mess of cold mud and some straw,
And the Jack Johnsons roar as they speed through the air
O'er my little wet home in the trench.

7. Cannadine, "War and Death, Grief and Mourning in Modern Britain," in T. Joachim Whaley, ed., Mirrors of Mortality: Studies in the Social History of Death (New York: St. Martin's Press, 1981), p. 204.

8. The Waste Land, in The Waste Land: A Facsimile and Transcript of the Original Drafts Including the Annotations of Ezra Pound, ed. And with an intro. By Valerie Eliot (New York: Harcourt Brace Jovanovich, 1971), p. 145.

9. "Green clumsy legs": Siegfried Sassoon, "Counter-Attack," in Collected Poems (New York: Viking, 1949), p. 68; "red wet thing": Ivor Gurney, "To His Love," Collected Poems, ed. P. J. Kavanagh (Oxford and New York: Oxford University Press, 1982), p. 41; "queer sardonic rat": Isaac Rosenberg, Collected Poems, ed. Gordon Bottomley and Denys Harding (New York: Schocken, 1949), p. 73; "monstrous anger" and "stuttering rifles": Wilfred Owen, Collected Poems , ed. C. Day Lewis (New York: New Directions, 1964), p. 44.

10. Leger, Une Correspondance de Guerre a Louis Poughon, 1914-1918 (Paris: Editions du Centre Pompidou, 1990), p. 70: "You're entered into the earth, you're absorbed by it, you stick yourself to it in order to avoid the death that's everywhere. . . . You hide behind someone who's been killed. You live with the dead like good friends. You don't bury them. What's the use? Another shell would dig them up" (trans. mine).

11. Hughes, New and Selected Poems, 1957-1994 (London: Faber and Faber, 1995), p. 274.

12. On T.S. Eliot and Gallipoli, see Sandra M. Gilbert, "'Rats' Alley': The Great War, Modernism, and the (Anti) Pastoral Elegy," New Literary History, Winter 1999 (?)

13. In parts of Europe, people still quite literally live with the grim remains of the war. For interviews with a few of the professional demineurs who to this day spend one week of every month out at sea, detonating some of the countless unexploded shells with which the French countryside is still littered, see Donovan Webster, Aftermath: The Remnants of War (New York: Pantheon, 1996), pp. 52-53; I am grateful to John Curie for bringing this work to my attention.

Introduction: The Quickening of Modernity

1. The shifting terms of scholarly debate related to questions of postmodernity are more fully articulated in works related to architectural and the urban environment of the twentieth century. See in particular David Harvey, The Condition of Postmodernity: An Enquiry into the Origins of Cultural Change (Oxford: Blackwell, 1989); and Edward Soja, Postmodern Geographies: The Reassertion of Space in Critical Social Theory (London: Verso, 1989). For a synthetic discussion of issues related to historical and literary Modernism whose focus is primarily sociological, see Stuart Hall, David Held, Don Hubert and Kenneth Thompson (eds.), Modernity: An Introduction to Modern Societies (Oxford: Blackwell, 1996); and for a summary and critique of the place of postmodernity in the discipline of history, see Alun Munslow, Deconstructing History (London: Routledge, 1997).

2. The terms of this debate with respect to aesthetic sensibilities and expressions are best explored through the work of Paul Fussell, The Great War and Modern Memory, (Oxford: Oxford University Press, 1976); and works which are revisionist or expansions of his posi-

tions, including more importantly Modris Eksteins, *The Rites of Spring: The Great War and the Birth of the Modern Age* (New York: Anchor, 1989); George L. Mosse, *Fallen Soldiers: Reshaping the Memory of the World Wars* (Oxford: Oxford University Press, 1990) and Jay Winter, *Sites of Memory, Sites of Mourning: The Great War in European Cultural History* (Cambridge: Cambridge University Press, 1995).

3. The bibliography of salient works on the questions of "total war" and the ways in which 1914–1918 utilized in the negative the very machinery and technology which had driven Europe's industrialization is understandably vast. For an entrance into that rich field, see Jay Winter and Jean-Louis Robert, *Capital Cities at War: London, Paris, Berlin, 1914–1919* (Cambridge: Cambridge University Press, 1997; T. Ashworth, *Trench Warfare 1914–1918. The Live and Let Live System* (London, 1980); Jean-Jacques Becker, *The Great War and the French People* (Oxford: Oxford University Press, 1985).

4. F. Scott Fitzgerald's *Tender is the Night* (New York: Scribner, 1933), together with works by Hemingway, Faulkner, Woolf, Maugham and others are a rich commentary on how the generations of the war and after, whether American, British or French, reckoned physically and psychologically with its meanings thought the 1920s and beyond.

5. Virginia Woolf, *Mrs Dalloway* (London: Harcourt, 1925).

6. Scholars have also adopted in many instances a view of 1914–1945 as a second thirty years' war. For some examples of this position see Raymond Sontag, *A Broken World, 1919–1939* (New York: Harper, 1969); Charles Maier, *Recasting Bourgeois Europe: Stabilization in France, Germany, and Italy in the Decade after World War One* (Princeton: Princeton University Press, 1975).

7. It is perhaps the same impulse to know about the nineteenth century and its confidences which helped the recent film "Titanic" to achieve its tremendous success not just in the United States but also all over Europe. The First World War has recently come into homes all over Britain and the United States as a television documentary, produced jointly by the B.B.C. and P.B.S, just as novels with the conflict as its them have achieved much popular and critical acclaim, notable among the works of Pat Barker, Mark Helprin and Sebastian Faulks.

8. Pat Barker's novels on shell shock and the First World War have received terrific critical acclaim and are an excellent literary point of entrance into the ongoing textuality of 1914–1918. See Pat Barker, *Regeneration* (New York: Penguin, 1991); for a recent and excellent edited collection focusing on war literature of the first generation, see Trudi Tate, *Women, Men and the Great War* (Manchester: Manchester University Press, 1995).

La Pudique Anastasie

1. I wish to thank the organizers and participants of the conference on "World War One and the Cultures of Modernity" at the University of Southern Mississippi for their helpful comments and suggestions. This piece also benefited from astute advice offered by Jeff Ravel and James Sweeney.

2. See carton Ba 697 for the correspondence and Ba 724 for the song text at the Archives de la Préfecture de Police, Paris. (Hereafter as APP) According to nineteenth-century regulations, prefects outside of Paris had their own authority to ban any performance piece, but a song or theatrical revue banned in the capital was also blocked everywhere else.

3. Songs submitted to the censor included pieces written before the war. The Archives de la Préfecture de Police in Paris houses the songs arranged in alphabetical order in 34 car-

tons: Ba 697–730. Cartons Ba 731–736 contain other modified songs and some duplicates. Songs were submitted in various forms: handwritten, typewritten, and as sheet music; some have visa stamps, and some have no indication of a final decision. Overall, the collection at the Police archives is quite complete for songs performed in Parisian entertainment establishments. The Bibliothèque Nationale also has sheet music, but, unfortunately, not all the songs which were registered with them are now in their collection.

4. During WWI, all belligerent powers examined the press and developed control of certain propaganda materials such as posters, but to date we know far more about censorship of newspapers than about any other form. Cultural censorship has attracted far less attention. On newspaper censorship see for instance, Phillip Knightley, *The First Casualty. From the Crimea to Vietnam: The War Correspondent as Hero, Propagandist, and Myth Maker* (New York: Harcourt Brace Jovanovich, 1975), 80–111; A.G. Marquis, "Words as Weapons: Propaganda in Britain and Germany during the First World War," *Journal of Contemporary History* 13 (July 1978): 467–498; M.L. Sanders and Philip Taylor, *British Propaganda during the First World War, 1914–1918* (London: The MacMillan Press Ltd, 1982); and Jean-Jacques Becker, *The Great War and the French People*, trans. Arnold Pomerans (Dover, New Hampshire: Berg Publishers Ltd., 1985), 29–63.

5. Although difficult to define precisely, *cafés-concerts* usually offered free access, drinking at tables, and men and women could talk, smoke and join in the program. In contrast, the music halls charged an entrance fee, often seated people on benches, and offered drinks at a separate bar.

6. Chamber of Deputies, 25 January 1916.

7. See, for instance, Kenneth Silver's discussion of Parisians' anxiety over their appearance and the need to be above suspicion. Silver, *Esprit de corps: The Art of the Parisian Avant-Garde and the First World War, 1914–1925* (Princeton: Princeton University Press, 1989), 5–6.

8. The state of siege declared on 5 August 1914 relied upon a set of laws dating back to 1849, which gave military officials broad and immediate responsibilities for all censorship. (More specifically, this meant the Ministry of War.) Along with the 8 August 1849 state of siege law, the legal basis for press censorship rested on the 29 July 1881 press law which had been updated in October 1913, and the 5 August 1914 law which "banned the publication of all non-official information of a military nature." Becker, *The Great War*, 48. Despite his contention that procedures for censorship were embryonic at the start of the war, Becker illustrates the power of having an established legal foundation. This quick imposition in the midst of a vast mobilization left little space for debate. The laws sanctioned any measures taken to "insure public order"—a very broad concept. See also Emile Mermet et al., *Annuaire de la presse* (Paris: E. Mermet, 1915), 37.

9. The French government was the only power to set up a centralized system for songs from the beginning, although the Germans also paid immediate attention to the possible inappropriateness of amusements. Gary Stark's article on German censorship of popular entertainment offers some interesting comparisons. The declaration of a state of siege at the beginning of August also triggered Germany's censorship laws, and authorities then linked public morality and morale in pushing forward an older agenda. In contrast, the Germans developed a decentralized system based in individual cities and regions and run mainly by military officials, reflecting how the "German military enjoyed extraordinary power over civil life." See Stark, "All Quiet on the Home Front: Popular Entertainments, Censorship and Civilian Morale in Germany, 1914–1918," in *Authority, Identity and the Social History of the Great War*, ed. Frans Coetzee and Marilyn Shevin-Coetzee (Providence, RI: Berghahn Books, 1995), 57–80, especially 60–62.

10. APP, Ba 1614 contains a review of events in August 1914 regarding police and military arrangements in Paris.

11. A larger staff had to have been necessary to examine all of the scripts for the musical revues and plays. Paris had four different prefects of police during the war: Hennion, Laurent, Hudelo, and Raux. Laurent was the most important figure since he oversaw the process during its formative stages (from September to December 1914) and then over the next two-and-a-half years. In the provinces, it was also the prefects' office who judged the suitability of songs. Overall, press censorship was far more fragmented than theater or music, but the censorship process for other media also evolved towards greater civilian participation.

12. The system had ended in June 1906 because of a lapse in funding, not because lawmakers had abrogated the laws or statutes. See Josette Parrain, "Censure, théâtre, et Commune (1871–1914)," *Le Mouvement Social* 29 (April 1972): 339. (This article reviews the archival sources for the period 1871 to 1906 including the F18 and F21 series in the Archives nationales.) In fact, these laws were not eliminated until October 1945. Philippe J. Maarek, *La censure cinématographique* (Paris: Librairies techniques, [1982]), 10–11.

13. Besides Parrain's work on censorship in the early Third Republic, see T.J. Clark, *The Painting of Modern Life: Paris in the Art of Manet and His Followers* (New York: Alfred A. Knopf, 1985), 227–234; Jacques Rancière, "Le Bon Temps ou la barrière des plaisirs," *Les Révoltes Logiques*, Spring-Summer 1978; Alberic Cahuet, *La liberté du théâtre en France et à l'étranger; histoire, fonctionnement et discussion de la censure dramatique* (Paris: Dujarric, 1902), 244–304; F.W.J. Hemmings, *Theatre and State in France, 1760–1905* (Cambridge: Cambridge University Press, 1994), 193–225.

14. According to a circular of May 1917, some theaters had permanent police surveyors, while others received only random visits. *Circulaires émanées du Préfet de Police, 1917–1918* (Paris: Imprimerie Chaix, 1919), 25–28 of 1917.

15. APP, Ba 697 and Ba 700; the lyricist published a very different version of this song which received approval starting sometime in 1916. See also "Il jouait des castagnettes," Ba 711.

16. Paul Allard, *Images secrètes de la guerre; 200 photographies et documents censurés en France* (Paris: La Société Anonyme les Illustrés Français, 1933), 27. According to an official's report to the prefect, quoted in Allard, "Ce mot, le spectateur le remplace, très vraisemblablement, par un autre d'une syllabe également et qui rime avec *ému*."

17. Lyrics published in newspapers were read by the newspaper censors and only occasionally passed on to the police. Even if songs banned by the police appeared in journals or newspapers, the song censors usually maintained their own block reflecting the different approaches to these modes of communication.

18. Paisian authorities supervised the material carried out to troops by Parisian entertainers (in a sort of proto-USO). They also reviewed all interviews and reports about these shows published for Paris consumption.

19. Stéphane Audoin-Rouzeau's work on trenchnewspapers also illustrates the lack of central control until at least 1917. He explains, "unbroken supervision on this scale of millions of men and in the living conditions which they endured remained difficult to exercise." Audoin-Rouzeau, *Men at War 1914–1918: National Sentiment and Trench Journalism in France during the First World War*, trans. Helen McPhail (Providence, RI: Berg Publishers, 1992), 20–33, especially 23. On military censorship of songs, see the documents in the Archives du service historique de l'Armée de terre, cartons 5N 342, 5N 346, 5N 371–373, 7N 951 (hereafter SHAT).

Notes

20. Silver, *Esprit de corps*, 83. The quote continues, "In effect, while the soldier is subject to the total regulation of his actions by the army, the subtleties of his thought process, having been rendered powerless to affect his life, are relatively ignored, while the mind of the civilian, still capable of instigating deviant and even subversive behavior, is given no such latitude." (83–84)

21. Paris was actually incorporated into the Army zone in 1914 and 1918. The rest of France (behind the lines) varied somewhat from Paris—for example, the war was much more remote in the southwest corner of France than in the capital. Although contemporaries (and historians) may have sometimes used the stark dichotomy of the home front and the front, it greatly oversimplifies the actual situation.

22. Stark has found this same protection of "public confidence" in the German government and in the officers corps especially, as well as support for the *Burgfrieden*, or temporary political truce. Stark, "All Quiet," 66–69.

23. Songwriters had previously found Italian neutrality a tempting target of derision; censors allowed some commentary up until negotiations for Italy's entry became imminent. See Enthoven's "Chanson Napolitaine," APP, Ba 697 for the lyrics and prefect's note.

24. See "On dit que" by Eugène Héros and Georges Baltha, APP, Ba 734 and "Voyage officiel," Ba 697. The latter's lyrics depicted a stereotypic government minister making inane speeches in the provinces—all normal grist for the pre-war mill.

25. APP, Ba 697.

26. "la Question des corps nus" by Fernand Dhervyl, APP, Ba 735 and "Vive le Roi!" by Dufleuve, copyright 1910, Ba 729.

27. The satirist Jean Bastia tried to circumvent the prohibition when he submitted a piece about "le Tigre" who directed an asylum where patients were not well treated. Monsieur Martin was not fooled, explaining in his memo to the prefect in March 1918 that "evidently, they wish to depict Monsieur Clemenceau [the Prime Minister] in a humorous way with pointed allusions to the *Instructions en cours*, without, however, any name being pronounced." APP, Ba 736. "A Votre Santé" by Paul Weil was also blocked in January 1917 because of the "allusions constantes à tous les scandales actuels," even though the lyrics were highly critical of the unpatriotic actions then under investigation. Ba 697 and 700.

28. Audoin-Rouzeau, *Men at War*, 20.

29. La Fusée, 5 November 1916.

30 This specific change was ordered for "Suivant le grade" by Léon Durocher. APP, Ba 735.

31. APP, Ba 712. Even after civilian leaders had recognized Joffre's weaknesses and had eased him out of power by early 1916, censors still monitored the representations of him. Cf. "Quand Joffre reviendra" which was questioned in September 1918. Ba 697.

32. One finds a remarkable overlap between songs and newspapers in the descriptions of poilus and early battles. See, for instance, the strange collection of newspaper quotes in Becker, *The Great War*, 29 –42.

33. APP, Ba 701. See also, the "dialogue militaire" "Baloche et Parigot" by Bouchaud (dit Dufleuve); Ba 700. On song genres of the *Belle Epoque* including the *comique-troupier*, see François Caradec and Alain Weill, *Le Café-concert* (Paris: Hachette-Massin, 1980) 44–46. Charles Rearick comments on the continuing popularity of this genre, but does not indicate that these songs would have been sung in a modified form. Charles Rearick, "Madelon and the Men—in War and Memory," *French Historical Studies* 17 (Fall 1992): 1008.

34. Becker, *The Great War*, 59.

35. The prefect of Seine-et-Marne in his report of August 30 [1914] signaled "falling morale" in his jurisdiction and offered a possible explanation: "'I believe that the stories of German atrocities which one can read each morning in newspapers from *Le Temps* to *La Guerre sociale* are the root of all the evil. No doubt the papers want to whip up feeling against the Germans, but in reality they spread fear and demoralize the population.'" Quoted in Becker, *The Great War*, 45. Newspapers were instructed to moderate the tales of atrocities, while they also had to cut all signs of pity, justice or love for the enemy. Allard, *Images secrètes*, 15–16.

36. "l'Embusqué" by Louis de Royaumont, APP, Ba 707. Here, the prefect expressed concern for the painful "sentiments d'une mère." (See the memo in Ba 697). In the end, the son chose "la France" as his true mother and went off to fight. See also, "Le Ruisseau" by V. Telly, Ba 697 and Ba 725.

37. "On dit que . . ." APP, Ba 734.

38. Pierre Bourdieu, "What Makes a Social Class? On the Theoretical and Practical Existence of Groups," *Berkeley Journal of Sociology* 32 (1987): 10–11.

39. Cf. "la Mauvaise graine," APP, Ba 716 and Robert Lanoff's "Jean Misère devant le Christ," Ba 733.

40. Cf. Robert Brécy, *Florilège de la chanson révolutionnaire de 1789 au front populaire* (Paris: Editions Hier et Demain, 1978); Robert Brécy, "Les Chansons du Premier Mai," *Revue d'histoire moderne et contemporaine* 28 (July 1981): 393–432; Laurent Marty, *Chanter pour survivre: culture ouvrière, travail et techniques dans le textile, Roubaix 1850–1914* ([Lille?]: Atelier ethno-histoire et culture ouvrière : Fédération Leo Lagrange, [1982]); Marie-Véronique Gauthier, *Chanson, sociabilité et grivoiserie au XIXe siècle* (Paris: Aubier, 1992); Serge Dillaz, *La Chanson française de contestation de la f Commune à Mai 1968* (Paris: Editions Seghers, 1973); Pierre Brochon, *La Chanson sociale de Béranger à Brassens* (Paris: Les Editions ouvrières, 1961).

41. APP, Ba 736. Not surprisingly, examiners also did not allow any complaints about the Republic or its institutions. A song which described the state's schools as prisons suffered cuts, while the army's habit of acting as strike breaker was erased. Song lyrics which worried about the army as a threat to the Republic would have had an extremely dissonant ring at a time when the nation was depending so heavily on its military.

42. Cf. the song "Bellevillois, prends ton Fusil!" APP, Ba 700 whose last refrain declared: "Bellevillois, prends ton fusil / Et pars au feu l'âme tranquille: / Pour sauver les tiens, nous voici, / Tous unis: 'Ceux de Belleville.'" The lyrics also promoted war aims for mothers and wives who sent men to avenge the atrocities committed by "le reptile."

43. "La Baïonnette," APP, Ba 700. The song was approved in February and March 1918 with the deletions. Josette Parrain, in her analysis of theater censors in the late nineteenth century and their treatment of the Commune, has noted officials' discomfort with the "*réveil populaire*" and any portrayals of the "people" in the streets and on barricades. Parrain, "Censure, Théâtre, et Commune," 30.

44. The third verse of Henri Maheu's "les Trois couleurs" sounded the "people" rising up in the Revolution to fight on the barricades for bread and vain dreams of equality. These lyrics had to be replaced, and the composer (most probably) created a rendition where the din came from the hateful invaders instead of the people, who now took up arms intoning the ultra-patriotic "Chant du départ." APP, Ba 736. An examiner also allowed the two verses of "un Soir de Paris" which described the love and mystery of Paris, but not the last verse which celebrated past Parisian uprisings with an exciting refrain: "C'est un soir de Paris / . . . / Ecoutez! . . . c'est Paris / Coeur du monde / Battant avec fierté / Un cri de liberté / C'est le bruit / Qui grandit / D'un peuple qui surgit / Et passe en chantant dans la nuit / Un grand

soir de Paris." Ba 735. This last song was submitted to the censor in 1917, when large labor strikes would have made the censors even more careful.

45. This part of the agenda was critical, as subjects involving formal politics and military strategy appeared less frequently in songs than did family relationships, love affairs or everyday incidents.

46. Again, my discussion here has been influenced by Pierre Bourdieu's work. See especially, "The Uses of the 'People'" in *In Other Words: Essays Towards a Reflexive Sociology*, trans. Matthew Adamson (Stanford: Stanford University Press, 1990), 150–155 and *Language and Symbolic Power* (Cambridge: Harvard University Press, 1991), chaps. 1, 3, and 11. For a useful, though critical, synthesis of Bourdieu's body of work, see Richard Jenkins, *Pierre Bourdieu* (New York: Routledge, 1992).

47. APP, Ba 697.

48. APP, Ba 697. (emphasis in original.)

49. One also sees this moralizing discourse regarding postcards where censors rejected certain cards as "incompetent, coarse, obscene or too frivolous." Marie-Monique Huss, "Pronatalism and the Popular Ideology of the Child in Wartime France: the Evidence of the picture postcard," in *The Upheaval of War: Family, Work and Welfare in Europe, 1914-1918*, ed. Richard Wall and Jay Winter (Cambridge: Cambridge University Press, 1988), 336.

50. For example, the supposedly amusing song "Histoire d'une puce," about a female and male lice meeting up, finding someone's head and making it their seaside resort, was judged not funny and was *non visée*—perhaps because of the aggravating problem of lice in the trenches. But lice and their adventures did remain a favorite subject in combatants' own lyrics.

51. The use of the word language here should be expanded to include the censors' attention to "body language" or gestures.

52. The word *miche* means round bread or in popular usage breasts. In a song about the desolate lives of German children, the censors removed the following two lines, eliminating the obvious indelicate rhyme: "Car vous aurez bientôt, pour que rien ne se perde, / L'air, en mangeant du pain, de manger de la m . . . . . !" "Fantaisie sur le pain K K." APP, Ba 708.

53. "Y a qu' l'amour," APP, Ba 736.

54. See, for instance, "Tâchez d'faire attention," APP, Ba 736, and "Affaire ratée," Ba 697. Huss has noted one illustrated example where "the censor rejected a postcard described as 'child urinating in Prussian helmet' (6 April 1916)," although she found others which had been sent. Huss, "Pronatalism and the Popular Ideology," 336.

55. Cf. "Oui! Mais Voila!" APP, Ba 734. In the song "le Train des conscrits" where young men departed for the front, the third verse ended with "Ah! oui, l'émotion était vive, / Guillaum' était traité d'bourreau; / Y'm'semblait qu'la locomotive / Criait: l'salaud, l'salaud, l'salaud!" This last line could have evoked a fervent, noisy reaction from the audience, but was cut for the 1915 and 1916 performances. Ba 728.

56. This name comes from Allard, *Images secrètes*, 3. Anastasie was a much older sobriquet for the censor. See Robert Justin Goldstein, *Censorship of Political Caricature in Nineteenth-Century France* (Kent, Ohio: Kent State University Press, 1989).

57. Allard, *Images secrètes*, 27. (emphasis in original) Note that the censors' search for aural double entendres was not limited to sexual jokes, but extended to their other areas of concern as well. Allard provides one case when a well-intentioned songwriter wanted to praise the "poilus, qui, en toute occasion, 'sont là et même un peu là'" The prefect cut the line, saying "Il y a équivoque. Le public pourrait entendre: 'un peu las!'" (28).

58. In "Absinthe et Picolo" by Stephane Morel, a performer would have gleefully explained that "Afin de respecter la loi / Chaqu' citoyen doit fair' comm' moi / J'ai remplacé chaque Pernod / Par un litre de Picolo / C'est plus cher mais ça n'y fait rien / Ça vous saoul' tout aussi bien!" (picolo meant petit vin.) APP, Ba 697.

59. The words "cocu" and "cornard" (popular terms for cuckold) were usually suppressed. Cf. "Bal de bienfaisance" by Eug. Joullot, APP, Ba 700; "Quand ils s'en vont" by Marc Hély and Virgile Thomas, Ba 735; and "Ah! C'qu'on se l'est tirbouchonné," Ba 697. Soldiers appear to have been regular seducers or objects of seduction in pre-war songs. Cf. "Folle complainte" by Bouchaud which was blocked "definitively" by the prefect, Ba 709.

60. See "Il était un pioupiou" by H. Gambart and H. Pichon. APP, Ba 711.

61. Cf. "Histoire Bruxelloise" by Mauricet which made fun of German leaders' sexual physiques. APP, Ba 711 and 697.

62. See, for example, "Faut supprimer les femmes" by Horace Delattre and A. Queyriaux which was at first *non visée* and then lost its worst verses. Its refrain had called women "cholera," and the lyrics explained that without women things would improve with no more marriage, divorce or mothers-in-law. Also, "les Femmes sont nos victimes" by Mellinger was about how women treat men so terribly and about a man who let his mother-in-law drown, killed and ate his wife, and threw his concierge out the window. It was blocked until February 1918. APP, Ba 709. Domestic violence, like the slaying of mothers-in-law (quite common in French humor) was also no longer funny. See "Hitchy Kou" written before 1912 by Lucien Boyer which had its second verse about mothers-in-law eliminated. APP, BA 733.

63. "Voilà la Parisienne!" by A. Deligny and Jules Combe. APP, Ba 736.

64. For example, "Hello hello Tommy!" APP, Ba 711.

65. Examiners suppressed references to cheap sex during regimental service in pre-war tunes about garrison life. Cf. "Vas-y mon pote!" by Jules Combe which had been "created" by Bach at the Eldorado, APP, Ba 736; or "la Femme au régiment" by Rimbault and Arnould, APP, Ba 709; the latter was *non visée* in September 1916. But in the song "Ah! Je l'attends," a "soldier" sang about how women should know they were to be free of charge and that "au régiment" one had as many as one wanted, and the censors allowed this song in December 1916 and November 1917. APP, Ba 697. See also, "la Permission" by Georges Millandy. APP, Ba 721.

66. In a more serious, but related, vein, one sees this conflict in the debates over what to do about the *enfants du barbare*, as they were called, who had resulted from the German rapes in 1914. See Ruth Harris, "The 'Child of the Barbarian': Rape, Race and Nationalism in France during the First World War," *Past and Present* 141 (November 1993): 170–206. It was, however, easy enough to prohibit songs which expressed an adversion to having children, which meant the song censors' efforts paralleled the government's confiscation of "neo-malthusian" pamphlets. Cf. "la Vertu de Madeleine" by L. Bénech, APP, Ba 736, and "la Mauvaise graine," Ba 716.

67. The aggressive pronatalist campaign of the pre-war period had been dominated by a vocal elite making this an important part of the conservative bourgeois ideology. As Marie-Monique Huss has explained, "Most pronatalist authors came from the professional classes: doctors, . . . , lawyers, . . . , politicians . . . , economists . . . , journalists and writers . . . ." Huss, "Pronatalism and the Popular Ideology," 330 331. See also Karen Offen's article, "Depopulation, Nationalism, and Feminism in Fin-de-Siècle France," *American Historical Review* 89 (June 1984): 648–676. Ken Silver has also noted the "vast wartime iconography of family and fecundity." Silver, *Esprit de corps*, 191.

68. See "On cherre, on cherre" by Jean Péheu and Paul Darny, APP, Ba 734; "les Quatre jours des poilus," Ba 735; "Bouscule pas le pot de fleurs!" Ba 701; "Qu'est-c' qu'on f'ra," Ba 735.

69. SHAT, 16 N 1529. For an example of a lieutenant leading his unit in rousing marching songs, see Georges Lafond, *Ma Mitrailleuse* (Paris: Arthème-Fayard et Cie, n.d.), 75.

70. See M. le capitaine Massy's *Moyens à employer pour maintenir et relever le moral des soldats en campagne*, quoted in René Thorel, *Un Cercle pour le soldat* (Paris: E. Sansot & Cie, 1909), 269.

71. Cf. the collection of soldiers' revues in the Fonds Rondel at la Bibliothèque de l'Arsenal. One particularly good example would be "En Embuscade" by E. Genval (Rf 82,359). The trench journals show how much French soldiers wrote and joked in their newspapers about their sexual interests. According to Audoin-Rouzeau, the combatants' "prolonged abstinence," fettered desires, and "a traditional military irreverence" explained the "vulgarity" in their newspapers. Audoin-Rouzeau, *14–18 Les Combattants des tranchées*, 145–156, especially 150.

72. French officials, pundits and composers adhered to claims that the more often a man had intercourse, the more virile one became, and cultural artifacts fostered the idea. This helps explain the army's support for prostitution near the front. As one general put it, following an older military tradition, "the prostitute and call girl are a necessary distraction, while a wife, who represents the home, weakens a soldier's heart. Quoted in Françoise Thébaud, *La Femme au temps de la guerre de 14* (Paris: Stock, 1986), 137, see also 138–140.

73. See Robert Isherwood's work for an analysis of popular culture and the French Rabelasian tradition in the eighteenth century. Isherwood, *Farce and Fantasy: Popular Entertainment in Eighteenth-Century Paris* (New York: Oxford University Press, 1986).

74. See Parrain, "Censure, Théâtre, et Commune," 327–342. She has noted that, at least in the case of the theater and other *spectacles*, the laws of the early Third Republic actually came from the Second Empire. (328)

75. Charles Rearick, *Pleasures of the Belle Epoque: Entertainment and Festivity in Turn-of-the-Century France* (New Haven: Yale University Press, 1985), 113–114 and 42–43. Rearick's chapter on "The Right to be Lazy and to Enjoy" discusses the campaign by "the cultural opposition" against "French prudes, hypocrites, and censors."

76. The serious preoccupation with using singing properly led to an assortment of books and government reports on the subject, including Albert Dupaigne, *L'Enseignement du chant dans les écoles* (Paris: Hachette, 1879); Amand Chevé, Ministère de l'instruction publique, *Rapport sur l'enseignement du chant dans les écoles primaires* (Paris: Imprimerie nationale, 1881); Camille Saint-Saëns, et al., *Rapports sur l'enseignement du chant dans les écoles primaires* (Paris: Imprimerie nationale, 1881); *Enseignement du chant. Travaux de la commission. Rapports et programmes* (Paris: Imprimerie nationale, 1884).

77. As far back as 1872, for instance, the Minister of Public Education had attributed some of the blame for the Commune's "depravity" to "the orgy of songs produced during that epoch" in the *cafés-concerts*. Quoted in Clark, *The Painting of Modern Life*, 210. See also the criticism of both the immorality and worthlessness of the lyrics by the bourgeois commentators Georges D'Avenel and Frédéric Passy, discussed in Rearick, *Pleasure of the Belle Epoque*, 111.

78. Weber, "Who Sang the Marseillaise?" in *The Wolf and the Lamb: Popular Culture in France*, ed. Jacques Beauroy, Marc Bertrand, and Edward Gargan (Saratoga, CA: Anma Libri & Co., 1976), 167–169. See also, Weber, *Peasants into Frenchmen, The Modernization of Rural France, 1870-1914* (Stanford: Stanford University Press, 1976), 441–442.

79. See Annie Stora-Lamarre, *L'Enfer de la IIIe République: censeurs et pornographes, 1881–1914* (Paris: Imago, 1990).

80. Susanna Barrows, "Venus and Bacchus in an Era of Mechanical Reproduction" (unpublished manuscript), especially 17, 25, 28. See also Barrows, "'Parliaments of the People': The Political Culture of Cafés in the Early Third Republic," in *Drinking: Behavior and Belief in Modern History*, ed. Susanna Barrows and Robin Room (Berkeley: University of California Press, 1991), 87-97.

81. The challenges continued throughout the war, but many times even repeated attempts failed. These debates highlight the points of contention and the strength of the police's position. Cartons Ba 737–740 at the Police Archives in Paris contain the music-hall programs for most of the music establishments within city limits. (Ba 741–743 have programs for the suburbs.) Censors crossed out the banned songs and made notes about mandatory modifications directly on the programs.

82. In the case of individual composers, who often had to absorb the costs of printing their own sheetmusic, even a modification meant a loss of income if the song had circulated before the war. Cf. the letter concerning the song "Opérations Russes" and the correspondence on the songs "Mirabeau Mirabelle" and "Tête de Pipe" in APP, Ba 697.

83. APP, Ba 697.

84. See APP, Ba 697 for correspondence and Ba 736 for songtext. Other performers also defended their reputations against the censors' readings. Emile Laurent of the Folies-Parisiennes, for instance, wrote to the prefect in August 1915 claiming that he had never had problems before and that this particular song ("les Pan pan") "had nothing uncalled-for or obscene" in it. "Besides," he asserted, "I ... do not have a habit of performing unwholesome songs." Despite these assurances, the song suffered some modifications. Ba 697.

85. The correspondence regarding the song "Chose et Machin" by D. Pinel is in APP, Ba 697. See also, the articles in Rt 900 and Rt 934(2), in the Fonds Rondel at la Bibliothèque de l'Arsenal. In Rearick's discussion of the groups which had "fought back by mocking the government, the ruling bourgeoisie, the censors, and the police," he also notes that the opposition defined the terms of the debate as French *gauloiserie* beating back foreign puritanism. *Pleasures of the Belle Epoque*, 43,46.

86. APP, Ba 697 from Moreau's letter filed under his son's song "Marmite et Crapouillot." See also the correspondence on the song "les Vaches."

87. Adding to the censors' confidence was the fact that in May 1917 as Parisian streets witnessed a rebirth of radical song repertoires, the music halls remained relatively quiet and uninvolved in the protests.

88. In November 1917 Clemenceau announced plans to suppress "la censure politique," and on 29 December 1917 he authorized new access to the military front and in canteens for all newspapers. This shift coincided with Clemenceau's avid attention to propaganda which included efforts to demoralize the enemy which he coordinated with Pétain and projects for raising civilian morale, for example with displays of captured enemy materiel on the streets of Paris. See Allard, *Images secrètes*, 49-53, and SHAT, 6 N 145. See also, Odile Krakovitch, "La censure des théâtres durant la grande guerre" in *Théâtre et spectacles hier et aujourd'hui. Actes du 115e congrès national des sociétés savantes* (Paris: Editions du CTHS, 1991), 331-353.

89. SHAT, 5 N 371. Another song seized during the same period was entitled "Révolution" and began with the ominous words "Révoltez-vous, parias des usines." In the fall of 1917, Pétain also tightened up the review of trench newspapers requesting that all copies be submitted to the central headquarters. Audoin-Rouzeau, *Men at War*, 22.

90. Brécy, *Florilège de la chanson révolutionnaire*, 237.

91. Guy Pedroncini, *Les Mutineries de 1917* (Paris: Presses Universitaires de France, 1967), 113–179. These events are also discussed in my book manuscript, entitled *Harmony and Disharmony: French Musical Politics During the Great War.*

92. APP, Ba 1614, from the early 1916 report and the November 1915 report. The former also noted that "as their primary task," the police had "striven to assure the maintenance of order by prohibiting shows which could excite the most violent feelings."

93. Stark, "All Quiet," 62–63, 76.

94. These are the guiding questions of Jean-Jacques Becker's work, for example.

Morale and Sexual Morality in the First World War

1. Richard Davenport-Hines, *Sex, Death and Punishment: Attitudes to Sex and Sexuality in Britain since the Renaissance* (London: Collins, 1990), 226.

2. Edward H. Beardsley, "Allied Against Sin: American and British Responses to Venereal Disease in World War I," *Medical History* 20 (1976), 189–202.

3. See Myna Trustram, *Women of the Regiment: Marriage and the Victorian Army* (Cambridge: Cambridge U. P., 1984), 1–20.

4. See Public Record Office file H.O.45/10724/251861 for a discussion of prostitution in London and port cities in Britain during the war, as well as the problem of the "amateur" prostitute, as they were referred to at the time. The introduction of women on to police forces in Britain was tied up with the policing of these women. See P.R.O. H.O. 45/10806/309485.

5. On the C.D. Acts see Trustram, 121–5; Judith R. Walkowitz, *Prostitution and Victorian Society: Women, Class, and the State* (New York: Cambridge, U. P., 1980).

6. *Prevention of Venereal Disease: Being the Report of and the Evidence Taken by the Special Committee on Venereal Disease* (London: Williams and Northgate, 1921), 5.

7. Minutes of proceedings at a conference regarding venereal disease and its treatment in the armed forces, 10 May 1918, P.R.O. W.O. 32/11404.

8. *Lancet* (9 Nov. 1918), 655–6.

9. P.R.O. W.O. 32/11404.

10. Charles W. Cathcart to *British Medical Journal* (24 Feb. 1917), 280.

11. The primary form of portable prophylaxis used during the First World War was not condoms, but disinfectant ointments that were to be smeared on the genitals after sexual contact. Although the German, Austrian, and French armies, as well as the British navy, had approved the use of disinfectant "packets" for their servicemen, their use in the British army (with the exception of some colonial divisions) were not approved for distribution until 1918. See David M. Simpson, "The Moral Battlefield: Venereal Disease and the British Army in the First World War" (Ph.D. diss., University of Iowa, 1998).

12. For an extended argument against the common stereotype of Victorian sexual morality, see Michael Mason, *The Making of Victorian Sexuality* (Oxford: Oxford U. P., 1994).

13. *Prevention of Venereal Disease*, 6.

14. J. E. H., *True Manliness*, quoted in Lesley A. Hall, "Forbidden by God, Despised by Men: Masturbation, Medical Warnings, Moral Panic, and Manhood in Great Britain, 1850–1950," *Journal of the History of Sexuality* 2, no. 3 (1992): 372.

15. *Prevention of Venereal Disease*, 52.

16. Ibid., 87.

17. Col. J. G. Adami, "The Policy of the Ostrich," *The Canadian Medical Association Journal* 9, no. 4 (Apr. 1919), 289–301.

18. Ibid., 291.

19. The great fears over hereditary syphilis at the time was a misunderstanding of the nature of congenital syphilis. Children could indeed be infected with the disease from their mothers, but fears of syphilitic families passing on a hereditary taint from generation to generation were wildly overstated.

20. P.R.O. W.O.32/5597.

21. See Kenneth Ballhatchet, *Race, Sex and Class under the Raj: Imperial Attitudes and Policies and their Critics, 1793-1905* (New York: St. Martin's, 1980).

22. Oriental and India Office Library, L/Mil/7/13890.

23. John Baynes, *Morale: A Study of Men and Courage: The Second Scottish Rifles at the Battle of Neuve Chapelle, 1915* (London: Cassell, 1967), 211.

24. L. W. Harrison, "Some Lessons Learnt in Fifty Years' Practice in Venereology," *British Journal of Venereal Diseases* 30, no. 4 (Dec. 1954), 184-190.

25. *A Straight Talk to His Men*, (Westminster: White Cross League, [n.d.]), 5.

26. O.I.O.L., L/Mil/7/13892.

27. Ibid.

28. Letter from H. Hudson, Lt.-General, Adjutant General in India, to the General Officers Commanding, Divisions and Independent Brigades, 25 Sept. 1917. O.I.O.L., L/Mil/7/13893.

29. "Venereal Disease in India. Report for the year 1916." O.I.O.L., L/Mil/7/13893.

30. Baynes, 212.

31. The First World War Memoirs of P. G. Heath, Imperial War Museum, DS/Misc/60.

32. Desmond Morton, *When Your Number's Up: the Canadian Soldier in the First World War* (Toronto: Random House of Canada, 1993), 239.

33. Paul Fussell, *The Great War and Modern Memory*, (Oxford: Oxford U. P., 1975), 270–309; Morton, 241.

34. Baynes, 214.

35. Denis Winter, *Death's Men: Soldiers of the Great War* (London: Penguin, 1978), 150.

36. G. Archdall Reid, *Prevention of Venereal Disease* (London: William Heinemann, 1920), 70.

37. Baynes, 203–4.

38. Quoted in Jane Tolerton, *Ettie: A Life of Ettie Rout* (Auckland, NZ: Penguin, 1992), 129.

39. J. G. Fuller, *Troop Morale and Popular Culture in the British and Dominion Armies 1914–1918* (Oxford: Clarendon, 1990), 180.

Sketches of the *Poilu's World*

1. The author wishes to thank Margaret Anderson, Susanna Barrows, Regina Sweeney, and Chad Bryant for their thoughtful criticisms of previous versions of this article. He also wishes to thank the Center for German and European Studies at the University of California at Berkeley for their financial support.

2. Such a "perhaps not fully conscious" articulation of anxiety is a common function of "reflective humor," as one historian has pointed out. Mary Lee Townsend, *Forbidden Laughter: Popular Humor and the Limits of Repression in Nineteenth-Century Prussia* (Ann Arbor: University of Michigan Press, 1992), 9–11. Townsend offers an extensive and insightful general overview of the kinds and functions of humor. See also, Sigmund Freud, *Jokes and their Rela-*

tion to the Unconscious, translated by James Strachey (New York: W.W. Norton and Company, 1960). And for discussion of the use of laughter in response to official seriousness, as well as humor's regenerating value, see Mikhail Bakhtin, *Rabelais and His World*, translated by Helene Iswolsky (Bloomington: Indiana University Press, 1984), chp. 1.

3. See, for example, Tony Ashworth, *Trench Warfare 1914–1918: The Live and Let Live System* (New York: Holmes and Meier, 1980); Eric Leed, *No Man's Land: Combat and Identity in World War I* (London: Cambridge University Press, 1979); Antoine Prost, *In the Wake of War: "Les Anciens Combattants" and French Society* (Providence: Berg, 1992), ch. 1; Leonard Smith, *Between Mutiny and Obedience: The Case of the French Fifth Infantry Division during World War I* (Princeton: Princeton University Press, 1994).

4. This is Weber's appraisal of Louis-Ferdinand Céline's *Journey to the End of Night*. Weber, *The Hollow Years: France in the 1930s* (New York: W.W. Norton, 1994), 19.

5. The limitations of various sources are nicely summarized well in David Englander, "The French Soldier, 1914–1918", *French History* 1:1 (March 1987): 50.

6. Stéphane Audoin-Rouzeau, *Men at War: National Sentiment and Trench Journalism in France during the First World War*, translated by Helen McPhail (Providence: Berg, 1992).

7. Audoin-Rouzeau, *Men at War*, 34, 20.

8. Audoin-Rouzeau, *Men at War*, 34. It is also important to note that these papers were not free from censorship. Trench papers were generally encouraged, as is indicated by an 8 March 1916 circular from General Joffre, because they attempted to boost morale. Official censorship was enforced, though sporadically; self-censorship within newspaper staffs was more likely, as editors used their best judgement in deciding what was inappropriate to print. Similarly, though many articles targeted official "eyewash," trench papers were not totally free of propaganda. See Audoin-Rouzeau, *Men at War*, 20–33. Further, with trench journalism, as with memoirs and diaries, there remain questions of authorship and authenticity. For instance, were those writers who rendered the most vivid description of life at the front truly representative of the average *poilu*?

9. The analysis of trench cartoons in this paper is based on a survey of approximately 75 trench papers in the Hoover Institute Library at Stanford University. Audoin-Rouzeau estimates that about 400 trench papers were published by French forces between 1914. and 1918, of which approximately half survive. Audoin-Rouzeau, *Men at War*, 8.

10. Claude Roger-Marx, "Caricatures Françaises et Étrangères d'Autrefois et d'Aujourd'hui", *Arts et Métiers Graphiques* 31 (15 September 1932): 57.

11. For example, Leonard Smith notes that "after a month of nearly constant maneuver and combat, the 5e DI took part in a total of only thirty-five days of pitched battles over the next seventeen months of the war, primarily in two attacks at Neuville-St. Vaast in the spring and fall of 1915." *Between Mutiny and Obedience*, 74.

12. For a discussion of the homefront's *poilu*, see Charles Rearick, *The French in Love and War: Popular Culture in the Era of the World Wars* (New Haven: Yale University Press, 1997), chp. 1.

13. It is interesting that moral character was so central to cartoons considering that French moral superiority to the enemy was perhaps the most common theme in printed official propaganda. See Stéphane Audoin-Rouzeau, "'Bourrage de Crâne' et Information en France en 1914–1918," in Jean-Jacques Becker and S. Audoin-Rouzeau (eds.), *Les Sociétés Européenes et la Guerre de 1914–1918* (Nanterre: Publications de l'Université de Nanterre, 1990), 165–166.

14. Ruth Harris, "The 'Child of the Barbarian': Rape, Race and Nationalism in France During the First World War", *Past and Present* 141 (November 1993): 186.

15. For an interesting discussion of the uses of female images as symbols of the nation, see Kenneth Silver, *Esprit de Corps: The Art of the Parisian Avant-Garde and the First World War* (Princeton: Princeton University Press, 1989), 11–27.

16. Jean-Jacques Becker, *The Great War and the French People* (Leamington Spa: Berg, 1985), 37.

17. See, for example, David Englander, "The French Soldier," 52; and Jay Winter, *The Experience of World War I* (Oxford: Equinox, 1988), 122, 138–42.

18. Quoted in Prost, *In the Wake of War*, 8.

19. Audoin-Rouzeau, *Men at War*, 10; Englander, "The French Soldier," 63.

20. Criticism was not accepted from the civilian press, either. The government shut down papers which questioned military strategy or criticized internal politics. Ross F. Collins, "The Development of Censorship in World War I France", *Journalism Monographs* 131 (February 1992): 12.

21. See, for example, Edward Said, *Orientalism* (New York, Vintage Books, 1978).

22. Englander, "The French Soldier," 57. French soldiers feared the presence of English and American soldiers for the same reasons. One cartoon explicitly represents the perceived sexual conquest of the English. In *Le Tord-Boyau* (no. 16, December 1917), a French woman is asked by military authorities if the English left anything behind. "Yes, sir, this!" she says, holding up a baby. It is interesting to note that while *poilus* feared the allies impregnating French women, a heated debate was taking place on the homefront over what to do with "children of the enemy"—babies born as a result of alleged German rape. See Stéphane Audoin-Rouzeau, *L'Enfant de l'ennemi (1914–1918): Viol, avortement, infanticide pendant la Grande Guerre* (Paris: Aubier, 1995).

23. François Déchelette, *L'Argot des Poilus: Dictionnaire humoristique et philologique du langage des soldats de la Grande Guerre de 1914* (Genève: Slatkine Reprints, 1972), 183.

24. A Private Legentil, Class of 1916, described in his diary the socializing between soldiers during periods out of the trenches: "We got to know the old-timers of the section, who were quite few, having left many comrades on the slopes of the fort of Douaumont." These old-timers, Legentil says, spent much of their free time getting drunk. Smith, *Between Mutiny and Obedience*, 165.

25. Sigmund Freud, *Civilization and Its Discontents*, translated by James Strachey (New York: W. W. Norton & Company, 1961), 46.

26. Déchelette, *L'Argot des Poilus*, 91–92.

27. See, for example, the first of the "Camp Festival" cartoons (Figure 6) discussed above.

28. John Horne, "'L'impôt du sang': Republican rhetoric and industrial warfare in France, 1914–1918", *Social History* 14:2 (May 1989): 203; and see Audoin-Rouzeau, *Men at War*, 135–143.

29. See Paul Fussell, *The Great War and Modern Memory* (New York: Oxford University Press, 1975); and for a discussion of the gendering of these dichotomies had on gender relations, see Mary Louise Roberts, *Civilization Without Sexes: Reconstructing Gender in Postwar France, 1917–1927* (Chicago: University of Chicago Press, 1994), chp. 1.

30. See Audoin-Rouzeau, *Men at War*, 135–43.

31. Although Audoin-Rouzeau examines soldiers' complex responses to the national press, he argues that a "national sentiment" ultimately kept them fighting. Audoin-Rouzeau, *Men at War*, pp. 182–188. For the importance of patriotism, *devoir*, and comradeship, see Modris Eksteins, *Rites of Spring: The Great War and the Birth of the Modern Age* (Boston: Houghton Mifflin Co., 1989), chp. 5; for a revision to some of some common as-

sumptions, see L. L. Farrar, Jr., "Nationalism in Wartime: Critiquing the Conventional Wisdom," in Frans Coetzee and Marilyn Shevin-Coetzee (Eds.), *Authority, Identity and the Social History of the Great War* (Providence: Berghahn Books, 1995), 133152.

32. Some *poilus* may have never known these comforts, as they were commonly associated with urban, bourgeois society. But they remained the symbols of French civilization. See Eugen Weber, *Peasants into Frenchmen: The Modernization of Rural France 1870–1914* (Stanford: Stanford University Press, 1976), 486.

The First World War and the Public Sphere in Germany

1. Jeffrey Verhey, "The 'Spirit of 1914': The Myth of Enthusiasm and the Rhetoric of Unity in World War I Germany" (Ph.D. diss., University of California, Berkeley, 1991), 229-31.

2. Jürgen Habermas, *The Structural Transformation of the Public Sphere* (Cambridge: Cambridge University Press, 1989), 25–26.

3. Ibid., 15–16.

4. Geoff Eley, "Nations, Publics and Political Cultures: Placing Habermas in the Nineteenth Century," in Craig Calhoun, ed., *Habermas and the Public Sphere* (Cambridge MIT Press, 1992), 290.

5. Roger Chartier, *The Cultural Origins of the French Revolution* (Durham: Duke University Press, 1991), 134–35; see also Arlette Farge, *Subversive Words: Public Opinion in Eighteenth-Century France* (University Park: Pennsylvania State University Press, 1994), 5.

6. Belinda Davis, "Reconsidering Habermas, Gender, and the Public Sphere: The Case of Wilhelmine Germany," in Geoff Eley, ed., *Society, Culture, and the State in Germany 1870–1930* (Ann Arbor: University of Michigan Press, 1996), 407.

7. Thomas Lindenberger, *Strassenpolitik: Zur Sozialgeschichte der öffentlichen Ordnung in Berlin 1900 bis 1914* (Bonn: Verlag Dietz Nachfolger, 1995), 67.

8. Lindenberger, 11; Davis, 407.

9. Davis, "Reconsidering Habermas," 406.

10. Davis, "Reconsidering Habermas," 412.

11. Erich Mühsam, *Tagebücher 1910–1924* (Munich: Deutsche Taschenbuch Verlag, 1994), 102.

12. Jean-Noël Kapferer, *Rumors: Uses, Interpretations, and Images* (New Brunswick: Transaction Publishers, 1990), 263.

13. Mark Cornwall, "News, Rumour and the Control of Information in Austria-Hungary, 1914–1918," *History* 77 (February 1992), 50-51.

14. Verhey, 178–79.

15. "Gerüchte," *General Anzeiger der Münchner Neueste Nachrichten*, Nr. 399, 6 August 1914.

16. "Eine Mahnung der Polizeidirektion," *Münchner Neuste Nachrichten*, Nr. 398, 6 August 1914.

17. "Die Gefahren der Spionenjagd," *BZ am Mittag*, Nr. 182, 5 August 1914.

18. "Spione und Pöbel," *Bremer Bürger-Zeitung*, Nr. 179, 4 August 1914.

19. "Blinder Eifer," *Berliner Morgenpost*, Nr. 214, 7 August 1914; "Ruhig Blut, *Vossische Zeitung*, Nr. 393, 5 August 1914.

20. An die königliche Polizeidirektion, 6 August 1914, BayHStA, Abt. II, Polizeidirektion München, #4562.

21. "Franzosenfeindliche Kundgebungen," *Rheinisch-Westfälische Zeitung*, Nr. 965, 25 August 1914.

22. "Weimar," *Rheinisch-Westfälische Zeitung*, Nr. 930, 7 August 1914.

23. Verhey, 176–180; Jeffrey Smith, "A People's War: The Transformation of German Politics, 1913–1918" (Ph.D. diss., University of Illinois, 1997), 199.

24. "Bericht der Abteilung VII," 17 February 1915, in Ingo Materna and Hans-Joachim Schreckenbach, eds., *Berichte des Berliner Polizeipräsidenten zur Stimmung und Lage der Bevölkerung in Berlin 1914-1918* (Weimar, 1987), 43-44.

25. "Bericht des Polizeipräsidenten Berlin-Lichtenberg," 16 October 1915, in Materna, *Berichte*, 89; see also Peter Fritzsche, *Germans into Nazis* (Cambridge: Harvard University Press, 1998), 67.

26. Jagow an den Minister des Innern, 16 October 1915, in Materna, *Berichte*, 90–91.

27. Fritzsche, 67.

28. "Bericht der Abteilung VII," in Materna, *Berichte*, 140–41.

29. Jagow, "61. Stimmungsbericht," 18 March 1916, in Materna, *Berichte*, 116.

30. Michael Balfour, *The Kaiser and his Times* (Boston: Houghton Mifflin, 1964), 357.

31. Ibid., 358.

32. "Der Kaiser im Kölner Dom," *Berliner Morgenpost*, Nr. 206, 26 July 1916.

33. Ullrich, "Kriegsalltag," 612–13.

34. George Mosse, *Fallen Soldiers: Reshaping the Memory of the World Wars* (New York: Oxford University Press, 1990), 128.

35. Hubertus Jahn, *Patriotic Culture in Russia during World War I* (Ithaca: Cornell University Press, 1995), 39.

36. Marie-Monique Huss, "Pronatalism and the Popular Ideology of the Child in Wartime France: the Evidence of the Picture Postcard," in Richard Wall and Jay Winter, eds., *The Upheaval of War: Family, Work, and Welfare in Europe 1914–1918* (Cambridge: Cambridge University Press, 1988), 334.

37. Jahn, 39.

38. Mosse, 125.

39. Jahn, 41; John Fraser, "Propaganda on the Picture Postcard," *Oxford Art Journal* 3 (1980), 41.

40. Rainer Rother, ed., *Die Letzten Tage der Menschheit: Bilder des Ersten Weltkriegs* (Berlin: Deutsches Historisches Museum, 1994), 137.

41. "Der Frankierte Kaiser: Posen fürs Volk," *Zeitmagazin* 44 (October 1990), 44; Rother, 146.

42. Ullrich, "Kriegsalltag," 612.

43. The term "patriotic fantasy" is used by Huss, "Pronatalism," in describing similar postcards in France.

44. *Simplicissimus*, 13 July 1915, 174.

45. T.W., "Die Erfolg der Revolution," *Berliner Tageblatt*, Nr. 576, 10 November 1918; see also Theodor Wolff, *Tagebücher 1914–1919*, vol. 2 (Boppard am Rhein: Harald Boldt Verlag, 1984), 814.

46. Laurence Moyer, *Victory Must Be Ours: Germany in the Great War 1914–1918* (New York: Hippocrene Books, 1995), 310.

47. Fritzsche, 85–86.

48. Verhey, 465.

Notes

The Paradox of Working Heroines

1. I would like to thank the Fulbright Foundation and the Mellon Foundation for their financial support, and Lou Roberts, Peter Stansky, Susan Porter Benson, and Jennifer Baszile for their helpful comments at different stages of the manuscript.

2. Peggy Bate to F. A. Brettell, 25 December 1915. Lt. F. A. Brettell, Imperial War Museum, Department of Documents (hereafter IWM-DD), PP/MCR/169.

3. Eleanora Pemberton to her mother, undated [received 12 April 1916]. Miss E. B. Pemberton, IWM-DD 85/33/1.

4. Angela Woollacott, *On Her Their Lives Depend: Munitions Workers in the Great War* (Berkeley: University of California Press, 1994), 183; Gareth Griffiths, *Women's Factory Work in World War I* (Phoenix Mill, UK: Alan Sutton, 1991), 13–14. Griffiths also points out the increasing mean age of domestic servants in the 20th century, which, along with its decline as a percentage of employed women, suggests that new female workers were not entering the field. The number of women entering munitions is difficult to assess, as different industrial categories included munitions production in addition to other kinds of work, but seems to be somewhere on the rough order of one million. See Woollacott, *On Her Their Lives Depend*, 18; Griffiths, *Women's Factory Work*, 13; Richard Wall, "English and German Families and the First World War, 1914-1918," 56; Deborah Thom, "Women and Work in Wartime Britain," 304; both in Richard Wall and Jay Winter (eds.), *The Upheaval of War: Family, Work and Welfare in Europe, 1914-1918* (Cambridge: Cambridge University Press, 1988).

5. Ethel Alec-Tweedie, in *The English Review*, April 1916; quoted in Ethel Alec-Tweedie, *Women and Soldiers* (London: John Lane, [1918]), 41–42.

6. See, for example, Alec-Tweedie, *Women and Soldiers*; see also Jenny Gould, "Women's Military Services in First World War Britain," in Margaret Randolph Higonnet, Jane Jenson, Sonya Michel, and Margaret Collins Weitz (eds.), *Behind the Lines: Gender and the Two World Wars* (New Haven: Yale University Press, 1987); and Krisztina Robert, "Gender, Class, and Patriotism: Women's Paramilitary Units in First World War Britain," International History Review , vol. XIX, no. 1 (February 1997), 52–65.

7. This was a subject of extensive debate. See J. M. Cowper, *A Short History of Queen Mary's Army Auxiliary Corps* (privately pub. by the Women's Royal Army Corps Association, 1967), 22.

8. Dorothy Loveday to Miss Robertson, dated only "Friday." Miss Dorothy Loveday, Peter Liddle 1914–1918 Personal Experience Archive, University of Leeds (hereafter PL), Women Collection.

9. It is worth noting that WAAC discharge forms gave ratings for both "work" and "personal character." See, for example, discharge papers of Miss M. I. Gilmore, IWM-DD 83/6/1; Miss J. G. Lambert, PL Women Collection.

10. Peggy Bate to "Brett" Brettell, 30 January 1918. Lt. F. A. Brettell, IWM-DD PP/MCR/169.

11. Peggy Bate to "Brett" Brettell, 15.January 1917. Lt. F. A. Brettell, IWM-DD PP/MCR/169.

12. Loveday herself had already been passed for foreign service. Dorothy Loveday to Miss Robertson, 30 December 1917. Miss Dorothy Loveday, PL Women Collection.

13. Alec-Tweedie, *Women and Soldiers*, 127.

14. Hilda M. Love, "America and the 'WAACs;'" newspaper clipping [no publication information] (emphasis in original). Miss A. Essington-Nelson, IWM-DD 86/48/1.

15. Dorothy Loveday to Miss Robertson, 14 January 1918. Miss Dorothy Loveday, PL Women Collection.

16. Dorothy Loveday to Miss Robertson, 6 February 1918. Miss Dorothy Loveday, PL Women Collection.

17. Dorothy Loveday to Miss Robertson, undated [first page missing] but probably January 1918. Miss Dorothy Loveday, PL Women Collection.

18. See Cowper, *Short History*, 42–51; quotation from commission, 45.

19. Dorothy Pickford to her sister Molly, 14 March 1918. Hon. D. F. Pickford, IWM-DD Con Shelf.

20. Quoted in David Mitchell, *Monstrous Regiment: The Story of the Women of the First World War* (New York: Macmillan, 1965), 226.

21. Dorothy Pickford to Molly, 24 February 1918. Hon. D. F. Pickford, IWM-DD Con Shelf.

22. Helen M. Beale to Dorothy Brown, 14 March 1918, Beale Family Papers, Cobnor Cottage, Chidham, Chichester (hereafter BP). I would like to thank the late Joan Edom, nee Beale, for giving me generous access to her family papers, and for her help. I also thank her daughter-in-law, Gillian Edom.

23. Helen M. Beale to Margaret A. Beale, 17 February 1918, BP.

24. Helen M. Beale to Dorothy Brown, 21 February 1918, BP.

25. Sybil Field to Helen M. Beale, 20 March 1918, BP.

26. Dorothy Brown to Helen M. Beale, 28 February [1918], BP.

27. Helen M. Beale to Dorothy Brown, 14 March 1918, BP.

28. Diary entry, 11 September [1917]. 'A Rose in Picardy': The Diaries of Gwen Ware (privately published, 1984), 24-25. British Red Cross Society Archives, Barnett Hill, Guildford.

29. See Gladys Pott, "Women in Agriculture," in Mrs. H. Usborne, *Women's Work in Wartime: A Handbook of Employments* (London: T. W. Laurie, [1917]), 117.

30. *Women's Land Army Handbook*, 5. See, for example, Miss D. Ferrar, IWM-DD, 92/30/1.

31. "Land Army Song - To the tune of 'Come Lasses and Lads'," *Women's Land Army Handbook*.

32. "Land Army Song - To the tune of 'The British Grenadiers'," *Women's Land Army Handbook*.

33. Pott, "Women in Agriculture," 125-126.

34. Quoted in Sharon Ouditt, *Fighting Forces, Writing Women: Identity and Ideology in the First World War* (London: Routledge, 1994), 54.

35. See Barbara McLaren, *Women of the War* (London: Hodder and Stoughton, 1917), 102. The real "prose" of land work, overlooked by Prothero and others but mentioned by McLaren (104), was that "in addition to their farm work, [most women land workers] do their own cooking and housework; therefore they are really doing a man's work outside, but without the prepared meal and the immediate rest that most men can look forward to after work."

36. Berta Ruck, *The Land Girl's Love Story* (1919); quoted in Ouditt, *Fighting Forces*, 65.

37. F. I. Hildrick Smith, in *Queen Mary's High School Magazine* (1916), 5. Miss E. T. Rubery, IWM-DD 85/7/1.

38. *Land Army Handbook*, 5.

39. F. I. Hildrick Smith, in *Queen Mary's High School Magazine* (1916), 5. Miss E. T. Rubery, IWM-DD 85/7/1.

40. Pott, "Women in Agriculture,"121.

41. Ruck, *Love Story*, 82, 24; quoted in Ouditt, *Fighting Forces*, 65.

42. Pott, "Women in Agriculture,"125.

43. McLaren, *Women of the War*, 16.

44. F. I. Hildrick Smith, in *Queen Mary's High School Magazine* (1916), 5–6. Miss E. T. Rubery, IWM-DD 85/7/1.

45. Ouditt, *Fighting Forces*, 56. Ouditt quotes some of the results of this effort: "Miss J. Barr, Hertford. For exceptional courage and devotion to duty in saving valuable pigs from drowning. . . . Miss A. Bohills and Miss K. Harrison. These two women were employed at a very lonely farm in Northumberland and have shown great devotion in sticking to their job under very difficult circumstances."

46. East & West Kent Women's Threshing Sub-Committee to Miss D. Ferrar, 22 August 1918. Miss D. Ferrar, IWM-DD, 92/30/1.

47. See letter from F. J. Heron Maxwell, Helen Rice, and F. S. W. Cornwallis to Miss M. Britton. Mrs. M. Harrold, IWM-DD, 86/20/1.

48. Food Production Department to Miss D. Ferrar, July 1918. Miss D. Ferrar, IWM-DD, 92/30/1.

49. Walter Nevill to his family, 19 April 1917; Commander W. H. Nevill RNR, IWM-DD Con Shelf. Frank Ennor to Kathleen La Fontaine, 16 July 1917; Lieutenant F. H. Ennor, IWM-DD 86/28/1.

50. Katharine Furse to Lord Selbourne, 18 May 1916. Dame Katharine Furse, PL Women Collection.

51. Quoted in Ouditt, *Fighting Forces*, 65.

52. Ina Scott, "The Land," in Gilbert Stone (ed.), *Women War Workers: Accounts Contributed by Representative Workers of the Work done by Women in the More Important Branches of War Employment* (New York: Thomas Y. Crowell, [1917]), 57.

53. Medicine would be the obvious other example where men and women were performing the same tasks as part of the war effort. However, since it required extensive training, it was not an option to anyone seeking "war work," but instead created different professional tensions between men and women.

54. McLaren, *Women of the War*, 54, 29.

55. See L. K. Yates, *The Woman's Part: A Record of Munitions Work* (New York: George H. Doran, [1918?]), 13.

56. See L. Keyser Yates, "The Open Road: Women's Opportunity in the Munition Factory" in Usborne, *Women's Work in War Time*, 115.

57. Alec-Tweedie, *Women and Soldiers*, 34.

58. Ian Hay, *Carrying On - After the First Hundred Thousand* (Edinburgh and London: William Blackwood & Sons, 1917), 311–312.

59. See Jane Lewis's discussion of *England's Effort* (1916) and other writings of Mrs. Humphrey Ward in *Women and Social Action in Victorian and Edwardian England* (Aldershot, UK: Edward Elgar, 1991), 252.

60. See Monica Cosens, *Lloyd George's Munition Girls* (London: Hutchinson, [1916]; Woollacott, *On Her Their Lives Depend*; Ouditt, *Fighting Forces*; Gail Braybon, *Women Workers in the First World War* (London: Routledge, 1989 [1981]). In fact, it could be easier to use military language in reference to munitions workers than to the women's auxiliary organizations, as the munitions workers were not a threat to the existing military structure.

61. T. Hall Caine, *Our Girls: Their Work for the War* (London: Hutchinson, 1916); quoted in Woollacott, *On Her Their Lives Depend*, 6.

62. Yates, *Woman's Part*, 9. The prevalence of this theme is demonstrated by the disconcerting similarity between Yates's description and one employed earlier by Barbara McLaren.

63. Yates, *Woman's Part*, 9.

64. Woollacott, *On Her Their Lives Depend*, 180.

65. Woollacott, *On Her Their Lives Depend*, 40.

66. Thom, "Women and Work ," 304.

67. Woollacott, *On Her Their Lives Depend*, 115. See also Thom, "Women and Work in Wartime Britain," 305; Braybon, *Women Workers*, 167.

68. Alec-Tweedie, *Women and Soldiers* , 77, 67. She also argued (42–43) that the "poor" were wasting their newfound wealth on pianos, carpets, fur coats, and silk petticoats.

69. Braybon, *Women Workers*, 167.

70. Cosens, *Munition Girls*, 119–120.

71. Naomi Loughlan, "Munition Work," in Stone, *Women War Workers*, 32–33.

72. Cosens, *Munition Girls*, 80–81.

73. Loughlan, "Munition Work," 33.

74. McLaren, *Women of the War*, 11.

75. Alec-Tweedie, *Women and Soldiers*, 18. See also similar claims in Mary Frances Billington, *The Roll-Call of Serving Women: A Record of Woman's Work for Combatants and Sufferers in the Great War* (London: The Religious Tract Society, 1915), 207; and McLaren, *Women of the War*, 52, who refers to the "excellent leadership of the educated women who have entered the works."

76. McLaren, *Women of the War*, 13.

77. See, for example, Dorothea Proud's discussion of "Welfare Work" in Stone, *Women War Workers*, 239–253.

78. Yates, *Woman's Part*, 37. Yates also referred to the Lady Welfare Supervisor as a "modern Florence Nightingale," and averred that "the faces of rows of women light up as [she] passed through their shop;" 40.

79. Alec-Tweedie, *Women and Soldiers*, 20–21.

80. Lewis, *Women and Social Action*, 263.

81. Woollacott, *On Her Their Lives Depend*, 154–155.

82. Thom, "Women and Work," 314.

83. Dorothy Brown to Helen M. Beale, 4 February [1919], BP.

84. Helen M. Beale to Dorothy Brown, 23 February 1919, BP.

85. Margaret A. Beale to Helen M. Beale, 7 May [1919], BP.

86. Helen M. Beale to Margaret S. Beale, 7 May 1919, BP.

87. Helen M. Beale to Margaret A. Beale, 10 September 1919, BP.

88. Helen M. Beale to Margaret A. Beale, 18 September 1919, BP.

89. Margaret S. Beale to Helen M. Beale, 21 September 1919, BP.

90. Helen M. Beale to Dorothy Brown, 14 October 1919, BP.

91. See Woollacott, *On Her Their Lives Depend*, 181-185. See also Thom, "Women and Work ," 315-317.

Marketing Modernism

1. Quoted in Humphrey Carpenter, *A Serious Character: The Life of Ezra Pound* (New York: Delta, 1988) 279.

2. Quoted in A. Alvarez, review of *The Life of Ezra Pound* by Noel Stock. *Saturday Review* 18 July 1970: 27–9.

3. Quoted in B. L. Reid, *The Man From New York: John Quinn and His Friends* (New York: Oxford University Press, 1967) 280.

4. For more details on this, see Timothy Materer, "Make it Sell! Ezra Pound Advertises Modernism," in Kevin J. H. Dettmar and Stephen Watt, eds., *Marketing Modernism: Self-Promotion, Canonization, Rereading* (Ann Arbor: University of Michigan Press, 1996).

5. See Lawrence Rainey, "F. T. Marinetti and Ezra Pound," *Modernism/Modernity* 1.3 (Fall 1994): 195–215. See also Rainey's "Consuming Investments: Joyce's *Ulysses,*" *James Joyce Quarterly* 33.4: 531–67, and "The Real Scandal of *Ulysses,*" *TLS* Jan. 31, 1997: 11–13.

6. Rainey, "Marinetti," 211.

7. Ezra Pound, TL to Peter Russell, 9-19-5?. (Ezra Pound Collection, University of Texas Harry Ransom Humanities Research Center, hereafter referred to as "HRC.")

8. Rainey, "Marinetti," 210.

9. *Ibid.*

10. See Joan Shelley Rubin, *The Making of Middlebrow Culture,* (Chapel Hill: University of North Carolina Press, 1992) as well as Richard Wightman Fox and T.J. Jackson Lears, *The Culture of Consumption: Critical Essays in American History, 1880-1980,* (New York: Pantheon, 1983).

11. Rubin 27.

12. In a letter to Felix Schelling of 17 Nov. 1916, in Ezra Pound, *Selected Letters 1907–1941*, D. D. Paige, ed. (New York: New Directions, 1971) 99.

13. *Publishers Weekly* March 11, 1916: 865.

14. Houghton Mifflin, perhaps urged on by the well-connected Amy Lowell, began issuing her *Some Imagist Poets* annuals in 1915.

15. Advertisement in *The New Republic*, Oct. 27 1917: xi.

16. Kreymbourg and Man Ray had begun plans for *The Glebe* in 1913; in 1914 the magazine began to be financed by the Boni brothers, and although Kreymbourg wanted to publish the Imagists in the first issue, the Boni brothers changed the plans.

17. Tom Dardis, *Firebrand: The Life of Horace Liveright,* (New York: Random House, 1995) 52.

18. Advertisement, *New Republic* 16 April 1918.

19. In 1925, Bennett Cerf, who was then a vice-president at Boni & Liveright, and his college friend Donald Klopfer bought the Modern Library for $215,000. With the Modern Library as a backbone, they later founded Random House.

20. After selling out the first printing of 1000 copies, a second run of 1000 had to be ordered by early 1923 (Sharpe 157, in Willison 1996).

21. Forrest Read, ed., *Pound/Joyce,* (New York: New Directions, 1968) 107.

22. Dardis 95.

Dangerous Neutrality

1. For example, A. James Gregor, *Young Mussolini and the Intellectual Origins of Fascism* (Berkeley: University of California Press, 1979).

2. Martin Blinkhorn, *Mussolini and Fascist Italy*, 2nd ed. (London, 1994), 17–8.

3. On the effect of World War I on Spain and on the Spanish intelligentsia in particular, see Gerald H. Meaker, "A Civil War of Words: The Ideological Impact of the First World War on Spain, 1914–18," in Hans A. Schmitt, *Neutral Europe between War and Revolution, 1917–23* (Charlottesville: University Press of Virginia), 1-65, and Francisco J. Romero Sal-

vadó, "Spain and the First World War: The Structural Crisis of the Liberal Monarchy," *European History Quarterly* 25 (1995), 529–54

4. Catalonia is slightly larger than Belgium and lies on the northeastern corner of the Iberian peninsula, between the Pyrenees, the Mediterranean, and the Ebro basin. Today it has about six million inhabitants, over five million of whom speak Catalan as their first language. As Catalans often point out, their language has a vast body of its own medieval and modern literature and should in no way be considered a mere dialect. Modern Catalan nationalism arose in the latter part of the last century as part of the overall rise in the recognition of small nationalities that had lost their independence as modern European states had formed. Well aware of other nationalist aspirations of the age, Catalanists declared solidarity with similar movements in Ireland, Greece, Finland, Norway, and elsewhere. But unlike these places, Catalonia has not yet achieved complete political independence. In many cases, moreover, nationalist aspirations in Catalonia rival those of peoples so often in the headlines today—especially those in eastern Europe for whom the First World War was also so important. While Catalan nationalism has not produced the sort of violence one sees these days in the Balkans, it still does have the power to make and break ruling coalitions in Spain. For a general if rather partial overview see Albert Balcells, *Catalan Nationalism. Past and Present*, trans. Jacqueline Hall (New York: St. Martin's, 1996). Daniele Conversi, *The Basques, the Catalans and Spain* (Reno and Las Vegas: University of Nevada Press, 1997), is a very comprehensive study of Catalan and Basque nationalism.

5. José Carlos Mainer, "Una frustración histórica: la aliadofilia de los intelectuales," in *Literatura y pequeña-burguesía en España* (Madrid, 1972), 141–64, cited in Josep Murgades, "Repercussions de la guerra en la cultura," *L'Avenç*, N. 69 (March 1984), 74.

6. Brief but extremely useful articles published in Catalan that discuss World War I and Catalonia include Enric Ucelay Da Cal, "Wilson i no Lenin: l'esquerra catalana i l'any 1917, *L'Avenç* 9 (Oct. 1978), 53–8, David Martínez Fiol, "Aliadòfils i Germanòfils a Catalunya: Elements per comprendre la mobilització catalanista durant la gran guerra, 1914–1918," which appears in the introduction to his collection of texts *El Catalanisme i la Gran Guerra (1914–1918). Antologia* (Barcelona: Edicions de la Magrana, 1988), v- xxxix, and the articles in the dossier on "Catalunya davant el món en guerra (1914–1919)," *L'Avenç* 69 (March 1984), 32–79. I have drawn heavily upon these works in writing the present article. See also Meaker, "Civil," 31–9.

7. Here I use the term "modernist" loosely to describe the outlook of fin-de-siècle intellectuals who rejected the dominant cultural values of nineteenth-century Europe—which rested largely on the Enlightenment legacies of rationalism and liberalism—in favor of radically new moralities and ways of looking at the world, such as those espoused by Nietzsche. Catalan *modernisme* does not equate to this sort of European-wide modernism or to Spanish literary *modernismo*; it initially arose as a way of describing the Catalan version of the "new style" art and architecture sweeping Europe, which in Catalonia functioned as a form of enduring conspicuous consumption and means of affirming rural background and local patriotism.

8. Joan-Lluís Marfany discusses this transformation—unfortunately with little mention of the impact of World War I—in his *La cultura del catalanisme. El nacionalisme català en els seus inicis* (Barcelona: Editorial Empúries, 1996). I follow Marfany's lead in using the terms "Catalanism" and "Catalan nationalism" interchangeably. On the interplay between socially conservative and more "radical" elements of Catalan nationalism during this period, see also Balcells, 35–82. Arthur Terry offers brief overviews of Catalan literary modernism and its continuation, noucentisme, in "Catalan Literary *Modernisme* and *Noucentisme*: From Dissidence

to Order," in Helen Graham and Jo Labanyi, eds., *Spanish Cultural Studies. An Introduction* (New York: Oxford University Press, 1995), and in chapters 3 and 4 of his earlier work *Catalan Literature* (London: Ernest Benn, 1972).

9. Although one British observer doubted that the Germans had much influence on the strike movement in Spain as a whole, he did suspect that German influence have been behind some labor disturbances in mines near Bilbao, aiming to hinder the supply of ore to the allies. Edward J. Newbigin to T. H. Carlton Levick, Bilbao, 16 Aug. 1917, Public Records Office, London (hereafter PRO), F.O. 371. See also Jorge Ventura Subirats, "La verdadera personalidad del 'Barón de König,'" *Cuadernos de Historia Económica de Cataluña* V (March 1971), 103–18. Activities of German agents in wartime Catalonia play a role in the Eduardo Mendoza's post-modernist historical novel *La verdad sobre el caso Savolta* (Barcelona, 1990).

10. Initially, Primo de Rivera received significant support from sectors of Catalan society most frightened by the threat of working-class revolutionary violence. Moreover, the *Juntas de Defensa*, a sort of trade-union for low-level military officers that also destabilized the parliamentary regime, was based in Barcelona. Carolyn P. Boyd, *La política pretoriana en el reinado de Alfonso XIII*. Trans. Mauro Hernández Benítez (Madrid, 1990). An earlier version of Boyd's work appeared in English as *Praetorian Politics in Liberal Spain* (Chapel Hill: University of North Carolina Press, 1979).

11. Balcells, *Catalan,* 69.

12. Balcells, *Catalan,* 67–72.

13. *Història dels moviments nacionalistes*, n. VII, VIII and XV (Barcelona, Societat Catalana d'Edicions, 1913–1914), cited in Martínez Fiol, *Catalanisme*, xii.

14. As Jordi Casassas argues, pragmatic concerns probably motivated Cambó here. In wartime conditions Cambó had to face a growing, increasingly radical working class, and he may well have seen Catalanism as a way of keeping the masses in line with the more "paternalist"—i.e. hegemonic—interests and cultural forms of the Catalan bourgeoisie. See Casassas' article "La radicalització del catalanisme," *L'Avenç* 69 (March 1984), 56.

15. Sir Arthur Hardinge to Arthur James Balfour, 9 Aug. 1917, San Sebastian. PRO, F.O. 371.

16. Stanley G. Payne, "Catalan and Basque Nationalism," *Journal of Contemporary History* 6 (1971), 29–30.

17. On d'Ors see Vicente Cacho Viu, *Revisión de Eugenio d'Ors* (Barcelona: Cuaderns Crema, 1997). As Joaquim Coll i Amargós shows in a recent article, the more radical, antipositivist ideas of French thinkers associated with the likes of Maurice Barrès had at least some impact on other Catalan intellectuals as well by as early as the late nineteenth century. See his "Brunetière, Barrès i el catalanisme finisecular," *L'Avenç* 232 (Jan. 1999), 8–12.

18. D'Ors eventually moved to Madrid and became a sympathizer of the Falange, a fascist political organization. Cacho Viu=s recent work, *Revisión*, examines d'Ors' writings and activities leading up to his embrace of Franco and Nationalist cause in the Spanish Civil War.

19. Ucelay, "Wilson."

20. Eugeni Xammar, "Contra la idea d'imperi," in Martínez Fiol, *Catalanisme*, 8–9. This selection first appeared in Xammar's *Contra la idea d'imperi* (Edinburg, New York, London and Paris: Thomas Nelson and Sons, 1916).

21. Posición de Catalunya davant el problema europeu," *Revista Anyal* (1915), reprinted in Martínez Fiol, *Catalanisme,* 8694.

22. Hardinge to Balfour, 18. July 1917, PRO, F.O. 371. Hardinge to the Managers of

London County and Westminster Bank and Anglo-South America Bank, 16 July 1917, PRO, F.O. 371. A. Rovira i Virgili, "La revolta irlandesa," *Renaixement*, 18 May 1916, reprinted in Martínez Fiol, *Catalanisme*, 103–7.

23. Gary W. McDonogh, "Other People's Nations: Towards an Interactive Model of Nationalist Movements," *Canadian Review of Studies in Nationalism* XIV, 2 (1987), 301–3.

24. David Martínez i Fiol, *Els "Voluntaris Catalans" a la Gran Guerra (1914-1918)*, prol. Enric Ucelay-Da Cal (Barcelona: Publicacions de l'Abadia de Montserrat, 1991).

25. For example, E. Cortade, *Catalunya i la gran guerra* (Barcelona: Rafael Dalman, 1969), 54–78.

26. See Ucelay da Cal's prologue to Martínez i Fiol, "*Voluntaris*," 7–13.

27. Martínez Fiol, "*Voluntaris*," 145.

28. Xosé M. Núñez Seixas, *Historiographical Approaches to Nationalism in Spain* (Saarbrücken and Fort Lauderdale: Breitenbach, 1993), 65.

29. Casassas, "Radicalització," 60.

30. Ucelay da Cal, "Vanguardia." On the "integral nationalist" and militarist strains of Catalanism, the "escamots," and related radical youth groups, see also Enrique Ucelay Da Cal, "Estat Català: The Strategies of Separation and Revolution of Catalan Radical Nationalism, 1919-1933" (Ph.D. dissertation, Columbia University, 1979), 279–326.

31. Ucelay da Cal, "Vanguardia," 61, 58.

Regaining the "Lost Provinces"

1. Marius-Ary LeBlond *L'alsace et la lorraine: glorifée par nos écrivains et nos artistes*, (Paris: Libraire Larousse, 1915).

2. Ibid.

3. Ibid.

4. Ibid.

5. Ibid. 12.

6. I have examined very few guides from the German perspective, but my incomplete research suggests that German authors (and indeed English and American writers who took the German position) had strong counter arguments to mount against French claims over Alsace and Lorraine. For a sampling, see Jules Froelich, *Le pangermaniste en Alsace*, (Paris, Berger-Levrault, 1913); and Franz Holtzendorff, *The Right of Conquest*, (Berlin, CG Luderitz, 1872).

7. Ibid.

8. I am indebted to the rich and thoughtful—if at times consternatingly odd—analysis of landscape offered by Simon Schama, in his *Landscape and Memory* (London: HarperCollins, 1995).

9. Among the more recent and important works related to travel and narratives of the tourist, my larger debt for background information and analytical grounding is to the following: Bruce Redford, *Venice and the Grand Tour*, (New Haven: Yale University Press, 1996); and several of the essays in Chloe Chard and Helen Langdon, eds., *Transport: Travel, Pleasure and Imaginative Geography, 1600–1830* (New Haven: Yale University Press, 1996).

10. I am consciously using "traveler" and "tourist" interchangeably, opposing what I take to be the less than useful distinction drawn by Paul Fussel in his *Abroad: British Literary Traveling Between the Wars*, (Oxford: Oxford University Press, 1980).

11. For an analysis of nineteenth-century guides to the spas of France, see Douglas P. Mackaman, *Leisure Settings: Bourgeois Culture, Medicine and the Spa in Modern France* (Chicago: The University of Chicago Press, 1998.)

12. Auguste Forestier, *Des promenades d'Aix-les-Bains ou le nouveau guide pratique, medical et pittoresque. Vade-Mecum*, (Chambery: printed by gouvernment, 1876) 123. Condescension in travel guides, if it had bothered bourgeois readers in the nineteenth century and would continue to do so into the twentieth, was surely no concern of most middle-class readers in this genre. The phenomenal publishing success of the Joanne, Hachette, Baedeker and Michelin series, all of which offered differently nuanced descriptions of history, culture and the natural sciences, agreed more or less in narrative style and objectives. People had not traveled much but were freed by the railroad and economic prosperity to do so. Mostly middle class, readers of these multi-edition series guides needed help in setting concrete schedules for their tours and holidays. Which trains to take, where to stay, what to eat and how to begin processing the cultural artifacts and political markers they would see and cross—these very real needs of the new traveler and uninitiated tourist were of the utmost concern to guide writers who sought to help masses of people be in-the-know as they were on-the-move.

13. For the still seminal discussion on tourism and the search for authentic experience, see Dean MacCannell, *The Tourist: A New Theory of the Leisure Class* (New York: Schocken Books, 1976). Building on both MacCannell and the interpretive genius of Edward Said, as well as offering a feminist and postmodern invigoration of debates related to tourism and its narrations, see Caren Kaplan, *Questions of Travel: Postmodern Discourses of Displacement* (Durham, North Carolina: Duke University Press, 1996).

14. The notion of the privileged optic in tourism is following Dean MacCannell.

15. Edwards 21.

16. Ibid.

17. Ibid.

18. Ibid.

19. Ibid. 91.

20. Ibid.

21. Ibid. 79.

22. Ibid.

23. Ibid. 80.

24. On authentic experience and the narrative dynamics of touristic seeing, see Kaplan's criticism of Paul Fussell, 50–55.

25. Hallays, 31.

26. Ibid.

27. Edwards, 207.

28. Andre Hallays, *The Spell of Alsace*, (Boston: The Page Company, 1919) 21.

29. Thomas Balch, *Some Facts about Alsace and Lorraine*, (Philadelphia Geography Club, 1895) 5 and Edwards 188.

30. I take a romanticist sensibility to be the point of departure for assessing the narrative tone and aesthetic interests of these books. My study of the relationship between tourism and nationalism is not far enough advanced yet to say to what extent a more modernist mood characterized travel writing and guidebooks for France, beyond Alsace and Lorraine. From the work I have completed on this project, in addition to the much more extensive and systematic readings of travel and tourist literature I did for *Leisure Settings: Bourgeois Culture, Medicine and the Spa in Modern France*, it is my strong inclination to suppose that a romanticist way of "seeing" is the tourist's optic of choice and meaning, not just up to but indeed through and beyond the Great War. In this thinking I am girded by Jay Winter, *Sites of Memory, Sites of Mourning: The Great War in European Cultural History*, (Cam-

bridge: Cambridge University Press, 1995), and, thus, in opposition to both Dean Mac-Cannell and Paul Fussell.

31. Few responsible tourists to Alsace and Lorraine could have visited the territory without at least being advised to read one of the seven volumes devoted to the provinces in the seventy-volume series, entitled *Voyage en France*, which were produced in the years immediately prior to and during the First World War. The author, Ardouin Dumazet, reveals in his introduction to each of the books on Alsace and Lorraine that he "has always dreamed of the day when these dear provinces will be returned to their mother country." If this general statement seems like what many people in France and beyond might have written in the latter years of the Great War, the author achieves great narrative intimacy with his readers as he goes on to explain why it so matters to him that "France regains its stolen soil." Dedicated to his son Maurice, the guides are expositions of the trips that the author and his boy had made to Alsace and Lorraine some years before the younger man went to St. Cyr, to begin fulfilling, the father tells us, "a destiny that would make Maurice lie forever among the flowers of the valley of the Thur." Ardouin-Dumazet, *Les provinces délivereés, Voyage en France*, (Paris: Berger-Levrault, 1919) v.

32. Hallays 2. But if the distressing and important history and unsure future of the provinces could be ascertained by careful touristic consideration, Hallays warns his readers that "all this, however, does not appear at first glance to the traveler, who, Baedeker in and, visits Mulhouse between two trains."

33. Edwards 82.

34. Ibid.

35. Ibid.

36. Ibid.

37. For a survey of the history of the cult of the fallen solider in European thought, see George L. Mosse, *Fallen Soldiers: Reshaping the Memory of the World Wars*, (Oxford: Oxford University Press, 1990).

38. Ibid 30.

39. For an account of the frenzied and commercial interest in battlefield tourism to the Somme and elsewhere (which emotions and signatures of the modern were not, it should be added, seemingly shared by the modest number of tourists or the larger groups of pilgrims who would travel to the western front), see Eksteins.

40. Ibid.

41. Charles D. Hazen, *Alsace and Lorraine Under German Rule*, (1917) 98.

42. Ibid.

43. Ibid.

44. Ibid.

45. For an important analysis of the language question in Alsace and Lorraine, see Dan P. Silverman, *Reluctant Union: Alsace-Lorraine and Imperial Germany, 18711918*, (The Pennsylvania State Press, 1972) 74.

46. Edwards 40.

47. The fact that linguistic Frenchification had made only partial inroads to Alsace and Lorraine is remarkable when one considers that the territory had been under French administration for some two centuries. Forcing the people of the Alsace and Lorraine to adopt German was apparently no more successful under the Germanization program. Scholars such as Stephen Harp and Dan P. Silverman are probably closest to the truth regarding language and the existence of linguistic oppositional practices in the territory, when arguing as Silverman

has that "what we are dealing with here is not a choosing of sides in favor of either France or Germany, but rather a particularist provincial revolt against the imposition of any uniform language by any central government." Silverman 76.

48. Balch 4.

49. Ibid.

50. On landscape and its historical links to memory and meaning, see Schama and Keith Thomas, *Man and the Natural World: Changing Attitudes in England, 1500–1800* (Oxford: Oxford University Press, 1983).

51. Hallays 21.

52. Ibid.

53. Edwards 26.

54. Ibid. 26.

55. Ibid. 71.

56. Ibid.

57. Edwards 334.

58. Ibid. 335.

Iniquities of the Fathers

1. Northrop Frye, Anatomy of Criticism (Princeton: Princeton University Press, 1957) 147–51. Paul Fussell has noted the applicability of Frye's archetypes to memoirs of the war (The Great War and Modern Memory (New York: Oxford University Press, 1975), Chap. IX.

2. Quoted by Geoffrey Moorhouse in Hell's Foundations (London: Hodder and Stoughton, 1992) 66.

3. Ibid. 72.

4. Ibid. 73.

5. See Leonard Scigaj, *Ted Hughes* (Boston: Twayne, 1991) 18.

6. Ted Hughes, "Dust as We Are," in *Wolfwatching* (London: Faber and Faber, 1989).

7. *Heart of Darkness*, 3rd ed., ed. Robert Kimbrough (New York: Norton, 1988) 36, 20, 29, 75.

8. Ted Hughes, review of *Men Who March Away: Poems of the First World War*, in *The Listener* 5 Aug. 1965: 208.

9. Ted Hughes, *The Hawk in the Rain* (London: Faber and Faber, 1968).

10. Wilfred Owen, *Collected Poems*, ed. C.Day Lewis (Norfolk, Conn.: New Directions, 1964).

11. "Ted Hughes and Crow," interview with Ekbert Faas in Fass, *Ted Hughes: The Unaccommodated Universe* (Santa Barbara: Black Sparrow Press, 1980) 199.

12. "The Tyger," in William Blake, *Selected Poetry and Prose*, ed. Northrop Frye (New York: Modern Library, 1953).

13. Hughes, *Lupercal* (London: Faber and Faber, 1960).

14. Frye, *Anatomy of Criticism* 149–50.

15. Hughes, "Men Who March Away."

16. Hughes, "The Crimes of Fools Exposed," review of *The Collected Poems of Wilfred Owen*, in The New York Times Book Review 12 April 1964: 4.

17. Faas 200.

18. See Faas 37.

19. C.G. Jung, *Psychology and Alchemy*, trans. R.F.C. Hull (New York: Pantheon, 1953) 86.

20. Ibid. 136.

21. Scigaj, Ted Hughes 54.

22. Frye 150.

23. Ibid. 149.

24. Ibid. 147.

25. Hughes, *Wodwo* (Faber and Faber, 1971).

26. King Lear, in *The Complete Works of William Shakespeare*, ed. W.J. Craig (London: Oxford University Press, 1962) 4.1.36-37.

27. Frye 239.

28. Ibid. 238.

29. T. S. Eliot, *Collected Poems* (London: Faber and Faber, 1963).

30. Ibid. 1.22-24.

31. R. M. and C. H. Berndt, *The World of the First Australians* (Chicago: University of Chicago Press, 1965) 188.

32. Mircea Eliade, *Australian Religions* (Ithaca: Cornell University Press, 1973) 64, 66.

33. William Wordsworth, *The Prelude*, in *The Poetical Works* (Boston: Houghton Mifflin, 1982) 1.301.

34. *The Waste Land* 1.35-42.

35. Faas 204.

36. William Blake, "Preface" to Milton, in *Selected Poetry and Prose*.

37. Leonard Scigaj, *The Poetry of Ted Hughes: Form and Imagination* (Iowa City: University of Iowa Press, 191986) 256.

38. Ibid. 235.

39. Alan Watts, *Tao: The Watercourse Way* (New York: Pantheon Books, 1975) 44.

40. Hughes, *Remains of Elmet* (London: Faber and Faber, 1979). Hughes identified the utterance as a Taoist proverb in a conversation with Leonard Scigaj (see Scigaj, *The Poetry of Ted Hughes* 335).

41. Watts, *Tao* 41.

42. Blake, "The Chimney Sweep," in *Selected Poetry and Prose*.

43. Owen, *Collected Poems*.

44. W.H. Auden, "As I walked out one evening," in *Selected Poems*, ed. Edward Mendelson (New York: Vintage, 1979).

45. *The Waste Land* 1.62-63. Interestingly, Bertrand Russell suggested that this passage was inspired by his telling Eliot about watching the troop trains depart London, and afterwards having hallucinatory visions in which the city's inhabitants seemed unreal (Fussell, *The Great War and Modern Memory* 326).

War, Memory, and the Modern

1. I thank the Social Sciences and Humanities Research Council of Canada for funding much of the research for this essay. Nigel Steel of the Imperial War Museum; Roger Dalley and Jeremy Gee of the Commonwealth War Graves Commission; Peter Slosse and Jan Dewilde of Ieper; and my colleague John Warden made special efforts to assist my work, for which I am most grateful.

2. With this argument I follow in the footsteps of Paul Fussell and Eric J. Leed,

who, after their stimulating interpretations of the Great War, proceeded to write their next books on traveling and tourism: Paul Fussell, *The Great War and Modern Mind* (New York: Oxford University Press, 1975) and *Abroad: British Literary Traveling Between the Wars* (New York: Oxford University Press, 1980); and Eric J. Leed, *No Man's Land: Combat and Identity in World War I* (Cambridge: Cambridge University Press, 1979) and *The Mind of the Traveler: From Gilgamesh to Global Tourism* (New York: Basic Books, 1991). George L. Mosse has much to say that is relevant to this topic in *Fallen Soldiers: Reshaping the Memory of the World Wars* (New York: Oxford University Press, 1990).

3. See Richard White, "The Soldier as Tourist: The Australian Experience of the Great War," *War and Society* 5/1 (May 1987), 63–77; and "The Promised Land, the Old World," *The Age Monthly Review* 7/2 (June 1987), 6–8; as well as the riposte by James Wieland, "There and Back with the Anzacs: More Than Touring," *Journal of the Australian War Memorial* 18 (April 1991), 49–56.

4. Quoted by Edmund Blunden, in his introduction to Fabian Ware, *The Immortal Heritage: An Account of the Work and Policy of the Imperial War Graves Commission during Twenty Years 1917-1937* (Cambridge: Cambridge University Press, 1937), 20–21.

5. Letter, 23 December 1915, J. W. Gamble, Imperial War Museum, London.

6. *Guides illustres Michelin des champs de bataille: Ypres et les batailles d'Ypres 1914–1918* (Clermond-Ferrand: Michelin, 1919), 69.

7. In Philip Longworth, *The Unending Vigil: A History of the Commonwealth War Graves Commission 1917–1967* (London: Constable, 1967), 87.

8. The placard is part of the First World War collection of the Imperial War Museum, London. It was loaned in 1992 to the Historial de la Grande Guerre, Peronne.

9. Miss 0. Edis, typescript, p. 17, Imperial War Museum, London.

10. When the guide for the first battle of the Marne appeared, the French army was, ironically, on the verge of collapse from mutinies. The German offensive of 1918 then brought the battlefield back to this same gentle farming terrain, and, in view of the assertion in the 1917 guide that "the country over which it leads the reader has long been freed," *(Illustrated Michelin Guides for the Visit to the Battle-Fields: Battle-Fields of the Marne 1914* [Clemont-Ferrand: Michelin, 1917] one may wonder how many thrill-seeking tourists were caught in the German advance.

11. See, for example, Leon Auscher, *Le Tourisme en automobile* (Paris: Dunod, 1904), and for some interesting historical detail, Ren6 Duchet, *Le Tourisme A travers les Ages: Sa place dans la vie moderne* (Paris: Vigot, 1949). In his 1927 guidebook, *Through Europe On Two Dollars a Day* (New York: McBride), Frank Schoonmaker could still write: "It is hard for a Frenchman to understand that restless urge that makes a person want to wander, hard for him to realize that you and I would rather have a trip to Europe than four or five hundred dollars in the bank" (140).

12. Pickfords' brochure *Seeing the Battlefields* (London, n.d.), 3. Pickfords picked up more than the idea of battlefield tours from Michelin; it also borrowed some prose verbatim from the Michelin guides.

13. Some of the difficulties are described in John W. Dafoe, *Over the Canadian Battlefields: Notes of a Little Journey in France, in March, 1919* (Toronto: Thomas Allen, 1919), 14–15.

14. One of the sets of the Guides *Michelin pour la visite des champs de bataille*, 19 vol. (1917–20), in the Biblioth6que Nationale in Paris, is the gift of ttienne Moreau-N61aton, the distinguished art collector, whose son was killed near the end of the war.

15. Letter of 22 January 1919, Miss P. E. Goodliff, Imperial War Museum, London.

16. Miss O. Edis, typescript, pp. 12–13, Imperial War Museum, London.

17. Diary entries, 24 April, 19 May, and 31 July, 1919, Mrs. A. Mullineaux, Imperial War Museum, London.

18. Letter of David Milne to Alice and Vincent Massey, 20 August 1934. The original is in Massey College, University of Toronto. I thank my colleague Professor Lora Carney for drawing my attention to this material.

19. Pierre Chabert, *Le Tourisme americain et ses enseignements pour la France* (Paris: Hachette, 1919), ix, 126–132.

20. Leon Auscher, *La Prosperite de la France par le tourisme* (Bar-le-Duc: Comte- Jacquet, 1920), pp. 6–11. The arguments presented after the Second World War were virtually the same: see Georges Villette, *Tourisme, facteur essential de redressement de l'economie nationals* (Paris: G. Lang, 1950).

21. Schoonmaker, *Through Europe*, 129–30.

22. Quoted in *St. Barnabas Pilgrimages 1924* (London: Eyre & Spottiswoode, n.d.), 27.

23. In his introduction to Fabian Ware, *The Immortal Heritage*, 18.

24. In his introduction to Philip Longworth, *The Unending Vigil*, xxiv.

25. Sidney C. Hurst, *The Silent Cities: An Illustrated Guide to the War Cemeteries and Memorials to the "Missing" in France and Flanders 1914–1918* (London: Methuen, 1929).

26. *War Graves of the Empire* (London: Times Publishing Company, 1928), 40.

27. Duchet, *Le Tourisme*, 172–74; also Louis Damblanc, *Le Tourisme francais* (Paris: Rassemblement Republicain, 1938).

28. H. A. Taylor, *Good-Bye to the Battlefields: To-Day and Yesterday on the Western Front* (London: Stanley Paul & Co., 1928), 30.

29. Gerhard Schinke, "Eine Reise an die Kriegsgraber in Flandern im Jahre 1927," MSg2/1731, Bundesarchiv-Militararchiv, Freiburg im Breisgau.

30. Taylor, *Good-Bye to the Battlefields*, 127.

31. Christopher Isherwood, *Kathleen and Frank* (London: Methuen, 1971), 359. Edmund Blunden has a similar reaction: *The Mind's Eye* (London: Cape, 1934), 47.

32. R. H. Mottram, *Journey to the Western Front: Twenty Years After* (London: Bell, 1936), 1–2.

33. Most guidebooks maintained a reverential tone. One such successful volume which had two printings within a year of publication in 1935 was Graham Seton Hutchinson's *Pilgrimage* (London: Rich & Cowan).

34. Useful guides to a tour of the Western Front include Rose E. B. Coombs, *Before Endeavours Fade: A Guide to the Battlefields of the First World War*, rev. ed. (London: Battle of Britain Prints International, 1990); Martin and Mary Middlebrook, *The Somme Battlefields: A Comprehensive Guide From Crecy to the Two World Wars* (London: Viking, 1991); chapter 13, "Visiting the sites," in Edwin Gibson and G. Kingsley Ward, *Courage Remembered: The Story Behind the Construction and Maintenance of the Commonwealth's Military Cemeteries and Memorials of the Wars of 1914–1918 and 1939–1945* (London: HMSO, 1989); Nigel H. Jones, *The War Walk: A Journey Along the Western Front* (London: Robert Hale, 1983); Chrisje and Kees Brants, *Velden van weleer: Reisgids naar de Eerste Wereldoorlog* (Amsterdam: Nijgh & Van Ditmar, 1995); and Stephen O'Shea, *Back to the Front: An Accidental Historian Walks the Trenches of World War I* (Toronto: Douglas & McIntyre, 1996).

35. The Belgian and French offices of the Commonwealth War Graves Commission, at Ieper and Beaurains respectively, assembled several hundred visitors' books from its cemeteries and memorials for me to peruse in 1991. Most contained entries from the previous year or two,

usually 1989–91, but in a few cases, where the books came from less frequented sites, entries spanned a longer period, in several instances going back to 1986. I personally visited more than a hundred cemeteries in the course of a tour of the Western Front in 1991 and consulted the then current visitors' books in not only the Commonwealth but also French, Belgian, American, Italian, and German cemeteries.

36. The Commonwealth War Graves Commission, responsible for some 23,000 burial sites around the world, has not, given the volume of material involved, retained the visitors' books. The Historial de la Grande Guerre in Peronne has become the repository of recent visitors' books.

Contributors

Regina Sweeny is assistant professor of history at Middlebury College. She is completing a book on the cultural history of French singing, morality, and mass entertainment in the epoch of the First World War.

Greg Barnhisel is a doctoral candidate in English literature at the University of Texas at Austin, working on research related to the publishing industry, Modernist literature and the career of Ezra Pound.

Jeffrey Smith, a recent Ph.D. in modern German history from the University of Illinois at Urbana-Champaign, is working on a book on the transformation of German politics during the First World War.

Geoffrey Jensen is assistant professor of history and director of international studies at the University of Southern Mississippi. He is completing a book about the cultural modernism of the Spanish military and its links to the origins of Franco's Spain.

James P. Daughton received his M.Phil. in European studies from Cambridge University and is a doctoral candidate in history at the University of California at Berkeley.

David Simpson is a graduate of the School of Foreign Service at Georgetown University and is now a doctoral candidate in history at the University of Iowa. He is working on a history of venereal disease and the British army during the First World War.

Janet Watson is assistant professor of history at the University of Connecticut, where she is completing a book on the history of class, gender relations and their representations in wartime Britain.

Douglas Mackaman is associate professor of history and director of French area studies at the University of Southern Mississippi. Building on his first book, *Leisure Settings: Bourgeois Culture, Medicine and the Spa in Modern France*, he is researching a study on the relationship between tourism and national identity in Europe during the period 1750–1930.

Dwight Eddins is professor of English at the University of Alabama. He is engaged in literary research related to modern poetry and culture.

Michael Mays is associate professor of English and co-director of the Institute for the Study of Modern Life at the University of Southern Mississippi. He is working on a book about the literary and cultural terms of Irish nationalism in the twentieth century.

Modris Eksteins is professor of history at Scarborough College, University of Toronto. The author of works in German history and European history, his *Rites of Spring: The Great War and the Birth of the Modern Age* has become a classic text to students of the war and interdisciplinary inquiry.

Index

Index

Joyce, James, 151

Larkin, Philip, xi
Leed, Eric, x
Leisure, 49, 51, 70, 150–60
Lindenberger, Thomas, 70
Literature: cartoons as examples of, 37–45; travel guides as, 124–35; and war, xxi; and women's wartime experiences, 91, 94–96

Mackaman, Douglas, x, xii
Mail, 58–62, 77–80
Mass culture: cartoons as examples of, 35–52; and the politics of the public sphere, 69–75, 77–80; and wartime censorship, 3–20
Mays, Michael, x, xii
Medicine, 34, 150–60
Memory and memorialization, 145, 147–50, 151, 155–60
Milne, A. A., ix
Modernism: and Ezra Pound, 104–10; literary marketing of, 104–15; in poetry, 140–50
Morale: cultural politics and the maintenance of, 4–16, 35–50, 63–67, 72–75, 83–99; prostitution and front line, 21–30
Morality: bourgeois expressions of, 10–13; cartoon commentaries on, 40; drinking as a reducer of, 23–25; empire and military regulations of, 30; and sexual activity, 20–34; and women's work, 85–90
Mosse, George, 77
Mourning, 9150–60
Muscular Christianity, 30
Music Halls, 6–15
Mussolini, Benito, 117

Nationalism, 117–24, 126–34
Newspapers, 38, 44, 72–75

O'Neill, Eugene, 152
Owen, Wilfred, x, xiii, 104, 137–38, 147

Pilgrimage, 130–35, 150–60
Postcards, 77–80
Pound, Ezra, 104–16
Propaganda: and cartoons, 35–47; homefront reactions to, 70–77; trench culture and appeals to, 42; wartime songs as expressions of, 8–18; and women's work, 83–95
Prostitution: and British soldiers, 20–30; hygiene and governmental regulations of, 22; in London, 21–24; wartime manifestations of, 21–33

Race, 47–49
Reproduction: venereal disease and fears about, 23–32; and women's wartime work, 84–90
Romanticism: aesthetics of, xx; and nationalism, 127–34; women's farm work and the construction of, 88–92

Sassoon, Siefried, 137
Sexuality: British soldiers and front line expressions of, 2–28; cultural politics of, 3, 20–34; and drinking, 23; in empire, 29–33; and self control, 25–30; and song lyrics, 12; and women's wartime work, 83–86
Silver, Kenneth, 6
Social class: cartoons and the absence of references to, 46; drinking as an indication of, 23–26; entertainment and cultural constructions of, 2–17; sexuality as figured by, 23–27
Spain, 117–24
Spies, 71

Thom, Deborah, 97
Total war: cultural mobilization for, 3–17, 35–50; and women's work, 81–103
Tourism, xiv, 124–35
Trenches: cartooned depictions of, 36–50; city street names for, x; the community of, 46–53; poetic references to, x; songs and singing in, 6–14; tourist writings about, xiv, 124–35, 150–60

196

Index

United States of American, 104–16

Venereal disease: empire and concerns about, 30; prewar appearances of, 22–24; and prostitution, 23–30

Verdun, xix, 49, 156

Women: as representations of civilization, 58–61; soldiers and fantasies about, 56–62; wartime work of, 81–103

Woolf, Virginia, xxi

Ypres, 152–53